To War with

A Tank Gunner Remembers

1939-1945

Jack Merewood

1ST THE QUEEN'S DRAGOON GUARDS

For my family

First published in Great Britain 1996
by 1st The Queen's Dragoon Guards
Maindy Barracks, Whitchurch Road
Cardiff CF4 3YE

Typeset in Sabon by The Typesetting Bureau
Allen House, East Borough, Wimborne, Dorset
Printed and bound in Great Britain
by Biddles Ltd, King's Lynn, Norfolk

Produced for the Regiment
by Michael Russell (Publishing) Ltd
Wilby Hall, Wilby, Norwich NR16 2JP

Contents

Acknowledgements

These memoirs would never have been written had it not been for my wife Sheila and my daughter Anne. It was their idea, and at times when I flagged a little, their enthusiasm and encouragement revitalised me. I couldn't have done it without them and all the work and time they gave.

They are written from memory, and with constant reference to small diaries I kept during the war. Without these the task would have been impossible, but often a few lines were enough to bring back vivid memories.

I wish to thank Bishop Michael Mann for his invaluable help and advice. Also Ian McMillan for his enthusiasm and help with the maps and the computer. I am indebted, too, to Bob Moss who loaned me a book on the history of the Bays; to my daughter-in-law, Sarah, who helped with the first chapters; and to my son, Stuart, who introduced me to the intricacies of a computer.

This is not a history, it is merely a record of my personal experiences. Reliving them has brought back to me the pain – and the pleasures – of those years.

JACK MEREWOOD

Foreword

Jack Merewood joined the Army in October 1939 as a militiaman and did his training with the Royal Armoured Corps at Catterick before joining the Queen's Bays in April 1940. The following month he found himself with the Bays in France when the 1st Armoured Division was sent as part of the abortive British attempt to bolster French resistance following the German breakthrough at Sedan. The Bays returned to England to re-equip and train, and in 1941 they arrived in the Western Desert in time to take part in the battles around Knightsbridge and the Cauldron. Jack Merewood served as a member of a tank crew all through the North African campaign, winning the Military Medal at Mareth; and later fighting in Italy, where the Bays suffered heavily at Coriano Ridge before the winter's fighting on the Gothic Line. But Jack also took part in the final successful offensive when the German Army in Italy surrendered some days before the end of the fighting in North West Europe.

Jack tells his story as the fighting soldier that he was. Throughout his service he kept a diary, mainly for the benefit of his family; and now they have encouraged him to recall for future generations the feelings generated by his experience of war and especially of the close-knit comradeship of a tank crew facing danger and death together.

Jack's regiment, the Queen's Bays, was joined to the King's Dragoon Guards in 1959, to form the new regiment of 1st The Queen's Dragoon Guards. The QDG, like its forebears, the KDG and the Bays, has carried on their tradition of being a family regiment, and, whether you were a Bay, KDG or QDG, once you wore their cap badge, you were always a QDG. Jack is an old and valued member of that regimental family. It is that family which is honoured to support him in adding his experiences to the tapestry that makes up our regimental story, for that story is the inspiration and example to every member of the family, whether he be an old comrade or a serving soldier. This is the stuff that builds up the regimental tradition and pride which is the backbone of the British Army and the envy of other armies.

MICHAEL MANN

I

1939: Joining Up

In September 1938 Neville Chamberlain came back from his meeting in Munich with Hitler, waving his famous piece of paper and declaring 'Peace in our time'. However, neither he nor the Government must have been 100% sure of this because they decided to introduce conscription in Great Britain in 1939. In that year all young men aged twenty were required to register to serve six months in the Army and three-and-a-half years on the reserve. This meant an employer must release a young man for six months, after which he would go back to work; then he had to be given a month off each year for the next three years to go back into the Army to 'brush up' on his training.

I was twenty in February 1939, and in due course received notification that I was to report to the Drill Hall in Huddersfield one Saturday afternoon in June. I remember the occasion well, because it was a lovely hot sunny day and I had reluctantly to leave a cricket match I was watching at Lockwood cricket field.

My mother's two youngest brothers were both in the Territorial Army in the Royal Artillery. I told the interviewer that I worked in a bakehouse.

'Oh – you'll be just right then for an army cookhouse,' he said.

'No,' I replied.

If I had to spend six months in the Army I wanted to get away from baking and cooking and wanted to be outside. He asked if I had any preference when going into the Services. Not knowing one from the other and with my two uncles in mind, I said I would choose the Royal Artillery.

At 11 o'clock on that fateful Sunday morning, 3 September 1939, I was still at home. We listened to Neville Chamberlain on the wireless. When he said we were now in a state of war with Germany, my mother burst into tears. Only twenty-one years since the last war finished – and now another one.

A month or so later I received my calling-up papers, and had to report to Catterick Camp in North Yorkshire on 30 October. With the papers came a railway ticket to Richmond Station, the nearest one to Catterick Camp, two or three miles away. I duly arrived at Richmond with seemingly hundreds of others, and we were loaded into the waiting army trucks. There were many camps of different regiments at Catterick and we were delivered to one of them. We were then taken to the medical centre and given inoculations in both arms and a vaccination, then paraded to the canteen where we were given our 'tea' – two thick slices of bread with a slice of corned beef between and a mug of tea, then allocated to different barrack rooms. It was a cold night and the single stove in the middle of the room was unlit. Everyone was cold and miserable.

Next morning we were awakened at 6.30 a.m. by the strident notes of a bugle – reveille – a sound we would hear every morning for several months to come. Then breakfast – bacon, porridge, tea, and more slabs of bread; after which we all paraded on the square, I don't know how many, perhaps a hundred or so. A sergeant stood in front with a list of names in his hand.

'As your name is called out, go and stand over there,' he said.

The names were called, and everybody stood 'over there' – everybody that is except for one man who was left standing on his own, isolated from his fellow men. The one man feeling very conspicuous and embarrassed was – me! The sergeant asked my name, checked through his list again – I wasn't on it. He gave instructions to all the other men, then told me to follow him. He went into an office and I waited outside. When he came out he said I shouldn't be here in the R.A., but across the road in the R.A.C.

The R.A.C. turned out to be the Royal Armoured Corps where men were trained to fight in tanks. He explained how to get there, diagonally across the road about 300 yards away, and to whom to report; they would be expecting me. I did as I was told, and on reporting was informed that I should have been there yesterday, and now to join everybody else as they were just about to have their vaccinations and inoculations. This was a little disconcerting, but fortunately I was able to produce my paybook, which confirmed that I had all these things last night.

And so began my army career at Catterick – in the Royal Armoured Corps.

2
Training at Catterick

Life at Catterick was not easy. Young men from all walks of life with different natures and outlooks, here together (hopefully) to be moulded into well-trained and disciplined soldiers. Johnson had been brought up on a fairground. He could neither read nor write, but one of his jobs had been to help maintain the vehicles and steam engines, and when it came to mechanics he was a marvel. Ted Ryan from Wakefield had worked in a grocer's shop. Jimmy Turner, along with his father owned two fish-and-chip shops in South Kirkby. Lin Wood worked in a drawing office in Newcastle and Ronnie Cross from Alnwick was a newspaper reporter, earning when he was called up, the princely sum of £6 a week. My wage in the bakehouse at that time was £2.13s, to be increased to £3 a week when I was twenty-one.

We were divided into squads with about twenty men in each – Ronnie and I were in No. 33 squad and soon became firm friends. Most of the boys in the squad were 'Geordies', the rest were from Yorkshire. I can think of no one who actually liked the army life, but Ronnie hated it. Like all of us, he missed his home and family, but most of all he hated being away from his girl friend, Emily. I too was terribly homesick.

These first days were miserable ones. Ronnie and I wrote home every night. What we were able to write about I don't remember, but writing home was a kind of solace. There was a reasonably good writing-room in the NAAFI, and that is where we spent most evenings. (Every camp had its NAAFI – always cups of tea and buns, sweets, cigarettes etc. to be had there.) Of course we had letters from home all the time too; my mother and my sister Jessie did more than their fair share of writing.

The barrack-room in which we lived was an uninviting place, containing the twenty beds of our squad. These were just plain wooden frames on four legs, the frames being joined together with a lattice-work of leather straps and a canvas covering. Then on top of these we put three 'biscuits'. These were like small mattresses, and placed side by side they covered the length of the bed. Three rough grey army blankets and a pillow made the rest of the bed. One blanket covered the biscuits, the others covered you. There was a stove in the middle of the barrack-room, for which we were allowed wood and coal, but as winter wore on it became colder and once the stove went out at night it was necessary to add our greatcoats on top of the blankets to keep warm. Each morning our beds had to be 'made up', the biscuits piled at the bed head, blankets folded neatly on top of them and the pillow on top.

We had a troop sergeant, 'Chesty' Morris, who put the fear of God up us every time we heard his gravel voice. He was what one would imagine a real tough Regular Army sergeant to be like, stocky, of average height, and back as stiff and straight as a ramrod. He had a ruddy face, as though he had lived outdoors for years. The rough red complexion would turn a slight shade of purple if he got mad at us, which was fairly regularly. He carried a short cane or baton tucked tightly under his arm, and every morning he rapped on the barrack-room door with it and rasped out 'On parade' – and if it was perhaps a morning after the night before for him he would add 'at the double', which meant we then ran everywhere until he decided we'd had enough.

Regularly we had kit inspections. The biscuits were laid on the bed, a blanket spread on top of them, the other blankets folded and, with the pillow, placed at the bed head. Our kit was then laid out on the blanket in the correct order, as per Army regulations – gas-masks, shirts, socks, shaving kit, boot-brushes, holdall etc. A rap on the door with the cane, followed by a gruff 'Stand by your beds', announced the arrival of Chesty accompanied by an officer. Each man then stood smartly at the side of his bed. We could only wear army boots, never shoes. We had two pairs of boots, one pair for daily wear, the other pair with the toes 'spit and polished' for special occasions like guard duty or church parade. In the holdall (always pronounced 'hod-all' by the Quartermaster) were needles, cotton, wool, etc. We were required to darn our own thick grey socks, something that needed doing often. Only when socks had been darned and re-darned and were obviously beyond any more repair were we able to take them to the Quartermaster's store, where the

QM would exchange them for a new pair. Sometimes when tired of sewing on buttons we bought 'bachelor buttons' – buttons which could be clipped together through a hole in the trousers. The object of kit inspections was to check that we had all the kit with which we had been issued, to make sure nothing had been lost (or sold!). Chesty and the officer walked down the room inspecting each bed, and if something was missing would want to know the reason why. Generally excuses were accepted, after a ticking off, then it meant a visit to the stores, and another ticking off by the QM before being supplied with a replacement. If there were serious discrepancies, penalties were handed out, such as extra duties in the cookhouse (potato peeling for example) or other unpleasant duties.

On kit inspection days it was necessary not just to stand by one's bed but also to keep a close watch on everything on it; otherwise a holdall you felt sure you had might suddenly not be there, and someone who you were sure had lost his holdall would miraculously have acquired one. Not everyone was honest, but generally these incidents were few and far between, and in general there was a pretty good feeling of harmony in the barrack-room. If there was any trouble it was usually caused by men who liked to drink. I remember one incident of a boot being thrown across the room one night in the dark and the recipient, a boy called Oliver, sporting a black eye next morning. But all in all there was more of a feeling of comradeship than antagonism, so life in the barrack-room ran reasonably smoothly.

Drilling on the square was an almost daily part of our training, often with rifles, and woe betide anyone who dropped one. He was made to pick it up and run round the square, rifle held at arm's length above his head, till told to stop. The troop corporal was Corporal Payne, and though Chesty eventually knew us all by name, if anyone committed any misdemeanour the voice rasped out 'Take his name, Corporal Payne.' As time went by and we got used to it, this became something of a joke between us – and eventually we found that Chesty's bark was worse than his bite. But although at times he was really rough on us, he was, to give him his due, a fair man. He was never spiteful. If he gave us a rough time it was usually because we deserved it. I don't think, though, that he realised that butchers, bakers and candlestick makers can't be transformed into soldiers overnight.

[15]

It was a bitterly cold winter that year, and mothers, sisters, and girlfriends were busy knitting as many comforts for us as they could. Ronnie used to go to bed wearing a balaclava, scarf and socks! It was cold too, drilling with guns, especially pistols, and though we wore mittens when we could, at pistol drill our fingers used to be freezing. We learned to fire just about every gun there was – .38 pistols, .45 pistols (heavy pistols those were), tommy-guns, rifles, machine-guns. There was one gun we feared – it was an anti-tank rifle. You lay on the ground to fire it, and it was essential to hold it tight into your shoulder because of the recoil. Even held correctly the recoil could knock you back a foot. Not held tightly, and your shoulder got a nasty shock.

We learned about poison gases, we learned to assemble hand grenades. Dummies at first, and then the real thing. Then learned how to throw them, a fairly dangerous practice.

We also learned to drive. The first vehicle I ever drove was a bren-gun carrier, a small open-topped tracked vehicle, steered with a steering wheel as opposed to a tank which was steered by tiller bars. Tiller bars were levers, one connected to each track, so that when the right hand one was pulled, for example, this slowed down the right hand track. The left track continued at its original speed, so the tank turned to the right. From bren-gun carriers we graduated to tanks – mostly Crusaders and Stuarts.

The man who taught us to drive was a Corporal Weaver – and we thought he was mad! Out on the moors round Catterick, where we learned to drive, was one favourite place of his he called 'The Big Apple' – I never knew why – where the ground sloped upwards then dropped away at the other side. He used to get a fiendish pleasure out of running a Crusader up the slope as fast as he could, then 'taking off' at the top as though flying and falling to earth at the other side with a bang.

Crusaders were British tanks, low, sleek-looking and capable of speeds up to 40 m.p.h. Unfortunately the armoured sides were very thin. They had a crew of four – driver, wireless operator, gunner and tank commander. The guns were two-pounders (2 lb weight of the shell) and a machine gun, both in the turret, both loaded by the wireless operator, but fired by the gunner, the gunner sitting at one side of the breech and the wireless operator at the other.

The Stuarts were American tanks and were like sardine tins.

Hopeless things they were. The crew was similar to that of a Crusader, but the 'heavy' gun was a 37 mm bore, more like a peashooter than a gun. And whereas the turret on a Crusader was operated by the gunner just turning a 'spade-grip' (a device shaped like a spade handle which when gripped could be turned to the left or right to traverse, power-driven, the whole turret), in the Stuart the gunner had to stand and rotate the turret by turning a big wheel – very similar to that of an old mangling machine. This meant that at times he found himself climbing over the back of the driver. Imagine coming up against the Germans in these tin boxes – but we found ourselves doing just that two years later in North Africa.

In the tanks we wore headphones and received instructions from the tank commander over a microphone; otherwise with the noise of the engine and the guns it was pretty near impossible to hear. However, sometimes when later we were in action we would dispense with them and just shout at each other. We also had to see where we were going through periscopes. There were periscopes in the cupolas (lids) of the tanks, but these were never used, because we never travelled with the lid closed, the view would be too restricted. So the tank commander always stood with his head and generally half his body out of the top of the tank.

Sometimes with the tanks we'd drive into Leyburn, park in the square there and have a cup of tea and a bun in a nearby café. We had by necessity occasionally to drive on the roads. When we did so, it meant being especially careful not to turn quickly, for this could result in a track digging into the road surface.

But there was a lighter side to life too. Near the camp were a few shops and a post office, a cinema and swimming baths. As time went by, dances were held in a local hall. The girls were almost always ATS, and like us they enjoyed these welcome breaks. We also spent hours playing cards, usually brag (three, four, seven or nine card), or pontoon or Nap. Money not spent in the NAAFI generally ended up on card tables or beds or anywhere else we could play. In the beginning the stakes weren't high because our pay was 7/6d (37½p) a week. This was paid on Fridays, but instead of 7/6d each week, we were paid 5/- (25p) one week and 10/- (50p) the next. Over the following months we were given rises (one was sixpence a week – cigarette money), so the card stakes would rise a little. Nobody ever missed pay parade of course. Unless it was raining or snowing, a table was set up outside. The paymaster sat at it and as your name was called you went up to the table, saluted, and the officer handed you your pay.

We could go out at night, but had to be in for 'lights out' at 10.30 p.m., at least we were supposed to be. At weekends we were allowed as far as Richmond without a pass but it was not the most exciting of towns. There were two cinemas there, and it had its historic castle, but apart from the cinemas there was no entertainment for soldiers. To go further than Richmond without a pass brought the risk of being caught by the Redcaps (Military Police). They regularly stopped vehicles on the Great North Road and asked to see passes. Caught without one meant being reported, up later before the C.O. and sentence passed – usually a week or so C.B. (confined to barracks).

We were occasionally allowed weekend passes. I always used mine to go home. Like everyone else I would hitch-hike a lift down the road from the camp to Catterick village about two miles away and on the Great North Road. The Great North Road in those days was just an ordinary two-lane highway, the A1. The Romans built the original road, and it connected all the towns on the way. Nowadays it is a four-lane highway, and over the years all the towns have been bypassed.

It was always easy to get a lift from Catterick village, sometimes in private cars, but more often in army vehicles. Generally I could get a lift to Wetherby, then to Leeds, and then one from Leeds to Huddersfield. One of these varied lifts particularly sticks in my mind. There was a convoy of jeeps coming. One stopped to pick me up. The driver was an ATS girl – I remember she had lovely auburn hair. It was in the winter, there was snow and ice about, and coming through Boroughbridge we got stuck on the bridge, and I had to get out and push. We sang songs most of the way – mostly Christmas carols, and in this particular instance I was exceptionally lucky because the convoy came through Huddersfield and the girl dropped me off at Folly Hall, about a mile from home.

If I could get away early and get a good lift, and if I was in time, and Huddersfield Rugby League team were playing at home, I'd go straight to Fartown to the match. I knew my father would always be there, I'd find him, and after the match was over, we'd come home together. Oh – it was heaven to be home. There was always a dance on somewhere in town on Saturday nights, and that is where I generally went.

On Sunday, to get back to Catterick, it meant catching a train to Darlington. From there special trains for the soldiers ran straight to the camp. On Sunday nights these would be packed. The train stopped quite near to the RAC barracks, so once off the train it was only a few hundred yards' walk to the camp.

Many weekends Ronnie would go home with or without a pass, and sometimes I went with him (always without a pass – but we were never caught). Going to Alnwick meant going north now on the A1 as far as Newcastle. Often Lin Wood would go too and we'd leave him in Newcastle and then catch the train to Alnwick. Alnwick was on a small branch line, and the line ended at the station there. Sometimes Emily came down to Newcastle, and we'd meet her and Lin's girlfriend Joyce, and spend a little while with them before going on to Alnwick.

Ronnie was a great sportsman, he seemed to be good at almost any sport. He played cricket for Alnwick, and football. His father was steward at the billiard hall in Alnwick – so Ronnie was almost born with a billiard cue in his hand, and he was an excellent player, as was his brother Ian. He was also a very keen golfer and sometimes he'd take me to the golf course. Emily had a brother, John (later killed in action), who was in the RAF and I'd borrow his clubs. I was useless at golf, but we'd spend a bit of time at the course with Ronnie giving me some instruction. Like me, Ronnie was a keen card-player too, so we often played cards.

Ronnie's parents were marvellous people, and so was his granny (his mother's mother) who lived with them. They made such a fuss of us, fed us well and when we left we always came away loaded with buns and cakes and pies.

On the way back to Catterick from Alnwick, as from Huddersfield, it was change trains at Darlington. Often it was a bit hazardous there as the place swarmed with MPs and a considerable amount of time was taken in dodging them if we were without passes.

Just down the road from the barracks was Hipswell gym. Here we had a lot of PT. We were also kept fit by having to deliver coal. There was a big coal bunker in the barracks from which we loaded coal into metal tubs with a handle on each side, then to be delivered in the back of a wagon to the houses of officers who lived in the area.

One Saturday night there was a sergeants' dance at the gym. I was one of a number of men detailed to get the piano from the NAAFI in the camp, and take it there and set it up on the stage. There was a corporal in charge of us and when we came for the piano the NAAFI manageress impressed on him that we *must* handle it with care.

On the Sunday morning we went to collect the piano and return it to the NAAFI. We got it down from the stage but had to take it the length of the gym to load it onto a wagon. Once we got it moving, we really began to pick up speed, and were soon travelling at a pretty good lick. Then disaster! There were some brass rings let in holes in the floor. One of the casters caught in one of these, and the piano came to an abrupt halt. I was at the end of the piano, with my shoulder to it, and it split from top to bottom. With a musical twanging of strings the whole piano fell apart. We picked up the pieces and loaded them onto the wagon.

When we arrived back at the NAAFI the corporal, in fear and trembling, said to the manageress: 'Er – we've – er, brought back the piano.'

'Well bring it in,' she said.

Another man and I led the way, carrying the keyboard. As more men trooped in with the rest of the remains, the manageress looked to be on the verge of a heart attack. The corporal was held responsible, and the rest of us beat a hasty retreat. The NAAFI was piano-less the rest of the time that I was there. Whether or not they ever got another one I don't know.

Guard duty came round every two or three weeks. Seeing your name on the notice board to be on guard meant that night you reported to the guard room smartly dressed, complete with rifle (no bullets!) at 5.30 p.m. Six of you each night. You teamed up in pairs, then tossed up to choose the relief you wanted to be on. First relief was 6 p.m. to 8 p.m. then again midnight to 2 a.m.; second relief 8 p.m. to 10 p.m. and 2 a.m. to 4 a.m.; and third relief 10 p.m. to midnight, then 4 a.m. to 6 a.m. We spent the time on guard walking round the barracks, sheds, the huge garage etc. If anyone approached they had to be challenged 'Halt, who goes there?' 'Friend' was the acceptable answer. Life would have been exciting if anyone had answered 'Foe' – but no one ever did. There was a sergeant in charge of the guard – and when the orderly officer came round, usually about 10 p.m. to 10.30 p.m., the sergeant bellowed 'Turn out the guard', and the four remaining men were 'turned out' and in-spected by the officer.

We survived the harsh winter of 1939/40. I spent my twenty-first birthday at Catterick. I could have thought of a thousand other places I'd rather have been for that celebration. In fact I can't remember having any celebration in particular. I got some cards, and I had a really nice parcel from home – and one from Ronnie's parents too. So far as I recall that was the extent of it – perhaps I had an extra bun in the NAAFI that night.

There *had* been a celebration at Christmas. By army tradition, Christmas dinner was always served to the ordinary soldiers by the sergeants and officers. Christmas at Catterick was no exception. Tables were set in long rows, the food was good, turkey, pork and all the trimmings and Christmas pudding, and it was quite an enjoyable novelty to have the sergeants and officers waiting on us. At night there was a dance in the local dance hall. It wasn't like being at home – but at least there was the feeling of Christmas.

April 1940 came. Our training was finished. We could all now drive, operate the wireless or handle the guns, although some were more efficient than others. Every night lists of names appeared on the notice board, headed by the announcement 'The following are to be posted to' . . . and then the name of the regiment.

One night Ronnie's name was on the board, his future regiment to be the Queen's Bays. My name wasn't on the list. I quickly found our Squadron Leader, a Major Porter, and asked if I could be sent to the Bays to go with Ronnie. I was rather astonished when he put his arm around my shoulders, treating me as if I had done something very brave and said 'Yes'. The only other men to go from 33 Squad to the Bays were Ted Ryan and Jimmy Turner.

A few days later we were marched down to Richmond Station, led by Captain Pedder. Half way there, we stopped for a rest and were allowed to sit on the grassy bank at the side of the road. To my great surprise and embarrassment, Captain Pedder stood in front and told of my volunteering for this draft because of my friend. His first words were 'There is a man amongst us. . . . ' Apparently this was something unheard of. It caused me extreme embarrassment and to this day I can't understand the fuss it had caused.

3

1940: The Queen's Bays and France

After the march from Catterick Camp we boarded the train at Richmond Station, bound for Poole in Dorset and the Queen's Bays.

When the train arrived at Poole we were paraded in one long line. Someone of authority walked down the line. He stopped and said: 'You men, over there.' Then he walked further along, stopped and repeated this. We didn't realise what was happening, but then were enlightened: 'The first group will join 'A' Squadron, the second group 'B' Squadron, the third group 'C' Squadron, and the last 'HQ' Squadron'.

At Richmond Station Captain Pedder had left us and had gone back to the camp at Catterick. Here at Poole no one knew of my heroic volunteering act. Ronnie and I were separated in the general mêlée that resulted after we got off the train – and Ronnie found himself in 'B' Squadron and I was in 'C' Squadron. After all the fuss I now realised that I wasn't so important any more. We both felt very unhappy about being separated, but had no time to talk it over or commiserate with each other, because we soon found that the squadrons were located in different towns. So Ronnie stayed in Poole, and before I knew where I was, I and other men were loaded into trucks and carried off to Wareham, about ten miles away. Ted Ryan and Jimmy Turner were also in 'C' Squadron. Our other friend, Lin Wood, wasn't posted to the Bays, but sent to the 4th Hussars. Later he was taken prisoner and sent to Stalag XVIIIA in Germany. Unfortunately after a while I lost touch with him. Ronnie and I wrote to each other but didn't meet again for about six or seven weeks. We were then in France.

The Bays were a cavalry regiment formed in 1685 and as the name implies had bay horses. They remained a mounted regiment right up to 1936, when the horses were replaced by tanks and the Bays became a 'mechanised cavalry' regiment. In the South of England there were numerous cavalry regiments – many famous Hussars and Lancers amongst them – and the Bays were one of three such regiments who formed the 1st Armoured Division, the other two being the 10th Hussars and the 9th Lancers. The cavalry regiments regarded themselves as élite army units and many officers were from the landed gentry. In 'HQ' Squadron there was Lord Knebworth and in our squadron we had Lord Erleigh. This of course was to change when the war started, with the influx of enlisted men.

We 'rookies' had been sent from training corps to increase the strength of these old regiments, and at first the regulars were a little resentful of us. We weren't too keen on some of them either, particularly the NCOs, who were forever telling us what it was like 'when we had horses'. This wore a bit thin after a while so we all began saying 'Oh yes – but when we had horses.' However, we got used to each other, and eventually we integrated.

On arrival at Wareham we were allocated to different troops. A troop consisted of three tanks. The tank commanders were usually an officer, a sergeant and a corporal. There were five troops in a squadron, Nos. 1, 2, 3, and 4 which were fighting units, and 'HQ' (Headquarters) which was in control of the squadron. In addition to the tank crews there were other soldiers, administrative staff, fitters, technicians, cooks, lorry drivers, spare crews and others on general duties, so that the strength of a squadron would be about 120 men.

Ted and I were both in No. 1 Troop, Jimmy was in No. 2. A regiment consisted of four squadrons, 'A', 'B', 'C' and 'HQ'. 'A', 'B' and 'C' were fighting squadrons and were all controlled by the Commanding Officer in 'HQ' Squadron. 'HQ' Squadron always brought up the rear – as did the 'HQ' Troops in the squadrons. And so the total strength of the Regiment would be about 550 men – although this figure could fluctuate.

Ordinary soldiers were not privates but, not surprisingly, troopers.

Wareham was a small, average, country town, very quiet with no entertainment for young soldiers, although there were some pleasant walks along the river bank. Lawrence of Arabia was killed while riding a motorbike near Wareham and is commemorated in the church.

We were billeted in houses, some occupied, some empty, there being no barracks in the town. Our troop was in an empty house on East Street. Walking along the river bank wasn't the most exciting way to occupy one's time, but of course there were girls in Wareham, and young soldiers in uniform were an attraction – as were the girls to young soldiers in uniform! A teenage girl, whose name I forget, seemed particularly attracted to me, and when we left she pleaded with me to write to her. I didn't feel particularly inclined to keep in touch, but because of her insistence I half-heartedly agreed to write – but I never did. Looking back now all these years I'm sorry I didn't write, at least a couple of times, but being a teenager and with more soldiers moving into Wareham after we left, she probably soon got over it.

However, we didn't stay in Wareham long enough to get attached to anybody. After about a fortnight we were sent home on a ten-day embarkation leave, which meant we would soon be going abroad, though we weren't told where we would be going and when.

The Colonel-in-Chief of the Queen's Bays was the Queen (now the Queen Mother), and when we were back from leave she came to see us. We had lined up the tanks and stood beside them. One tank had some wooden steps at the side of it and the Queen climbed up and looked inside. She walked along in front of us, and then we made an informal circle around her. She gave a friendly, encouraging speech, and wished us luck now we were going abroad.

We spent three more weeks at Wareham, before we were moved by train to Southampton, then across the Channel to Cherbourg, where we arrived on 20 May 1940.

We new recruits were sent as spare crews, to replace anyone who might be killed or injured. At one time we met up with 'B' Squadron, and I saw Ronnie. He had been made squadron office clerk, and was driving a small truck set up like an office. That particular night we spent in a wood – and soon found it was swarming with mosquitoes. Next morning after a miserable night everybody was covered with itchy lumps.

We spent our time bumping about in the back of a lorry, sleeping in woods or fields. We never saw the tanks. From Cherbourg we had made our way east and were in the area of Abbeville and Amiens, and the tanks were fighting somewhere along the River Somme. Once I got into Rouen and saw the cathedral. We only had trickles of news. We lost some tanks and men – our Troop Leader, Lieutenant Aitken, who looked like a young boy, was killed. We thought we were advancing – even winning maybe, but we were in for a rude awakening.

One night we were sleeping in a barn near a small town on the outskirts of Le Mans. At about 4 a.m. we heard banging and shouting: 'Get up, get up! Get your kit together and get in a wagon!'

In the dark I hastily stuffed some belongings into my kitbag, climbed aboard a truck, and then we were off, heading west all day. We finally stopped in some fields outside the port of Brest on the north-west coast in the early evening. It suddenly struck me that, far from winning the war, we must be losing. The Germans had us on the run.

We stayed in the fields until dark, then drove down to the docks in Brest, where several boats were moored. We climbed out of the lorries, then the drivers took them to the docks, smashed the engines with sledge-hammers, and pushed them into the harbour. We assembled with relative calm on the dockside, ready to board the boats. Without warning, German planes zoomed low over our heads, strafing the whole area. Tracer bullets were flying everywhere. Everybody dived for cover. Some were bound to have been hit, but I was all in one piece.

'Get on any boat you can,' shouted someone.

I ran across the dock and scrambled on to the nearest boat, the *Lady of Mann*. All was quiet, and in the pitch dark we sailed for England.

4
Stuarts and Crusaders on Salisbury Plain

The *Lady of Mann* sailed into Plymouth in daylight on 20 June. On the dockside we were handed postcards to send to our families, to tell them we were safe and back in England. We then went by train to the village of Longbridge Deverill in Wiltshire on the edge of Salisbury Plain. We had no tanks, no trucks, no equipment – nothing except a few belongings we had managed to cram into our kitbags on the hurried departure from the French barn. We were under canvas, and after having been there about three days were sent home on leave for eleven days – kitbags and all.

I had to change trains in London during the Blitz. Bombs were falling, and sirens wailing. There was an unreal atmosphere – the whole City seemed to be on fire. The journey from Paddington Station to King's Cross was by necessity partly on the tube, then by bus. People were trying to sleep in the underground stations. Wooden structures had been erected, and the platforms were lined with bunk beds. Over the next few months I came through London a number of times. They were always traumatic, harrowing experiences – especially at night.

On the train home from London there was another soldier in the same carriage as myself.

'Bad thing about Dunkirk, wasn't it?' he said.

I had no idea what he was talking about, but I was obviously expected to know.

'Er – yes,' I mumbled.

I reached Huddersfield at last, then arrived home to great celebrations. My family had given me up for lost weeks ago. And it was then I learned why I was supposed to know about Dunkirk.

About three weeks before we left Brest, after the collapse of the French and Belgian armies, the British forces had to retreat, and the huge evacuation from Dunkirk had taken place. However, while all this was going on our Regiment was still fighting, and we had little idea of what was happening. Somebody must have suddenly realised we were still in France and organised the headlong flight to Brest, and back across the Channel. How we escaped capture, I don't know.

Our families thought that once everyone had been evacuated from Dunkirk, any other soldiers had either been killed or taken prisoner. They had no news of us until our postcards arrived from Plymouth, so to them it was something of a miracle to learn that we were in England.

Home for over a week! I immediately changed into civilian clothes. This was strictly against Army rules, but it was a relief to get out of my uniform – also to be wearing *shoes*. I went into town with some trepidation, because there were MPs about and if I had been stopped I could have been in trouble. Very few young men wore civilian clothes and ones dressed like this were regarded with some suspicion. However I escaped notice.

With my parents I went to Blackpool for a few days. In Stanley Park there were some young soldiers doing rifle drill. We stopped to watch them, and one turned to me and said: 'It's alright standing there watching – it'll be your turn soon.'

My leave was over all too soon and it was with a feeling of despair that I left home again to return to Longbridge Deverill to rejoin the Regiment. We were only there a few days before we were moved again, this time to be under canvas on the outskirts of nearby Warminster, still in Wiltshire.

Now we were issued with new kit and new tanks – still Crusaders and Stuarts, and it was back to training. This time instead of driving the tanks on the moors round Catterick we were driving on the plains round Warminster. There was little to choose between the two, they were equally uninteresting, and Warminster was about as exciting as Richmond. But at least it was summer now. We were often out in the tanks very early in the mornings, and would collect mushrooms, take them back to the cookhouse and the cook would fry them for us with bacon for breakfast – delicious!

Now there was more of an opportunity for men in No. 1 Troop to become better acquainted. I was quite friendly with Bob Buckland from Swindon and Harold Balson from Earlston in Scotland. Both had joined the Bays as regulars, and were in the Regiment before I arrived.

Ronnie and I only saw each other occasionally these days. He was firmly established in 'B' Squadron office, and was obviously doing a good job. One day he told me he was going home on leave – to marry Emily. I had a round baby-face, and Ronnie christened me 'The Cherub'. Emily and I wrote to each other regularly and she began starting her letters 'Dear Cherub'. I was also being called 'Jackie' and everyone soon knew me by this name, which stuck to me for the rest of my army career.

One day on Salisbury Plain tragedy struck. A burly rugby player named Page was riding on the outside of a Stuart. This was nothing unusual, we often did it as we drove and changed drivers. This time the tank was travelling pretty fast, hit a bump and Page was thrown forward into its path. It ran over him. The driver had stopped and poor Page lay on his back with the track of the tank across his stomach. I was in another tank nearby, saw the accident and with others ran to the scene. Page was still conscious.

'For God's sake get this off me,' he said. But before anyone could make a move he had died. We were all very shaken by this terrible accident.

Occasionally we went by truck to Aldershot, about fifty miles away, passing Stonehenge on the way there and back. At Aldershot, a building was set up with replicas of tank turrets at one end, and at the other end a miniature rolling countryside with little tanks moving about on it. There were small guns in the turrets. In the turret would be someone acting as tank commander, and a gunner. According to strict army instructions, the commander gave an order something like this: 'Traverse right, traverse right, traverse right. Stop. German tank on the horizon at approximately 1,000 yards. Fire!'

We then shot at the miniature tanks. Later when there was a real German tank in front with guns blazing, the translation of this was: 'Over on the right – can you see him, Jackie? Let him have it!'

At Aldershot they also had pistol and rifle ranges, where we practised. I was pretty good at the shooting, and my destiny was to be that of a gunner.

As we were in camp we daily watched the formations of bombers on their way to Germany – and the German planes on their bombing missions to England. At night we could hear them too, but no bombs were ever dropped near us.

One night there was a heavy air raid on the city of Bristol, and next day we were sent to help clear up. Bombs had fallen in an area of shops and offices. Now they were piles of rubble. We searched for any victims who might be trapped, but found no one, and we helped to load the debris into lorries to be taken away. Something there left a lasting impression on me. In the middle of the ruins the Salvation Army had set up a table and were handing out free cups of tea. It was heartening to see the determined spirit of everyone there. That incident endeared the Salvation Army to me for the rest of my life.

At the end of October we made a long train journey to Linney Head, about five miles from Pembroke in South Wales. We were billeted in an old house near the cliff tops. A cold wind blew straight into the draughty house from the sea, and most of the time it rained. It was a desolate spot and we spent a miserable week there, firing the bigger guns out to sea. We were glad to get back to our tents near Warminster, but soon after our return to camp we were on the move again. This time it was to Tilford near Farnham in Surrey.

5
1940–41: Tilford and Marlborough

Tilford had a village green and a cricket field, surrounded by big old trees, pleasant houses and a couple of public houses. An idyllic setting. We were billeted a mile or so from the village in a lovely area of big country homes, on the road in the direction of Hindhead. Only 'C' Squadron was at Tilford, the other squadrons being in other towns and villages in the area. Ronnie in 'B' Squadron was at Godalming.

There were no barracks here, neither were we under canvas. Some troops occupied empty houses, but our troop was in 'The Studio' behind the house, lived in by an old lady, a widow, Mrs Donald. Her husband had been an artist, and ours was the building where he used to paint. It was big enough to hold about twenty 'beds', a bed being a waterproof ground sheet with a palliasse (a big cotton bag, stuffed with straw) on top. There was the luxury of an old carpet and also a small stove in which we could burn wood in the winter. Somebody produced a dartboard. A step ran across the building – so it was two levels. It had just one drawback: no running water. Our water supply was a big barrel outside the door that collected rainwater. At the other side of the door was a table, so when we wanted a wash, we dipped a bowl in the barrel, then stood it on the table. In the winter this meant breaking the ice on top of the barrel, so a morning wash soon had you feeling fresh – or frozen! One morning Bob Buckland came in and said: 'Brrr . . . that was a good wash.' I pointed out that he still had a cigarette behind his ear.

About three hundred yards up the road was a very big house, Eden Lodge. It had once been the home of Philip Snowden, a prominent Labour MP of the 1920s. It was empty now, and the officers, sergeant major and sergeants lived there. On the extensive lawn at the back of the house marquees were erected and the cookhouse established. We could take a path through the Studio garden and then through a small wood to get to the cookhouse, so didn't need to walk along the road.

Next door to The Studio, going in the opposite direction, was another big house, The Grange. Major and Mrs Campbell lived here, and also Mrs Campbell's mother. Major Campbell, a Scotsman, was a retired officer, who had served in the Argyll and Sutherland Highlanders; a big man, bald on top with grey hair at the sides. He was a pleasant, though soldierly man. Mrs Campbell was a small correct lady with an almost regal bearing. She was also very kind and they had made the generous gesture of opening one of their rooms for the soldiers. This was an extremely big room with a fireplace at each end, a table-tennis table in the middle, a grand piano, numerous writing tables and chairs, and easy chairs. There was also a radio. In fact after the places we had been for the last year, this really was luxury. Besides a gardener they employed two maids and a cook. The older maid was Marian, aged about fifty, the younger one Audrey, aged eighteen, and Louie was the cook. The two maids lived at The Grange, but Audrey's home was only three-quarters of a mile away, so she would go there on her time off and help her father with his milk round.

We only had to step over a very small wire fence to be in the adjoining grounds of The Grange, then into the house. Soon I was spending most of my evenings there. There was a warm, comfortable atmosphere, ideal for letter writing. Every evening about 9 p.m. Audrey and Marian brought a tray into the room with cups and saucers, tea and biscuits.

The grounds of The Grange stretched a long way back from the house, and in part of them chickens were kept. It was Audrey's job to go and see that they were all in the coops and locked up for the night. I felt that she might need some help and protection in doing this, so I offered my services. They were accepted, and we regularly spent pleasant evenings locking up the chickens. She had a boy-friend, George, who was in the Army. I enjoyed her company and occasionally we went to the pictures together. She and her brother both had bicycles, and he would lend me his, and she and I in the nice weather sometimes went for rides. When we left Tilford, Audrey and I wrote to each other – and now, fifty-four years later, we still do, at Christmas and birthdays. Audrey married George, and they have visited me and my wife, staying at our house, and we have also spent some time with them at their home near Hindhead. I got on well with Marian too, and after a while began helping with the tea and biscuits, and then with the washing up.

I also enjoyed Mrs Campbell's company. Sometimes she invited me to go into one of the lounges, and there we'd sit and talk. She was a member of the Oxford Group, a rather sophisticated society something like Toc H. They were a charitable group and Mrs Campbell certainly lived up to this image with the hospitality she showed us. A member of the group was the writer Daphne Du Maurier; she and the Campbells were friends, and she had stayed at The Grange a number of times.

A few new recruits joined our troop here, among them Jack Emery from Birmingham and Bob Weightman from London. Both agreeable, friendly young men.

Mrs Campbell also extended her generosity to the families of Bob and myself. She invited my sister Jessie, who was seventeen at the time, to stay at The Grange for a week, and also Bob's wife, Len.

Not all the boys went to The Grange at nights. There were the ones who liked to drink – and most of their evenings were spent at the Barley Mow.

We were given a week's leave approximately once every three months, so I had a couple of leaves from Tilford – each time encountering the London Blitz.

If soldiers arrived in Huddersfield late at night, it was only a short walk from the station to the YMCA. There, staying up all night, were members of Toc H, waiting with their cars to give anyone a lift home. This service was greatly appreciated by me more than once.

I was disappointed not to get leave at Christmas, but Mrs Campbell put on a Christmas party at The Grange. The table-tennis table was put away. We had a buffet tea and then in the evening sang carols and played games – postman's knock was out of the question, but charades and one or two similar games we enjoyed. One member of our squadron was called Reg Boler. He was a brilliant pianist, and before the war had played the piano in Jack Jackson's band. When he came into the room, if the wireless was on he'd sit at the piano and join in, no matter what tune was being played or in what key.

Farnham itself was a pleasant town, with two cinemas and several good shops. One Saturday afternoon I was in one of the cinemas when a message was flashed on the screen ordering all soldiers to return immediately to their regiments. I hurried out, as did others, stopped a civilian car, which we were allowed to do, and told the driver to take me to our squadron. We assembled in the main road, certain that the Germans were about to invade. However, after a short while the panic was off and we were dismissed. We never knew if there had been an attempted invasion or not.

Our social activities came at nights and weekends unless we were on guard duty, or some other duty, but they were a most welcome change after Richmond and Warminster. There were dances in the village hall at Beacon Hill near Hindhead most Friday nights. They were well attended, plenty of girls there – and naturally Audrey used to go too.

Work was still to do – training, PT, driving the tanks, no longer on Catterick Moors, or Salisbury Plain, but Frensham Common. We made occasional trips again to Aldershot firing on the ranges there.

I had once volunteered to play rugby at Catterick. I played one game and that was enough for me – far too rough. But I enjoyed soccer. As part of our PT we picked troop football teams to play each other. I was in our troop team. I was no Stanley Matthews, but with only twenty men to choose from, they had to pick somebody.

Our landlady, Mrs Donald, had a sister who used to come and visit her every Friday, and they invited two of our troop to have tea with them. It was always sardine sandwiches. They were very nice ladies and pleasant to talk to, but some of the boys *hated* to go, especially the Barley Mow fraternity. However, so as not to hurt Mrs Donald's feelings, we drew up a rota of who should spend an hour or two with them on Fridays. I personally didn't mind even if the sardine sandwiches did get a bit monotonous. I liked both the old ladies, so sometimes I would do someone else a favour by going in his place. Whether Mrs Donald noticed I was a rather more regular visitor than some of the others, I don't know. I didn't however care for their big, old, ugly bulldog. It was perfectly harmless, but the sight of it waddling and slobbering about was a bit off-putting when eating sardine sandwiches. We would have these get-togethers in their very pleasant front garden if the weather was nice, otherwise we had them inside. When *Dad's Army* came on television, whenever I saw Private Godfrey and his sister Dolly, both quite old people, Mrs Donald and her sister inevitably came to mind.

The time spent at Tilford was pleasant but the pangs of home-sickness came with regularity, and most nights I wrote home, as did some of the other boys like Ted Ryan and Bob Weightman.

We were at Tilford until 2 June 1941. The evening we left was a sad and tearful occasion. We all paraded in the middle of the main road, then climbed into lorries, to the goodbyes and kisses of many of our friends who had turned out to see us leave. Many of us had a genuine feeling of sadness as we made for our next destination – to Marlborough, back in Wiltshire. Not a studio as a billet, but this time a racehorse stable. There are a lot of such stables around Marlborough. They had taken the horses out of this one, and in the stalls had made bunk beds. Our palliasses went with us.

Marlborough has an unusually wide main road, with shops on either side, and at one end the Town Hall. When on guard duty we were taken by truck into the town where we paraded in front of the Town Hall, and with plenty of noise and ceremony were fallen in by the sergeant of the guard, and then inspected by the orderly officer. So far as we could see, this was just a bit of show for the benefit of the local people. There was nothing to guard in Marlborough, so after the parade we were fallen out, climbed back into the truck, and were taken back to our stables, where we proceeded to spend the night guarding them.

The whole Regiment was soon billeted around Marlborough; biding time prior to being sent abroad. The Green Dragon became a popular alternative to Tilford's Barley Mow, and no doubt the beer sales shot up when the Bays arrived. We were driving, shooting and doing almost anything to keep us occupied. Once we were taking some bricks from one place to another. Someone threw one out of the wagon and it hit me on top of the head. There was a fair bit of blood. A man called George Mobley was ordered to take me to the doctor's nearby. It was decided I'd have to have some stitches in my head. I sat down, the doctor started to stitch – and George fainted!

The Regiment got a cricket team together to play a team from Marlborough College. Ronnie and Harold Balson were selected to play. I volunteered to be scorer. We played just two or three matches but they were very enjoyable occasions.

Mrs Campbell asked me to keep in touch with her and I did so for many years until she died in the 1970s. She wrote regularly and it was always a pleasure to get her letters. While we were at Marlborough she wrote and invited me to spend a weekend at The Grange. A weekend pass wasn't difficult to get, so I accepted her offer and had a very agreeable time back at Tilford.

In July came the ominous news that we were to be sent on

embarkation leave. Another much appreciated week at home, but this time there was the feeling when, and even if, I would see home again. With very heavy hearts my family and I said goodbye to each other.

Back to Marlborough, guarding the stables, doing menial work, and then on 23 September 1941 the anticipated move. 'Killer' Wyatt and Ned Reeves wrote a song. I can only remember a few verses, and the first went like this:

'Twas on a Sunday morning
　　We took that long train ride.
We ended up at Gourock,
　　To board the *Empire Pride*.

6

The Empire Pride

It was a long train ride from Marlborough to Gourock in Scotland. When we arrived, we saw anchored out on the River Clyde what was to be our home for the next nine weeks – the *Empire Pride*, a new ship, especially built as a troopship. It was too big to sail up to the dockside, so we were ferried out to it on small tenders.

This was to be the ship's maiden voyage. After a couple of days at anchor, we sailed out to sea in the morning and came back later in the day. It wasn't explained to us why, we assumed it was perhaps a trial run. We went a few miles out, the sea was quite choppy and the ship tended to roll a bit, but nothing compared to what was to come. We came back and anchored once more in the river, then on 30 September 1941 we sailed in earnest – having already been on board a week. It was 9.15 p.m., and a lovely moonlit night. The Bays had a band (they were in 'HQ' Squadron), and as we sailed down the Clyde everyone was up on deck, the band played, and we sang 'Abide with Me', 'There'll Always Be an England', 'Just a Song at Twilight', 'Land of Hope and Glory' and other songs.

The accommodation on the *Empire Pride* could hardly be described as first class, or even third class for that matter. Where we lived and ate below decks was also where we slept at night.

We were all issued with hammocks, and what a performance it was getting into them. There were hooks in the ceiling on which to sling them, but there were more hammocks than hooks, so some men slept on their hammocks stretched out on the floor, while others made their beds on the tables. Each table, with a form down either side, seated ten men or so. One end of the table was up against the side of the ship, so the men sitting at the other end went to collect the food on trays for the whole table. We took turns on this duty. The food, at least at first, wasn't too bad, but the lack of variety after a while tended to make it pretty monotonous. For one thing we got tired of fish, fish and more fish.

Then – we were out into the Atlantic. Apparently we went about two thirds the way west across the ocean before turning south, in an effort to avoid submarines. We were in a convoy (it was said there were thirty-seven ships) and we had an escort of destroyers patrolling between and around the convoy, on the lookout for submarines. We regularly heard depth charges being dropped; sometimes they were near enough to make our ship vibrate.

Well out into the Atlantic, and the weather was terrible. The second verse of the song went:

> After we'd been sailing
>> Some twenty hours or more,
> The ship she started rolling,
>> And the boys were sick and sore.

The first week or so, many of the men were sick because of this very rough weather. Though I got headaches – and sometimes felt a bit off colour – I was never seasick, but poor Ronnie was never anything else. Whenever I wanted to find him, I knew where to look – in the toilets! One day I found him, a pale green in colour, and he said all he wanted to do was to die. He meant it too, because he felt he just couldn't survive any longer in these conditions. But survive he did.

There was always plenty of food, because, especially the first couple of weeks, hardly anyone wanted to eat. No words can describe the misery and discomfort. To make matters worse, because of the crowded conditions it began to get very hot downstairs. One day I went on deck to get some fresh air. There was plenty of that. The wind was howling through the rigging. The ship bounced like a cork, and the waves were coming right over the top.

The weather deteriorated to such an extent that we weren't allowed up on deck and the conditions were getting unbearable. So much so that there was almost a mutiny. Suddenly one evening everybody started to 'moo' and 'baa' like animals. The noise and shouting got louder and a group of senior officers came down the steps and made a great effort to calm things down. The ship was built to carry 1,600 troops – but there were about 3,000 on board. After some efforts at cajoling and also threats of the consequences if this didn't stop, we calmed down, but it was an uneasy peace.

Fortunately I had found a place to sling my hammock, and after a few nights of wrestling with it and occasionally falling out onto someone sleeping on the table below, I began to get the knack of it, and slept – but it wasn't a very comfortable sleep. It was entertaining to lie in one's hammock and watch all the others swing in unison one way and then the other as the ship rolled.

During the rough weather very little work of any kind was done – in fact few people were capable of doing anything, except the ship's crew. The officers were English, but the ordinary crew were Lascars (Indian seamen) and they amazed us with their agility, climbing up the ship's ropes as nimble as monkeys.

We did however have to do guard duty both night and day. Sometimes the duty would be inside the ship – fire duty, and you were given a certain area to patrol. Up on deck you could be on submarine watch – on the look-out for submarines or periscopes. It was an eerie feeling, walking the deck in the dark, with the thought that submarines could be lurking down below.

We turned south and east, and the weather calmed down. One of the ships had developed engine trouble, so the whole convoy slowed down to its pace. We found ourselves sailing to Freetown, the capital of Sierra Leone, on the African coast. The third verse of the song, which unfortunately is the last one I can remember, went:

> Our first port of calling,
> Not a ripple nor a wave.
> The heat it was terrific,
> And they called it 'White Man's Grave'.

The heat *was* terrific. Ronnie had emerged from the toilets and one night we stood on deck dressed only in shorts, and saw an electric storm over the shore. We'd never seen anything like it. Thunder roared, and vivid sheet lightning lit up the whole of the countryside. It was an amazing spectacle, one we would never forget. We felt lucky it didn't reach our ship.

From the ship the hills of Sierra Leone appeared to be completely covered with tropical growth. It was steaming hot, and below decks it was extremely uncomfortable, especially at night. During the day dozens of the local population came out in small boats, some of them laden with fruit which we weren't allowed to buy. Also they shouted for money and when we threw coins they would dive overboard for them. One man who called himself Charlie came out in a boat, wearing a bowler hat and tie and sang songs like 'South of the Border' and 'Lambeth Walk.' So we had quite a bit of entertainment, and in fact our Regimental Band got out their instruments and entertained us too.

Before we left Freetown some officers from the squadron went ashore and bought fresh fruit, so we had quite a treat when this was shared out.

We were in Freetown harbour for five days. When we left on 19 October, the sea was very calm and a beautiful blue. We saw lots of flying fish and schools of porpoises, and life began to get more bearable. We did have some rougher weather from time to time, but it was never as rough again as it had been that first week or so.

Three days after leaving Freetown we crossed the Equator. The weather had been unbearably hot, but rather disappointingly this particular day it was dull, cool, and wet. There was a 'Crossing the Line' ceremony where one of the officers had his face lavishly covered with 'shaving soap', was shaved with a huge cutthroat 'razor', then dumped in a tub of water.

As we went further south and into the open sea the weather was colder and we hit the waves again. We passed Ascension Island, and the next day on the horizon saw the island of St Helena.

Now we were able to 'work'. We had PT – not easy on a bouncing deck; there were also lectures and discussions. From time to time there would be a quiz, sometimes on army life (guns and tanks, even out at sea) and sometimes general knowledge. Funny how some little things stick in your mind. I was on a team once and was asked: 'Who was the Greek philosopher who lived in a barrel?'

There was a ripple of surprise when I knew the answer: 'Diogenes.'

I felt quite pleased with myself!

At nights we would write letters – to be posted sometime, somewhere, and play cards. A game of nine card brag in which I was playing comes to mind. There was a big kitty. Ned Reeves said in as steady a voice as possible:

'Four sevens.'

He laid them on the table and started to rake in the money when another quiet controlled voice came from Paddy Flanagan:

'Hold on.'

And he dramatically laid down four eights. We couldn't believe it – least of all poor Reeves.

[39]

Of course with nine card brag the maximum school you could have was five players. Three card brag was popular because more people could be in the school. So every night below decks it was like a miniature Las Vegas. You're not supposed to play for money in the Army, but that was a rule never enforced. Some men from another regiment produced a roulette wheel and a crown and anchor board, – actually a canvas sheet painted green, divided into six squares with a heart, diamond, club and spade in the corner squares and a crown and anchor on the middle squares. The men running the game shook two dice. On the six sides of the dice were not numbers, but heart, club, diamond, spade, crown, and anchor. Bets were placed on the squares, and odds given accordingly. For myself, I enjoyed playing cards, but it was always with people I knew. Crown and anchor and roulette are not good games to play with strangers.

We knew we were heading for South Africa. On 30 October we sighted land. After rounding the Cape of Good Hope the convoy split in two: one half went on to Durban, our half went to Cape Town. After five weeks on the *Empire Pride* – shore leave. Heaven! We were all a little unsteady on our feet – it took some time to adjust to walking on dry land, and we probably rolled when we walked, like sailors. Also, for five weeks we had been made to wear pumps. Now it was back to boots, and this didn't help at first. But, we were on land, and this was a blessing.

Once on shore, we found the good people of Cape Town waiting to greet us, sitting at tables just two or three hundred yards from the docks. Soldiers were standing in a queue and as their turn came they were taken off to be entertained.

Ronnie and I had vowed that the first thing we would do when we got ashore was to find a restaurant and have a good meal. So, anxious to put our vow into practice, we gave the queue a miss and found the Waldorf Restaurant and had eggs (two each!), chips, peas, bread and butter and tea – and strawberries and cream for dessert. Afterwards we walked about, looked around the shops, and then went to the cinema to see Leslie Howard in *Pimpernel Smith*. We felt great. There was no blackout in Cape Town, so in the evening the lights were a sight to enjoy.

At night it was back to the ship. We were given no indication, for obvious reasons, as to when we would be sailing, but next morning we were still there, so Ronnie and I joined the queue to the tables. It was our good fortune to be the guests of two middle-aged sisters, the Misses Store, who turned out to be marvellous people. That day they took us to a coastal town called Muisenberg a few miles away. There was a long white sandy beach, the sea was blue, the weather was warm and sunny, and we had a wonderful day with them. They took us back to the ship in the evening with the promise that they would look out for us next day. We certainly wanted them to – what we didn't want was the ship to sail in the night. It didn't, and true to their promise they met us next morning. This time they drove us up Table Mountain. When we got as far as we could drive, we could have ridden the cable car to the very top, but unfortunately the top was covered with a cloud – 'the tablecloth' they called it. We were still high up on the mountain however, and the view from there of the city, the wide expanse of Table Bay, and the ships, was out of this world. Once again we had a marvellous day with them, then back to the ship and a promise to see us tomorrow. On board the talk from everyone was the same – of the fantastic hospitality being shown by these South African people.

The next day we met the ladies again. They took us for a drive, then to their lovely home, with a beautiful garden filled with an abundance of flowers. They fed us like kings. That was the first time I had ever tasted passion fruit. We also had a bath – in a proper bathroom, a real luxury.

Back to the ship at night with a promise to meet tomorrow. We had been there four days – but tomorrow never came. In the early hours of the morning we heard the ship's engines start to throb, and we were on the move. One of the sisters, Miss Gladys Store, wrote home to my parents. She and I continued to write to each other for many years, until one day in the early 1970s I received a letter from someone in Cape Town to say that she had died. She and her sister were wonderful ladies. The way they took care of us those few days in Cape Town could never be forgotten.

We sailed up the east coast of Africa and were joined by the rest of the convoy from Durban. For two days we had an albatross following the ship. One day the *Repulse*, a battleship which had been part of our escort, sailed slowly up and down between the ships of the convoy and very close to them. The sailors lined the decks and waved to us. We all waved back and cheered. It was a very emotional occasion. The *Repulse* sailed east, and a short time later we learned she had been sunk in the battle for the defence of Singapore.

The weather began to get warm – then *hot*, so hot that for several nights, the sea being calm, many of the men, including Ronnie and myself, slept up on deck.

Sight of land again, and this time it was the port of Aden (then a British possession) at the southern end of the Red Sea. We stayed in the port (not allowed on shore) for a couple of days, and then the *Empire Pride* sailed up the Red Sea. The sunsets were beautiful, and at times we could see colourful, but barren, land on both sides.

On 25 November 1941 we docked at Suez, the southern end of the Suez Canal. Except for the four days in Cape Town we had been on board the *Empire Pride* for nine weeks. Now we had to get used to dry land again.

7
1941–42: Desert Encounters

By the time we had disembarked at Suez it was early evening. The weather was cold. We were back to wearing boots and had to walk (it could hardly be called a march) about a mile to a temporary camp, where we were allocated to small round tents. There were ten of us in our tent, with just enough room for us all to stretch in a circle on the floor with a couple of blankets each.

We had each carried our own kit and the first thing we did was to get out our mess-tins. We then lined up where an Arab was ladling out stew from a huge stew-pot. Our two mess-tins (the smaller one fitted upside down in the other, and the handles folded neatly over so that when packed they looked something like a box) were to prove invaluable; we ate and drank from them for years.

That first night on Egyptian soil was not one to write home about. We were cold, uncomfortable and dusty – but at least the stew was hot. Next morning we went by train, our 'carriages' being cattle trucks, to Amariya not far from Alexandria.

Our tanks and trucks had not travelled with us on the *Empire Pride*. Some of the drivers went to the docks to collect them and we were under canvas in that area for a couple of weeks or so. It was terribly sandy and dusty, and one night there was a terrific sandstorm that brought down one of the tents. If there was a good point, it was the lemonade they sold in one of the big marquees. I drank gallons of it.

Once the tanks arrived, it was necessary to give them a good 'going over'. My job, as with the other gunners, was to make sure the guns were cleaned and in good working order. We went out in the country and fired on a range. Off duty, being only a few miles from Alexandria, Ronnie and I got into the town a couple of times. There was very little going on; we looked around and went to the cinema. Lorries were laid on to take us into town and then pick us up at a certain point and time at night.

Eventually, we loaded our tanks onto a train, which took us to

Mersa Matruh, about 200 miles west of Alexandria, and about 150 miles east of the Libyan border, where we joined up with the rest of the Regiment. When the Regiment was together like this, a cook-house was set up, which moved about with the administrative element of the squadron – the squadron office, the trucks used to carry supplies, the water wagon, the fitters, spare crews and the rest of the non-fighting personnel.

Once we moved away with the tanks, we were on our own, and sometimes wouldn't see the cookhouse for weeks or months. We had to make our own meals. The tanks looked like travelling hardware shops, with tin cans and a frying pan hanging from the rear. To make tea we half filled a can with sand, poured on petrol, then placed another can holding water on top. A lighted match dropped on the petrol gave a good fire. A wooden matchstick dropped in the water helped to stop it from tasting smoky. When the water boiled, in went the tea, and we had 'brewed up'. All the pots and pans were black with fumes from the fire.

Most days we were up at 5 a.m. and out on schemes – these were manoeuvres in the desert, getting used to the conditions under which we were to live and fight. Sometimes we would cover sixty or seventy miles and stay away from the base one or two nights. Usually different squadrons (fifteen tanks each) were on a scheme of their own, but sometimes it might be the whole Regiment.

We spent Christmas in this area and had a couple of days off. There was very little to celebrate, though the Queen did send us all a packet of Player's cigarettes, something of a luxury. At night, when we bedded down at the sides of the tanks, Christmas carols could be heard coming from some of the other tanks. We joined in the singing too. On Boxing Day we were given a bottle of beer each.

We endured a few sandstorms here. The wind whipped up the stinging sand, sometimes reducing visibility to only two or three yards. All we could do then was to lie low and wait for the storm to pass. Needless to say the food was pretty gritty. There was no escape from the sand – in food, hair, bed; it is a constant memory of that whole campaign.

Although the Regiment was together, the squadrons were around three-quarters of a mile apart, but as the area was pretty flat they could all be seen from any one point. So I hadn't anticipated any problem when I decided one afternoon to walk over to 'B' Squadron to see Ronnie who was at the Squadron Office. We talked for a while and then, as it was almost dark, I thought I should be getting back. There were no lights of course, but I knew in which direction 'C' Squadron would be. The moon was up (not a full moon) and it was just a case of walking in a straight line, with the moon over my left shoulder.

I walked . . . and walked . . . and walked. I began to get a sinking feeling. This was much further than I had walked in the afternoon. I must have walked past the top end of the Squadron, so, if I turned round in a half circle, walked back the way I had come, only to the left as well, I should hit the Squadron. With hope in my heart I set off again. I walked and walked, and then the realisation began to dawn on me that I was hopelessly lost. I stood still. There was no sound, except the wind blowing sand through the bits of scrubby vegetation. I had no idea which way to turn, so I decided the only thing to do was to lie down and wait for the daylight – I should see *something* then. I found a hollow in the sand, with a bit of scrub on top of the little ridge, and lay there for a while. There was no light now from the moon, the wind blew, and it was cold. I had no idea of the time, but I knew it was still long before dawn. 'I'll freeze to death if I stay here all night,' I thought, so I decided to have another try. I took a guess at the direction in which to go, and set off again.

By this time I was tired. I'd heard of people being lost in the desert and walking round in circles. Was this happening to me? Every few yards I bent down to see if I could see any tanks on the skyline; it was light enough for that if I was near enough. For what seemed like ages, I walked and stooped and walked and stooped again, and again and again. Then at last, to my great relief, I saw the silhouette of a tank. I walked straight towards it – and was challenged by a guard. I didn't recognise the man. Was this 'C' Squadron? No, this was 'A' Squadron. He pointed out where 'C' Squadron was.

'Just go in a straight line.'

Another straight line, but this time I got it right. I saw more tanks on the skyline, and soon I was challenged again by a guard. This time I knew the voice and the face, an Irishman, Paddy Collins. I never thought I'd be so glad to see Paddy Collins. He knew me of course, and asked why I was walking about in the middle of the night. I cut my long story short, found our tank and gratefully crept between the blankets. It was 2.30 a.m.

There had been little fighting in North Africa until 1941. The enemy troops were Italians, and there were skirmishes with them from time to time, but the Italians had little heart for fighting. When the Germans began to send troops, however, and with the arrival of General Rommel in February, the fighting started in earnest. From April onwards there were numerous encounters, especially between Tobruk and Sidi Barrani, these culminating in a tremendous battle at Sidi Rezegh in November.

Soon after Christmas the tank units left the rest of the Regiment and headed west, travelling around sixty to seventy miles a day. We crossed the border into Libya and headed for an area south of Benghazi, in the region of Agedabia and El Agheila, about another 350 miles west of the border, where the fighting was taking place.

Once in the desert we had to get our bearings with the aid of a compass. Except for the coastal towns and a few scattered towns south of the coast, there was nothing marked on the map, simply because there was nothing there – except in some cases trig points, places marked with either oil drums or piles of stones. Many times a meeting point was just a map reference, in the middle of nowhere. Back at Catterick Camp, which now seemed years away, map-reading had been one of the things we had to learn – and now we realised how essential that training was. To take a bearing with a compass it was necessary to walk at least twenty yards away from the tank, because the metal of the tank could play tricks with the compass needle.

Into January 1942, and we were still moving west. I was in a Crusader and our tank commander SSM 'Beefy' Webb was replaced by Captain Patchett, second-in-command of the squadron. We were glad to have him as commander, as he brought food with him from the officers' mess, including tinned fruit, sauce, rice – and some whisky. The rest of the crew besides myself were Dick Rowney, the wireless operator, and Jack Emery, the driver, one of the young men who had joined us at Tilford (he inherited the name 'Jim' as there was a character on the wireless called Jim Emery). Sometimes crews were switched around, but Jim, Dick and I were in the same tank for a long time, though when Captain Patchett took over our tank he brought his own wireless operator, Les Haycroft, and Dick was moved to another tank.

To quote from my diary of 4 January 1942:

[46]

Up at 5.30 a.m. and did 81 miles. When we set off we were 30 miles south of Tobruk – moved west. Terribly bad going in places. Some places very stony others very soft sand. Writing this in semi-darkness in bivvy. Got on fine with Captain Patchett.

5 January: Up at 5 a.m. moved straight on and stopped from 7.30 a.m. to 8 a.m. for breakfast. No other halt till 5.45 p.m. Should have done 85 miles today but held up by a big minefield and only did about 55 to 60 miles. Went 20 miles through minefield in single file. Terribly dusty, everything thick with dust. Bitterly cold. Light meal. Cocoa and tinned fruit.

Our Royal Engineers had cleared a track through the minefield, but it was still hazardous going. Always on the move by dawn, we would sometimes stop a day or so in one place, but then it was off again. At night it was always someone's turn to do guard duty. We were on duty in pairs, and one night when Bob Buckland and I were on guard together, we were leaning against a tank, then set off walking. We were engrossed in talking about what we would do when we got back home, when we realised to our amazement that the tank in front of us was the one we'd been leaning against before we started walking. We had walked round in a circle without realising it.

One day we came across an Arab with a herd of sheep, and Captain Patchett bought one from him for £1. The Arab turned the sheep over on its back, cut its throat, and put it on our tank. At night Corporal 'Ginger' Hopkins, who had been a butcher, skinned and cut it up, and it was shared out. I refused my share, preferring to continue living on tinned sausages and rice. Another day we saw several Arabs with a herd of about forty camels, but most of the time we saw only sand, stones and scrub.

After a while we halted and stayed in the same place for over a week. My diary notes on 12 January 1942: 'Had first wash and shave for six days. Oh what a shave!! Still it felt grand after – washed hair too.' It had rained heavily and we had dug a little reservoir. Although it dried up by the next day, it gave us some very welcome water, both for drinking and washing.

Usually when we were on the move, and always when in action, we went into close leaguer at night. If we were fighting, we would pull back about four miles from the front line. Close leaguer meant all the tanks forming a square, close together. Then we'd replenish our supplies from wagons bringing ammunition and petrol, rations and water. We were allowed four pints of water each a day, so would fill our water cans from taps on the wagon.

On 22 January we close leaguered about ten miles from the enemy, and the next day we were to see our first action against the Germans. My diary for that day says: 'Set off from close leaguer at 6.30 a.m. No time for breakfast. Searched round for enemy all day, then towards evening saw him disappearing over a ridge in front of us. We were shelled, and the Squadron Leader's tank was hit. We picked up the crew who had bailed out, and withdrew.'

The following day we were in action again, and this time took the initiative and succeeded in pushing the Germans back. We took some prisoners too – they were taken care of by the infantry who were always with us. All the different infantry units who fought alongside us were, without exception, good fighters. On this occasion it was the 4th Indian Division. The infantrymen always said they would much rather be out on the ground than in a tank; we in the tanks felt the opposite. We also had the support of the artillery, who often fired their shells over the top of us.

For two or three days we were in and out of some sporadic fighting. We tank crews rarely knew what the plans were. We would move towards the Germans, engage them, perhaps knock out anti-tank guns, or machine-gun troops and lorries. Then our tank was hit.

When your tank is hit you have two options: one is to sit tight, the other to bale out. Both are dangerous. The tank is liable to catch fire and, with all the petrol and ammunition on board, could blow up. To bale out is to risk being machine-gunned, something the Germans often did. We didn't stop to think. We baled out, ran and dived behind a small ridge, held our breath and laid low. Captain Patchett had run in a different direction and we didn't see him. We waited a while, the Germans withdrew, so Jim, Les and I decided to go back and see if we could find the tank. When we found it, a tank from No. 2 Troop, commanded by Corporal Freddie Minks, was towing it. It wasn't badly damaged and Jim did some work on the engine and got it started. So next day we went into action again – and were involved in a terrific battle, our heaviest fighting yet. Things were going well. We had come across some vehicles and infantry a few hundred yards away, and were shelling and pouring machine-gun fire into them. We really sorted them out and had their soldiers frantically running in every direction, but then German Mark 4 tanks turned up. Our tanks were no match for them: their armour was thicker and they had bigger guns with a much longer range than ours. We returned their fire but with our 37 mm and two-pounders we just couldn't reach them. We tried to hold our ground but it was an impossible task and as the light began to fade we were forced to withdraw.

We suffered our first casualties here. When we pulled back, our tank stopped beside Freddie Minks's Stuart. Freddie had been killed. His crew got him out of the tank, and he was a sickening sight. Most of his head had been blown away. We wrapped him in a blanket, dug a grave and buried him. Captain Tatham-Warter read a short service over the grave. Another man called Young had also been killed when another Stuart was hit.

We were all required to wear a cord around our necks. On it were two hard Bakelite identification tags, one green and one red. If a man was killed, one of the tags was left with his body, and the other returned to the regimental base, citing where the man was buried. In the case of Freddie, this was taken care of by Captain Tatham-Warter, who was later himself killed at the Battle of El Alamein. One department of the Army took care of graves, and it was their un-enviable task to exhume bodies and give them a proper burial in army cemeteries. We marked Freddie's grave with a pile of stones. I wonder if it was ever found.

After we buried Freddie we kept moving until 4 a.m., and then were up again at 6.30 a.m. Unfortunately our tank had developed a radiator leak, and it was decided that we couldn't continue fighting. Jim and I took it back to the Ordnance Corps about fifteen miles away. When we arrived they examined it and found they couldn't do the job so we would have to take it to another RAOC depot twenty-five miles away. We loaded it on to a tank transporter and arrived there in the late evening. Jim and I slept in the tank on the transporter. The fitters inspected the tank and decided we had better take it to the main depot at Tobruk. So next day, still on the transporter, we travelled another sixty or seventy miles before stopping for the night. On the way we counted about twenty wrecked aeroplanes on the ground and hundreds of wrecked Italian wagons. Nine of the planes were definitely German, the others we couldn't identify.

Although during the fighting we had seen a considerable amount of aircraft activity, we had never been attacked ourselves. We saw many more German planes than our own – our aircraft support was very limited, though the pilots were very brave when overwhelmingly outnumbered. We saw a few dogfights and would raise a cheer if one of our Spitfires or Hurricanes brought down a German. We had machine-guns mounted on top of the tanks, and when we weren't moving one of us was always on ack-ack duty.

We arrived at Tobruk the next day and unloaded the tank straight away. There had already been a lot of fighting in and around Tobruk, and many of the buildings were in ruins. There was a YMCA there, but unfortunately we didn't have any money as we hadn't been paid for a long time. They did however give free cups of tea, so we took advantage of this offer – while looking rather wistfully at the sweets and biscuits which were on sale. We had rations on the tank, of course, but it would have been nice to have had a bit of a treat. Jim and I found an empty house and bedded down there for the night. Next day we went and had our free cup of tea again at the 'YM' and I noted in my diary: 'Won't we be glad when we get some pay, then we can buy some chocolate.' I also needed some money to buy stamps so that I could post some letters I had written.

Two days later we were still in Tobruk, and going into the 'YM' I was amazed to meet Joe Gagen, a young man who went to Hillhouse Central School when I did. He and his pal gave me sixty cigarettes and two stamps, so I could at least post two letters. He also gave me an old *Huddersfield Examiner* which I eagerly read. After five days in Tobruk we were informed that our tank was beyond repair, and they were giving us another one. To our dismay it was a Stuart. After the Crusader it was like moving from a Rolls-Royce to a Tin Lizzie. Of course we had no choice, so we transferred our kit and made our way back on a transporter to the Regiment. We had become really attached to our Crusader and were very sorry to lose it – especially for a Stuart.

We arrived back with the Regiment late the same day, only to discover that Captain Patchett and his whole crew were missing. We heard later that one of them had been killed and the others taken prisoner. Other news was that Dick Rowney, who had pulled his badly wounded commander out of his tank to safety, had been awarded the Military Medal, the first MM to be awarded to our Regiment in North Africa. We were also paid at last.

There had been other casualties, but now the Regiment had regrouped, we were soon in action again. We had a new tank commander, Lieutenant 'Joe' Radice, whom we didn't take to as we had done to Captain Patchett, and Dick Rowney was now back in our tank as wireless operator, with Jim and myself. We engaged German troops, tanks and vehicles, but with our 37 mm gun on the Stuart, we may as well have been attacking them with a peashooter. Then the fighting died down. The weather was warming up and our worst enemies now were the flies. They nearly drove us mad.

One thing we looked forward to was the arrival of a truck bringing the mail. Sometimes we'd go a week or two without mail and then get letters in batches. I was lucky that my mother and sister wrote almost daily, and Emily, Audrey and so many other people. It was marvellous to get all these letters.

On 6 March 1942 we were delighted to hear that we were now going to change the Stuarts in the squadron for Crusaders. They arrived the next day, and we were thankful to see the last of our Stuart. Our Crusader had done just under 400 miles, and on the side had the name 'Cagney' painted in large letters.

With the Regiment pulled back, our squadron found ourselves positioned on the top of an escarpment, where we were to stay for well over two months. We did our best to make things as comfortable as possible in the conditions. During the day the tanks could get too hot to touch, but at night it was cold.

On the ridge where we were the ground was solid, though sand blew about incessantly. Our tank crew dug a hole about four feet deep and nine feet long, with a sloping entrance at one end. In the walls we dug out squares to act as shelves and over the top we stretched a tarpaulin and put heavy stones on it all the way round to anchor it to the ground. It took a few days to make, but when finished it served as a shelter, and also a kitchen with shelves on which to keep our food.

A wagon came every few days bringing supplies from the base many miles away. The food was mainly tinned corned beef (bully beef) and tins of 'M & V' (meat and vegetables). We had a treat from time to time when we were issued with tins of bacon, sausages, potatoes and rice pudding. Besides our brewing-up tins we had a small, very well made stove. It consisted of a small cylinder which we filled with petrol, then pumped to compress it; we could then turn on and light a jet. Somehow I became cook on our tank. It being a Crusader there were four of us, but later on a Grant, where the crew was six men, and later still on a Sherman, with a crew of five, I always held this exalted position – probably because no one else wanted it, though from time to time I was congratulated on the concoctions I used to dream up with mixtures of our basic rations.

We had not seen bread for about three months. Instead we had packets of biscuits, very much like dog biscuits, extremely hard, and wearing on the gums. One day there was great excitement: the ration wagon had located a bakery in Tobruk and arrived with some *bread*. This was shared out between us. We had seen better bread. When sliced it was found to be grey in colour, and we had to dig the weevils out before eating it. It was bread though, a welcome change from biscuits, and this treat was repeated occasionally.

One day I was on ack-ack duty and some German planes flew over. I (and others) opened fire on them, but we didn't bring any down. Another morning, without warning, two Stukas appeared right out of the rising sun. They flew very low – one directly over our tank firing small explosive shells and bullets. I happened to be standing by our 'kitchenette'. I ducked inside and heard the splat of a bullet nearby. It was all over in seconds, and although we ran to our tanks and started firing our ack-ack guns, we were far too late to cause them any problems.

I went back to our dugout and found the bullet I had heard, flattened on one of the stones holding down our roof. It was no more than a foot away from where my head had been. I picked it up and carried it around with me for years; in fact I brought it home after the war but somehow it managed to get lost (probably thrown away by my mother). Jim and Dick had had narrow escapes too, standing near the tank, neither of them was hit – but two bullets had hit the Crusader. The other plane had flown directly over another tank about thirty yards away. Their crew hadn't been so lucky: Bob Weightman and Ted Ryan had both been injured, but fortunately neither of them seriously. Bob had been cut by bits of shrapnel on his neck and chest and Ted was hit in the foot.

Each crew slept at the side of their own tank. The wind, usually full of sand, would blow straight between the wheels and bogies of the tank, so you had to improvise some sort of protection. Each tank had a ground sheet which would be fastened to a bar that ran along the side, then draped down and stretched out on the ground to be slept on. We hardly saw any rain here, but on the odd occasion when we did, we slept with the ground sheet on top of us. At night it was deathly quiet and as we lay there by the tank, it was amazing how we could hear people talking on other tanks nearby – even if they whispered.

Water was a very precious commodity. The water wagon came every day and our four pints each had to suffice for drinking, washing and shaving. To try and keep the water cool, we'd dig a hole in the sand, bury the can there, and sometimes park the tank over it. This helped to some extent, but the water was always warm. If we decided to wash a shirt, we poured petrol into a big tin, dipped the shirt in, wrung it out, then hung it over one of the scrubby bushes to dry, which it did in no time.

From here we regularly went out on schemes. Sometimes for a change we'd take over the driving in turn, something I enjoyed. Joe used to refer to us as 'my demon drivers'. We would also fire the guns, which had then to be cleaned as soon as we returned to camp. It was a gunner's job to 'T. and A.' (test and adjust) the sights. On the end of the gun barrel were four small grooves, like points north, south, east and west. A length of cotton was stuck in each groove with a bit of grease, to make a cross at the end of the barrel. The gun was elevated or lowered until the cross was settled on something estimated at 1,000 yards away. Then the gunner looked through his periscope, inside which were markings in yards. If the 1,000 yard mark was adjusted to be on the same object as the cross on the gun barrel, then in theory the gun fired at something 1,000 yards away would score a direct hit. It didn't always work like that in practice, but in general it was a useful exercise.

Now that we were settled, at least for a while, the rest of the Regiment moved up, and Ronnie in 'B' Squadron was only about five miles away. I got a lift over to see him, and then he later brought me back in his squadron office truck. He came over a few times while we were there, and it was great to see each other again. On these occasions we always played cards.

So the weeks passed. . . .

One day the news came that we were going to be equipped with

American Grant tanks. Someone gave us a lecture on them, then a dozen men, including Jim and myself, and also a few of the officers, were sent back to Fort Capuzzo about seventy-five miles away on the Libyan/Egyptian border to collect them. My diary notes that before we left we 'scraped up all the rations we had left and managed to have some tea with no sugar, and bully beef, and a few biscuits, and found a jar of Marmite – a relic of Captain Patchett'. We left in a pick-up truck and arrived at a camp near Capuzzo. The tanks hadn't arrived yet and I noted in my diary: 'Slept in a *tent* last night.'

Fort Capuzzo is in the desert about eight or nine miles due south of a small town called Bardia, which is on a spur of land on top of cliffs overlooking the sea. The Grants still hadn't arrived, so we went off to Bardia, climbed down a path in the cliffs and went swimming in the beautiful warm blue sea. Seven Grants arrived next day, and they were the biggest tanks we'd seen (apart from German ones). They took a crew of six. The 75 mm gun was much the most powerful I had handled. We spent five days being instructed on the Grants, going off every day to swim in the sea afterwards at Bardia. It was like being on holiday.

Then it was time to take the tanks back to the Regiment. Shortly after, our squadron was to have all its tanks replaced by Grants while the other squadrons were left with Crusaders and Stuarts. We felt lucky to be equipped with these superior vehicles.

We withdrew several miles to the west, and put in a lot of practice with our new 75 mm guns. I have in my diary that on 11 May, when we were on the ranges, Lieutenant General Sir Willoughby Norrie, who was in charge of two armoured divisions (one of which was ours), came and spoke to all our crew. He asked me if I liked the 75 mm and understood it. My answer was 'Yes'. Our troop (three tanks) fired best of all. I took only three shots to knock down a target at 1,200 yards. Practice in driving and shooting went on, but soon the practising was to give way to the real thing.

8

In Action with the Grants

As the days went by, it was up early, usually about 5.30 a.m. and out in the desert for more practice. In addition to the original four of us, Joe Radice, Jim Emery, Dick Rowney and myself, two new men made up the rest of the crew. They were Corporal Tommy Gristock and a man called Hardwick. The crew arrangements in a Grant were very different from those in a Crusader. The gunner (myself) in charge of the 75 mm sat by the side of the driver and just slightly behind him. The man who loaded this gun (in our case Hardwick) was behind the gunner. Jim and I were unable to see the other three members of the crew because they were in the turret, above and behind us. In the turret were mounted a 37 mm gun and a Browning machine-gun. Gristock was in charge of these – loaded by Rowney who was also the wireless operator. The tank commander, Joe Radice, completed the turret crew.

In general, as a crew we got on pretty well. Dick and I didn't always see eye to eye, but we got along. Tommy was a very quiet man with little to say. Hardwick was cheerful. Joe Radice was brave, but a little odd in his ways. He seemed to make a habit of getting lost when walking about and was always knocking things over. He wore thick glasses and had rather a spotty face. Out of the whole crew Jim and I got on best together. He was a big young man, came from Birmingham, had a strong 'Brummie' accent and a dry sense of humour. He rarely got upset or annoyed and took everything in his stride. We had been in the same tanks (Crusader, Stuart and now Grant) together for the past six months. We had spent some particularly congenial days together with our broken down Crusader in Tobruk. He was a very good driver too. We had known each other since the day he and Bob Weightman and others had joined the squadron at Tilford in 1940. It was nice to be sitting beside each other now.

In the tank we had two types of 75 mm shells: A.P. (armour

piercing), olive green in colour, to be used against armoured vehicles; and H.E. (high explosive), coloured yellow and made to explode on impact. The Germans, always a few steps ahead of us, had a deadlier shell, an A.P./H.E., designed to go through the armour of a tank and then explode inside.

On 23 May 1942 we were woken at 4.30 a.m. by the guard and told to be ready to stand to by 5. There was tension and expectation in the air, for we knew that a German attack was imminent. But we didn't move. The next day this happened again, and this time we did move, about thirty-five miles west, to within only five or six miles from the front line. On the morning of 27 May the enemy launched the expected offensive, and were moving our way. We went to meet them. Our squadron was leading the attack, with 'A' and 'B' Squadrons behind and to our left and right. It was scorching hot and soon we could see German vehicles in front of us shimmering in the heat. We shelled them and really wreaked havoc among them. All hell was let loose as we exchanged fire; the noise was deafening and the dust rose in clouds. It was an exciting experience, but also very frightening. We were fighting with the best tanks we'd had so far, and had confidence in them, but our confidence was soon shattered. Through my periscope I saw a spurt of sand from the ground in front of us. Within seconds the next shell hit us. It was certainly an A.P./H.E. because it came straight through the front of the tank and exploded inside. I looked at Jim; he had taken the full blast of the shell in his face and was dead. I had blood on my face and arms but what was hurting most was my leg. It felt as if it had been hit with a sledgehammer. On looking at it I saw a hole in my thigh an inch or more across.

In a situation like this one doesn't stop to think, automatic reaction takes over. There was a door in the side of the Grant, behind the gunner, and also one above it. For some reason I crawled out of the top door, then lay on the back of the tank and rolled off on to the ground, a drop of about six or seven feet. Lieutenant Radice, Rowney and Hardwick had baled out. Radice was slightly wounded in the leg and Rowney in both ankles. They said that Gristock had been killed. Hardwick was unhurt. The battle was raging, another of our tanks nearby, commanded by Lieutenant Halsted, had been hit. He was wounded, and one of his crew, Harry Mounsey, a boy from Leeds, was killed. Our tank was still moving forward with Jim and

Tommy inside it. Then it caught fire, and the ammunition started to explode.

There were scout cars running about, and one driven by a very courageous Sergeant Harris picked me up and took me back several hundred yards, where medical soldiers were helping with the wounded. Sergeant Harris immediately left, to look for anyone else he could see in trouble. I owed him a great deal. The rest of our crew were picked up, though I didn't see them.

I was laid on the ground alongside some other men, none of whom I knew, and an M.O. gave me a shot of morphine to ease the pain. There were three ambulances there, and we were lifted into them on stretchers, perhaps six in each, the stretchers fitting in racks, like bunk beds. One man in our ambulance was a German soldier. It was late in the evening when the ambulances set off across the rough desert, and soon it was pitch dark. We came to a stop and I heard the drivers get out and start talking to each other. We were lost. In the distance they could see a few lights, and decided that with wounded men on board the only thing to do was to drive over to them. If they were Germans, we would give ourselves up. The bumpy journey continued, and we arrived at the lights to find that they were a few abandoned German vehicles with their lights left on. There was another conference on what to do next. If we drove north we would eventually hit the coast road, and if we got there without mishap, we should turn right and head for Egypt. The ambulances had no compasses, so which way was north? Fortunately there was a clear sky and someone had the bright idea of finding the North Star and following it. We had no idea where we were or how far it was to the coast, or even if there were Germans between us and it. After several more bumpy miles, out of the blackness in front of us there was a shout: 'What the hell are you doing here?' It was the voice of an officer of a Scottish infantry regiment. I heard the ambulance men explaining what had happened. The Scotsman said it was a miracle we hadn't been shot up but that we were now near El Adem, and would indeed hit the coast road if we kept going. He wished us luck.

The coast road at last! We headed east. It was nearing daylight and soon ahead of us was a casualty clearing station. This was one of many temporary units set up to deal with wounded soldiers who would be on their way, eventually, to a permanent hospital. This C.C.S. was a South African unit, and the men there were absolutely marvellous. I asked one of them about the German in our ambulance. He told me not to worry about him. He had died during the night.

I'd had a piece of shrapnel – which I'd pulled out – stuck in my left cheek, just below my eye. Another piece had cut my right temple, and they put stitches in this. Yet another piece had gone in my left wrist and was sticking out of the other side; they took this out too. My right arm was also cut, but none of these things bothered me as much as my leg, which was very painful. They bandaged me up, but didn't attempt to do anything with my leg. Later in the day I was on my way to another C.C.S. where the wounds were dressed, then another C.C.S., and another, and another, and five days after being wounded arrived at the railway station at Mersa Matruh in Egypt. From there I went by hospital train to a hospital near Ismalia, about seventy miles east of Cairo.

I will never forget the day I was wheeled on a stretcher into that ward. The 'ward' was a big marquee – and to me it looked like heaven. Bright, cheerful, flowers on the tables, and the sister was the nearest thing to an angel that one could imagine. Her name was Sister Furnival. How old she was I don't know. I was twenty-three and at that age anyone over thirty is old, but I would guess she was somewhere around forty. She was one of the most wonderful people I have ever met. I was given a bath, then five days' growth of beard was shaved off by an old Arab with a cutthroat razor.

I suppose there were about twenty beds in the ward. I was one of the first casualties to come in from the fighting, and I got on really well with everybody. Everyone was so kind and helpful – there were other sisters besides Sister Furnival, and all were marvellous.

I wasn't feeling too well, and after a couple of days' rest was taken to the X-ray department where they found I had some shrapnel in my thigh. On Thursday 4 June the surgeon told me they were going to operate next Monday, when my leg had settled down a bit. On Sunday they decided not to do the operation next day as my leg was 'unsettled'. Things were pretty painful, and I had trouble sleeping. They took the stitches out of my head, my leg was dressed daily, but it was Thursday 18 June before they finally did the operation. I have those dates in my diary, but didn't write in it again until the 27th, when I did my best to bring it up to date. They had taken two pieces of shrapnel out of my leg, one of them measuring well over an inch across, and a smaller piece, and they gave them to me as souvenirs. The small piece I lost, but I still have the other. And another piece too – left in my leg, which they must have overlooked.

I was very ill after the operation and had to have a blood transfusion. I then became delirious and came round to find what seemed like the rest of the army holding me down. My Commanding Officer wrote to my parents and told them I had been wounded and that a blood transfusion had saved my life. I couldn't eat. My legs were like matchsticks, and I thought I'd never be able to walk again. The sister tried to tempt me.

'Is there *anything* at all you would like?' she asked.

'Yorkshire pudding,' I said.

She left, and it wasn't long before she came back with a plate with a cover on it. And underneath the cover? Yorkshire pudding! She had got it from the officers' mess. She brought me ice-cream, lemonade. . . . With this sort of care and understanding I slowly improved.

During the time in hospital I had lots of mail. Some days I had little interest in reading the letters, but as I got better it was marvellous to go through them all. One day I got a wonderful parcel from Cape Town, listed in my diary are some of the contents: '. . . tins of fruit, custard powder, milk, coffee, six tubes of 'Lifesavers', shaving stick, four books, 160 cigarettes, razor blades, cotton, needles, socks, comb, [a comb! only a small item but how I needed one] – what a parcel.' How could I ever thank them?

On 27 June I wrote: 'On the 23rd (I think) a miracle happened – Ronnie walked in. Couldn't believe my eyes and ears.' Ronnie had his left arm in a sling. He had been diving into a slit trench as they were being bombed, and a piece of shrapnel had taken off the end of his thumb. As soon as I saw him I burst into tears, I just couldn't believe it. He had arrived here and been put in another ward but had found out where I was. I'm sure seeing Ronnie did me more good than any medicine could have done. He brought the awful news that Bob Weightman had been killed, machine-gunned after baling out of his tank. This was a great shock and very upsetting.

There was quite a lot of reading material in the ward, and there was also a library. Ronnie brought me books from there when he came round to see me every evening. But he was not the only visitor. I wrote in my diary that some ATS girls started coming to the ward.

One came a few afternoons and the diary says: 'The ATS sergeant came and sat with me again (to the envy of the boys). She's a Russian and really very beautiful, just like Sonja Henie. Told her so. . . .'

I was going to have to learn to walk again. Seven weeks after being wounded I gingerly got my feet on the ground for the first time – just for a few minutes. A note in my diary says: 'I'll be walking in two or three days.' That, to say the least, was over-optimistic. A week later, after daily testing, I walked a few yards with a crutch, then graduated to a stick, and eventually was going under my own steam.

The time passed, my leg was swollen from time to time, but it improved. There was an army cinema in a tent at the hospital, and sometimes Ronnie and I would go there. Then early in July we were separated, both moved to different nearby hospitals. We were destined eventually for convalescent camps, so we hoped we'd be reunited again soon. I really missed Sister Furnival, but when my walking improved I went back to see her.

While I had been in hospital the German push was gaining momentum and they had our forces on the run. As they advanced, General Auchinleck decided to dig in at El Alamein (150 miles west of Cairo) in the hope of holding them there. In view of this it was decided to evacuate the hospital.

The weather was now very hot indeed, and in the marquee wards it was very uncomfortable. On 18 July 1942 I was put on a train, bound for Palestine. We went alongside the Suez Canal for a few miles, crossed it in a boat, then boarded a train on the other side. We had left the hospital at 5 a.m. and arrived at our destination, a hospital in Jerusalem, at 2 a.m. next day, a long tiring ride, but interesting. I wasn't too keen on the hospital there, probably because I had become attached to the one near Ismalia. One thing I disliked intensely was that in a big room, with chairs and writing tables and playing-cards etc. were wickerwork chairs, and the minute you sat down on one, bugs came out and bit your legs. So before sitting down it was essential to lift up the chair, bang it on the floor and then tread on the bugs as they hit the ground. Some were as big as woodlice.

Every day I had to go for massage. My leg was stiff but the massage made it easier. Then, after being at the hospital for twelve days, I was sent to a convalescent camp at Nathanya. It was a beautiful place, right on the coast. There was a window near my bed, and I could see the blue sea from it about 500 yards away. It was marvellous to walk along the sea-shore, and sometimes to go in the sea which was very warm. The town of Nathanya itself was only small with nothing there of great interest.

Reveille was 6.15 a.m. during the week, but on Sundays we were allowed to lie in until 7. There was also a church service on Sunday mornings in one of the huts, which I went to. Most of the work we did was light duties – tidying up places, like the road, or the sergeants' mess, peeling potatoes and onions for an hour or so a day. We also did fifteen minutes' very light PT every morning before breakfast. We had to do the occasional guard duty as well, but it was an ideal convalescent camp. I made friends with a New Zealand boy, and we'd go for walks on the cliffs.

One day some more people arrived and I was amazed to find that one of them was Haydn Boothroyd, a boy who lived next door to me at home. We had lived next door to each other since we were children. It was a big surprise for both of us.

I'd been there eight days when a convoy arrived and I was delighted to see that one of the men was Ronnie. He was billeted in a tent, and soon I was moved to one about 300 yards away, so we saw each other regularly. There was a NAAFI there with a good reading room; also a hut which served as a cinema, so we saw a few films. More than anything we looked forward to the mail coming – but it only came spasmodically and one day there were twenty letters and two newspapers for Ronnie.

There were a lot of chameleons on some bushes nearby. We brought some into the tent, put them on our beds, and they entertained us by flicking out their long tongues to catch flies. We tied a string between two poles and they would walk along it, clinging with their 'hands' and tails. They were olive green in colour, but if you picked one up and put it on something red, it would take on a red tinge: move it to something yellow and it changed to yellow.

The camp had an old bus, in which the padre once a week ran a trip to Jerusalem and Bethlehem. Ronnie, Haydn and I went and thoroughly enjoyed it. We left the camp at 8 a.m. and arrived back at 9.15 in the evening. We saw the place in Jerusalem where Christ was tried by Pilate, many of the famous churches, the Temple, the Wailing Wall, and the Garden of Gethsemane, a sombre, almost gloomy place. It wasn't difficult to picture Jesus praying there. The padre said that some of the big gnarled olive trees were so old that they could have been there when Christ was alive. In Bethlehem we saw the star on the floor of the church where Jesus was reputed to have been born, and the fields where the shepherds 'watched their flocks by night'. We also went round a workshop where they were making souvenirs out of mother-of-pearl.

We were paid every week, but the amounts varied. One week we had 3,000 mils (about £3), the next 500 (about 50p). Money not spent in the NAAFI and on stamps was usually 'spent' on playing cards. At one time we decided I would look after both Ronnie's money and mine. I got involved in a game of three card brag. I had a good hand, ace, king, queen, and I bragged and bragged and when I bragged my last coin I had to see the other man's hand. He had an AKQ too, and having called him, I lost. For a few days we were completely broke. Ronnie treated it as just one of those things, though I felt very guilty about it.

One day we were granted weekend passes to go to Tel Aviv, which struck us as a clean and pleasant place. We found a good hotel, ate well, and walked on the sea front. I noticed a sign outside a building which had a man's name and then underneath TEACHER OF LAGUAGES. Another time six of us were invited to an exclusive club in Jaffa. Out on a lawn we had afternoon tea and the people there were really kind and friendly.

My leg wasn't getting better quickly enough for my liking so I volunteered to go on a PT course for an hour each morning. After three days my leg was sore and the instructor said I had to give up the leg exercises. Another three days and he said I must give it up altogether as it wasn't doing me any good.

On Monday 7 September 1942 Ronnie was told he would be going out of the camp on the coming Thursday. Also that Monday I had to go to the board room, where I was interviewed and told I might be sent to South Africa. I had heard that seriously wounded men were sometimes sent there to recuperate, and I later learned that was where Dick Rowney had gone. Ronnie went on the Thursday, and as I had heard no more about South Africa, I asked if I could leave. I did so the following Monday and noted in my diary: 'Handed borrowed kit in this morning, so that leaves me with one pair of socks, one pair of pants, one pair of shorts, one shirt and one towel!'

I caught Ronnie up at the transit camp at Benjamina (a very desolate spot). As it came dark the air was filled with the howling of wild dogs, and this lasted well into the night. There seemed to be hundreds, though we never saw them. After being there a few days and knowing that we were both bound for the Bays' base in Cairo, we asked if we could leave at the same time, a request which was granted. There were a group of us on the four-mile march to the railway station where we were then put on a train which was packed with civilians. There was no room in the carriages so we made ourselves as comfortable as we could in the corridor. The train left at 2.30 p.m. At 11 o'clock it stopped at a station and we were served some stew and tea on the platform. Next stop was Qantara about 6 a.m., where we had breakfast. My diary says: 'The Arabs were selling everything on the train – tea, chocolate, sun-glasses, books, lemonade and anything else you could think of.' We arrived at Cairo station at 10.30 a.m. after a very uncomfortable twenty-hour train ride. Here we waited for an hour or so, then a lorry came, picked us up and took us to Abbassia, our Cairo base.

We spent just over a week at the base and were put on 'escort duty' every day. This meant taking prisoners for walks, sometimes handcuffed to us. Ronnie, now a corporal, was put in charge of this operation.

They had their bugs in Cairo too. There were iron bedsteads in the barracks, and it was the weekly duty of an orderly to go round all the joints with a blow-lamp to burn them out. Also the 'biscuits' that made up the mattresses had the corners soaked with something like paraffin. In spite of this, some nights we were still bitten half to death.

I was issued with some new kit accompanied by much grumbling from the QM at my not having brought my kit with me when I baled out of the tank. He moaned particularly about having to give me a new gas-mask because I hadn't 'bothered' to take my other one with me. This really upset me. The people like him, back at the Cairo base we referred to rather contemptuously as 'base wallahs'. In their cosy Cairo offices they had no idea what it was like to be fighting in the desert. If you ever came across one somewhere else, he usually was telling everybody what the war was like.

We had been promised a week's leave in Cairo, but as we hadn't any money, not having been paid for some time, we couldn't go until the pay arrived. Finally it did and we set off. We stayed at a small hotel called the King George. There were a number of service clubs in Cairo, and in one of them were billiard tables where we had a few (very one-sided) games. At one of the clubs we arranged a visit to the Pyramids and the Sphinx, which fully lived up to our expectations. Our Arab guide was very good and knowledgeable. It was a real thrill to see these ancient structures. I climbed up just one of the huge stones of the Great Pyramid. It was an exciting day.

Cairo had several cinemas and one night we went to the Odeon to see Walt Disney's *Fantasia*. There were also good shops many of them French. I sent my grandfather a brass cigarette box lined with wood as a present. It had the Sphinx and the Pyramids and other Egyptian figures on it. When he died the box was handed down to me.

There were beggars everywhere – a particular nuisance were little boys running around as 'bootblacks'. While you were looking in a shop window they would sneak up and put a blob of boot-polish on your boots and then offer to clean them – for money of course. A gentle kick usually cleared them away, but often they would follow, pestering. We were not allowed to hit these tormentors, but it was a rule not always obeyed.

The back streets of Cairo were not a safe place for soldiers to go, especially at night, unless in pairs or more. There were gangs out to steal their money, but more importantly their paybooks to sell to German agents. It was said that there were thousands of swastika flags ready to be waved when the Germans marched into Cairo.

Our leave was over, so it was back to the base and the bugs. Next day we set out into the country, a rough ride on lorries, to be delivered back to our Regiment. I was dropped at 'C' Squadron, and immediately found myself back in No. 1 Troop as gunner in a Sherman tank commanded by our troop sergeant Nobby Clarke.

In less than three weeks we were in the Battle of El Alamein.

9
El Alamein

The Americans named their tanks after Civil War generals. We had General Stuart, then General Grant and now we had General Sherman. The Sherman tanks were the best we'd had, and we fought in them from the Battle of El Alamein in October 1942 to the end of the war. Although the big gun had a 75 mm bore like that of the Grant, it had a much longer barrel and was more powerful. With the Shermans we were getting nearer to matching the German tanks – though they were later to introduce the Tiger, with armour on the front about a foot thick and an 88 mm gun, a deadly weapon, the same as they used as an anti-aircraft gun. We held the Tiger tank in respect, and fear.

The arrangement of the crew in a Sherman was different from that of our previous tanks. There was a crew of five. Next to the driver sat the 'scatter-gunner', who had a Browning machine-gun. The 75 mm was in the turret, and to its left another Browning. The wireless was on a shelf across the back of the turret, and the operator also loaded both guns, which were fired by the gunner from two buttons on the floor by his left foot. The 75 mm had a recoil of about two feet, and a metal guard was attached to it for protection against being hit as the gun came back. A canvas bag was fastened underneath this. The breech had first to be opened by hand by pulling a lever to lower the breech-block. There were two small projections, one at each side of the breech and when a shell was pushed into the gun the protruding rim on the shell-case tripped these so that the breech block came up and closed the breech. When the gun was fired, it recoiled, and then the breech reopened automatically. The empty shell-case was thrown out, and with a clang hit the guard and dropped into the bag. The noise was deafening, and the tank would fill with the acrid fumes of the gunpowder.

In a circle all around the turret were 75 mm shells, held by spring clips so they could be quickly pulled out and loaded. A small framework at the side of the machine-gun held an ammunition box, the ammunition being in a belt which was threaded into the gun, and then as the gun was fired the belt automatically fed through. About every eighth bullet was a tracer which lit up when fired so that the gunner could see where the bullets were going. Two or three more boxes of ammunition were in the turret, then more boxes and 75 mm shells were stored underneath the floor – accessible by a trap-door. There was also a mortar in the turret, this to be used to fire smoke bombs if we wanted to cover up our positions or retreat.

While I had been away, the Regiment had suffered a considerable number of casualties in the retreat to El Alamein. When I rejoined I saw a lot of new faces – recruits who had arrived from England to bring the Regiment up to full strength. Among them was Colin Rawlins from Bridport in Dorset. I was glad to see Jimmy Turner, Ted Ryan, Bob Buckland, Harold Balson and other familiar faces. Besides Nobby Clarke, the tank commander, our driver was George Brooker, scatter-gunner Ted Ryan and wireless operator Ron Grist.

The days in October were spent driving the new Shermans and firing the guns. Because of the sand it was essential to be constantly stripping down, cleaning and oiling the guns. To clean the barrel we had a long rod with a brush on the end. The rod unscrewed into two pieces, and it sometimes came in handy when making a 'bivvy' at the side of the tank. When we stopped for any length of time camouflage nets were spread over the tanks to eliminate the shadow cast by the sun, this making it more difficult to be spotted by enemy aircraft.

We were told that on 23 October we were to launch an all-out offensive. On that date I wrote in my diary: 'Well, now dawns the great day. Troop Leader gave us all the "dope" at 8 a.m., then at 9.30 a.m. church parade. After dinner got tank all fixed up for the beginning of the fight. Played cards in afternoon. Supposed to sleep but none of us can.'

During the day we gradually moved forward, then along a track which had been cleared through one of our minefields. Ahead lay a German minefield, and when the Regiment came to it, the tanks lined up along the edge, nose to tail. By 8 p.m. we were in position, and I wrote in my diary:

There's a glorious sunset tonight. What a mad world. Who would think we're on the eve of a great battle – perhaps the fiercest we've been in yet. May it be God's will that I come through these few days alive. If I have to die, I'm not afraid, but my heart aches for Jessie and my mother and dad. God comfort them. Above all I pray to God that He will bring Ronnie through this safely, so that he and Emily will be able to live happily together for many years. God give me courage.

The enemy were at the other side of the minefield and our Engineers were clearing a way through it for the tanks to follow. Our Regiment was only part of the huge operation that was about to take place, for the whole front stretched for forty miles, from the sea in the north to the edge of the Qattara Depression, a big area of soft impassable sand in the south. This was the reason why this particular place had been chosen for us to dig in.

It was quiet. Then at ten o'clock our artillery opened up, firing over the top of us. The flashing of the guns lit the sky, the noise was deafening, and for four hours we sat in the tanks and listened to it.

Messages were given over the wireless in code, and the code to inform us we were about to advance was 'We'll now take a drink'. We sat there and waited for those words, tense, excited, and fearful of what was to come. The words came at 2 a.m. as the artillery barrage stopped. We started to move forward.

Our squadron was leading, and the first tank to negotiate the corner to go through the minefield misjudged it and hit a mine. It blew the track off, so that tank was already out of action. We had to make our way around it, and moved very slowly forward. The air was thick with sand and dust, and although we followed closely behind each other it was almost impossible to see the tank in front. The edges of the track had been marked with petrol tins, some of them with dim lights inside, to keep us from straying onto mines, for the track was little wider than a tank.

The plan was to be through the minefield by dawn, but because of the damaged tank and our slow progress it was already getting light before we reached the end of the track. We were being heavily shelled, but made the other side, and then spread out and gradually edged forward, firing as we went. The fighting grew fiercer and the barrel of our turret machine-gun began to glow red, and then became white hot as the bullets passed through it. Ron worked like a demon, and I was firing the guns as fast as he could load them. We moved like robots – no time to think. The noise both inside and outside the tank was horrendous, and added to this was the smell and sting of the burning gunpowder. The sky was alight as from a huge firework display.

Fighting alongside us was an Australian infantry unit, and we were cheered to see American planes come over. They dropped their bombs but we had advanced further than they realised and the bombs fell amongst us. Luckily none of the tanks was hit but the Australians suffered some casualties.

Late in the afternoon we came to a halt after what my diary describes as 'the worst day of my life'. The diary also notes: 'It is now about 5 p.m. There's stuff flying everywhere, George and I had a hectic half-hour brewing tea and dodging shells.'

We could only move back a short way at night to close leaguer, as we had the minefield behind us. It was a noisy, uncomfortable night, for the shelling from both sides continued and planes kept up their bombing raids. Next morning at first light we were back on the attack. We drove the enemy back, but then were held up by heavy anti-tank fire. Our tank was hit, but we were in the thick of the fighting and kept going. Once the clutch slipped, and for half a minute we were stationary until, to our great relief, the clutch gripped again. The day wore on – still fighting, firing, slowly but surely pushing forward. Then late in the day the 10th Hussars took over from us and our whole Regiment withdrew.

Now we had a chance to assess the damage to our tank. We had been hit in at least six places, and were in no doubt that we were the luckiest crew on earth because one hit had taken a huge chunk out of the side, right over the petrol tank. The hole was about a foot long and three or four inches wide – so big we could put a hand through it and swish the petrol around inside. Why the tank didn't catch fire we'd never know. We also found we had a few scratches and bruises between us. We were very upset to find that another tank from our troop had been hit, killing all five of the crew. Other troops had suffered casualties too. Pierson and Reeves from No. 2 Troop were there with their tank from which they were the only survivors. Their Troop Leader, Lieutenant Christie-Miller, and the other two crew members in the turret had been killed; Christie-Miller they said, had been 'cut in two' by the shell. The Regiment had suffered many casualties. We, with 'B' Squadron, had led the attack, and out of twenty-nine tanks between us only twelve were left. It was necessary for the Regiment to regroup with more tanks and men brought in to replace the casualties. We were to take our tank back to workshops about seven miles away, and one of us had to go with it, with George the driver. A new tank arrived for our troop and Nobby took this over. Ted and I tossed up to see who went back with George and who went forward with Nobby. The outcome was that I went with George. However, when we arrived at the workshops he wasn't well, and was sent to the hospital where it was found he had a burst eardrum. It was several months before he rejoined the Regiment, but instead of returning to the tanks, he was put in a scout car troop attached to 'HQ' Squadron.

Our tank, not surprisingly, was beyond repair, and that left me on my own, but not for long. I was sent in a pick-up truck back to where the tanks were, the crews were reshuffled and I was back with Nobby again. Ted was moved to another tank, to be replaced by Harold Balson, and our new driver was Colin Rawlins.

After a short respite, during which the Regiment was reorganised and reinforced, at 1 a.m. on 2 November we were under way, travelling all night. The choking dust was so thick it was impossible to see more than a yard or two – and was responsible for our having an accident. Our tank hit the one in front and the one behind ran into us. Though there was little damage to the tank, Colin was knocked unconscious, and Nobby had a bad cut on the head. The fitters' truck came up, the tank was left where it was, and we were all taken four miles back to 'B' Echelon (the area where the trucks etc. were) so that Nobby and Colin could have medical attention. The M.O. also said they needed a rest. We were sent a new tank commander, Lieutenant Dallas, and a driver, from 'B' Squadron, and told to stay where we were the remainder of the night we'd go back to the tank later. After just a couple of hours' sleep we were ready to move, but I wasn't feeling too good and Lieutenant Dallas sent for the M.O. who decided that *I* needed a rest as well, so another gunner was sent in my place. Jimmy Turner and Bob Buckland were also there on the sick list.

I had a welcome rest, but a brief one. Next day I was on the move with the fitters' truck, following the tanks. We caught them up and I was back in my old seat alongside the 75 mm. Meanwhile the enemy were still fighting but on the retreat, being harassed all the way.

As we moved forward the desert was a scene of destruction and desolation – burned out trucks and tanks, dead German and Italian soldiers, guns and equipment strewn everywhere. Then came hundreds of soldiers, mostly Italians, streaming across the desert shouting and waving their arms. We moved through them urging them past us for the infantry to collect and put in POW camps. The German supply lines had been stretched to the limit. Now they were short of vehicles, and as they retreated they just left the Italians behind.

We had little rest when it was dark, for enemy aircraft flew over and dropped bombs and flares all night long. Rockets were going up – another firework display, but though the bombs dropped near we escaped being hit.

We pushed on, the Germans fighting a rearguard action. From time to time we ran into pockets if resistance, one German anti-tank gun holding us up for half a day. They were a brave crew, but eventually the artillery silenced them. Another tank in our squadron was hit and all the turret crew killed, but except for occasional skirmishes we were now moving west, the advance was gaining momentum, and the enemy were retreating so fast that we lost touch with them. Thousands of troops besides ourselves were pushing forward and some were soon many miles ahead.

When we had to move quickly or a long way, we loaded the tanks on to transporters, and this we proceeded to do now. The transporters were similar to those one sees today carrying six or eight motor cars, only these were big heavy vehicles and it was one tank on one transporter, each with its own drivers. At the back there were two short ramps on hinges so that they could be dropped down easily. To load the tank, one man stood on the transporter and guided the tank driver up the ramps by shaking either his right or left fist to indicate which tiller bar to pull. The tank then slowly climbed the ramps, like some advancing monster. The front would go so high that the driver went out of sight, and then as it reached the point where it overbalanced, it came crashing down to be guided forward until completely on the transporter. Once a tank driven by Jimmy Turner was guided wrongly and fell off the transporter. Jimmy was very lucky to escape injury.

My diary for 13 November says: ' . . . Got news on the wireless . . . everything seems to be going OK. Still moving up coast road where there are plenty of lorries, guns etc. burnt and destroyed. Passed lorry loads of prisoners. Going all day with just a few minutes' halt here and there.'

That night we slept on the transporter at the foot of Halfya Pass (renamed by the army 'Hell-Fire'). This was a notorious pass, very narrow and steep, near the border between Egypt and Libya, so steep that we had to take the tanks off the transporters to climb it. My diary: 'What a climb. What an experience!' However, we made it and next morning: 'Up at 6 a.m. and moved off soon after . . . transporters left, so now travelling along coast road under our own steam. Bypassed bridge which had been blown up, saw biggest gun I've ever seen. Whew – what a monster! Bardia – that beautiful view we saw about six months ago. Very slow progress, thousands of vehicles on the road, can see them in front for miles . . . '

The weather turned cold now and it poured with rain, making life very uncomfortable as we made our way west. We had been bypassed by New Zealand units who were to carry on the chase, so now the fighting was far ahead of us. We listened to its progress on the wireless and a cheer went up when we heard that Tobruk had fallen.

On 17 November we were heading for Tmimi when to our surprise we were told we were going to hand over our tanks to the 22nd Armoured Brigade. They came and took all but three so that next day most of us travelled by lorry. My diary says: 'Buck and I rode on a lorry carrying diesel oil.'

Next day we went through Gazala where our Air Force were making good use of the airfield. There were dozens of destroyed German aeroplanes on the ground. Passing a German cemetery, on through what was left of Tmimi, finally reaching our destination, just another stretch of desert about twenty miles south of the coastal town of Derna, some ninety miles west of Tobruk. We were told we would be there for about three weeks and were to be equipped with new tanks.

Later, we learned that out of 600 tanks the Germans had at El Alamein they had lost 450. 20,000 soldiers had been killed and 30,000 taken prisoner. Our losses had amounted to about eight per cent.

10

1942: North Africa

We had finally arrived where we were going to stay for a while. The rest of the Division also moved into the area – 9th Lancers, 10th Hussars, and even a Free French regiment. We set to work as usual to make the place as comfortable as we could. The Germans and Italians had left equipment everywhere. Our troop salvaged a big German tent. My diary of 19 November: 'Very windy today and raining too. Cold. Buck, Bals, Colin, Nobby and me pitched the tent – big enough for the whole troop. Hard work but got plenty of laughs out of it with this strong wind. However, finally got it up and it proves to be a very good tent.' It was strong heavy canvas and good protection against the wind and rain. We rigged up different kinds of beds; I had found an Italian one which turned out to be very comfortable, and we also found some Italian tables and chairs. Our squadrons were just a few minutes' walk from each other, so Ronnie and I would visit one another regularly, to talk and play cards.

It was decided we should make a squadron football pitch (later we also made a regimental one). The desert took a bit of straightening out, but when finished the pitch wasn't too bad, just a few rough places. Matches between troops were arranged. I played for our troop, though not regularly as I had the occasional leg problem. Games between squadrons were good to watch, and our troop was well represented in the squadron team, sometimes supplying no less than six players, including Nobby, Bob Buckland and Ted Wanless. Jimmy was also in the team. Ronnie played for 'B' Squadron and for the Regiment too. When the regiments played each other there was always a crowd to cheer the sides on. I have notes about the matches. 27 November 1942: ' . . . 'C' playing 'B' Squadron in semi-final of knock-out . . . Ronnie played well, and Jimmy and Ted excelled themselves and we won 2-1!' A few days later we played 'HQ' in the final, an exciting match which we won 1-0. I also remember the sergeants taking on the officers and, to our delight, beating them 8-0.

Besides football we played baseball, basketball (though our version was more like rugby), and did some cross-country running.

Boxing matches were arranged and Dave Beauchamp, our troop corporal, who had been an amateur boxer, took part in them. Dave looked like a boxer, a real bruiser with a broken nose, and he was no mean fighter either. He spoke slowly with a thick Cockney accent. When he was fighting we'd all go along to cheer him on. One boxer from the Royal Horse Artillery, another regiment in the area, had the name of Garland; his nickname was not surprisingly 'Judy', though standing at the side of a boxing ring shouting 'Come on Judy' did seem a bit ludicrous.

Some more new recruits had joined the Regiment and two of them to come to our troop were Jack Ryder from Rochdale and Stan Tatlow from Solihull near Birmingham. Stan was a very quiet likeable boy and he and I got on well together. Jack was a really good card player so he fitted in nicely with our games of solo, and sometimes bridge.

Card schools were going on all the time in our leisure hours, and if it wasn't solo or bridge there were always games of brag in progress. Playing three card brag you had to be careful if two mates wanted to join the school, for it was easy for them to brag everybody out, so that they were the only two left. One would then 'see' the other, or he might even 'pack' and give the other the kitty, but there was the suspicion that afterwards they would share the spoils. So these mates were carefully watched and would often be refused entry into a game. Sometimes arguments arose.

I spent many hours writing letters to friends, relatives, Bob's wife Len, Jimmy's girl Doreen, and regularly to Emily. I wrote home every two or three days when I had the chance, and my mother and sister wrote as often – their letters were always eagerly awaited. Our letters were censored by one of the officers and anything written pertaining to the Army was blocked out. One of the boys, a big stubborn Welshman named Humphries, insisted on writing his letters in Welsh. When ordered to write in English he refused, but finally his Welsh letters were allowed to go through.

It wasn't all card playing, letter-writing and football. We regularly had drill parades, talks, lectures and PT. On Sundays there were church parades which were held out in the open. One Sunday it poured with rain, we were all soaked, and the service was abandoned. Sunday 29 November 1942: ' . . . after Church Parade Nobby got some flour and baking powder and I had a go at making some cakes. (Nobby made an oven.) They didn't come out too badly.' Nobby, besides being our troop sergeant, was also our barber, so now we all had haircuts. I couldn't remember the last time I'd had one.

Some days we were on 'regimental runner' duty. This meant going over to 'HQ' Squadron to be there to take messages to our own squadron if necessary. A typical day from my diary: ' . . . washed and shaved, on regimental runner at 8 a.m. Very cold wind. Monotonous job this. Came over to our Squadron about 4.30 for pay parade. Got £1. Back to 'HQ' and finished runner about 8 p.m.' There were quite a few books being passed around, and when on this duty I'd take one with me. One book I enjoyed immensely was Daphne Du Maurier's *Rebecca*.

Occasionally we were given 'comfort parcels' which were much appreciated. An example: 'Ten Gold Flake [cigarettes], packet of Bachelor Buttons, an egg, *cake* and books.' I also had another wonderful parcel from Cape Town.

Our new tanks were now arriving a few at a time, not up to full strength yet but soon would be. So now we were out driving and firing the guns. Once some soldiers from an infantry regiment were invited and we went over the tanks with them answering any questions we could. We also gave talks and instruction on the guns to some of our more recent recruits and gave demonstrations to the Free French too.

Ted Wanless, a Geordie who had been with the Bays since the Wareham days but in No. 2 Troop, had been made a lance-corporal and moved to our troop. He and a few others who were being groomed as possible tank commanders were sent out with us 'old gunners' to practice. One day I took my turn at commanding too.

As the war went on and we saw more and more action, the thought came to mind how the old tank crews were dwindling in numbers. Would there come a time when there wouldn't be any old ones left? When the next action came up, back they went with new crew members and inevitably we lost someone.

The fighting was now many miles west of us and we listened to its progress on the wireless in the tank. When we started the push from El Alamein the Russians launched their attack from Stalingrad, and we were heartened to hear that they too were making good progress. We'd also occasionally listen to 'Axis Sally'. She was a young lady with a very sweet voice, her English was perfect, and her broadcasts went something like this:

'Hello boys, how are you tonight – cold, miserable, homesick? How about a record to cheer you up? Let's hear Deanna Durbin singing "Beneath the Lights of Home".'

She played the record and then:

'Home. How long is it since you last saw home? A year, or two? Well don't worry, back in Blighty there are thousands of American and Canadian soldiers taking care of your wives and sweethearts. They've plenty of money, and gum for the children too. Let's have a Bing Crosby record now.'

And so on. Unfortunately for Axis Sally the propaganda didn't work, we'd make fun of her then switch off. The trouble was she played records we liked – which of course was the whole idea.

Into December and the weather turned really cold and wet, and sometimes we had torrential downpours. During one such storm, accompanied by thunder and lightning, our tent was flooded. A day or two later, to prevent a recurrence of this we dug a trench round it. The tent itself stood up very well to the weather, and we were grateful to the Germans for leaving such a good one behind.

I developed a boil on my wrist and eventually had to go sick with it. The M.O. put some drawing ointment on it and I had to have my arm in a sling. 21 December 1942: ' . . . couldn't play in football team today. Arm in sling. Paddy squeezed my boil, oooooh!!' By Christmas Eve I got rid of the sling and soon the boil got better.

Before Christmas we dug two long trenches about six feet apart. Out of the sides of the trenches we dug down so that it left them like long seats. The six-foot raised area left in the middle was the table. Our Christmas fare arrived in a wagon load, said to have come from Alexandria, 500 miles away. We sat on our home-made seats and true to tradition were served our Christmas dinner by the officers and sergeants. You couldn't have wished for a better meal, the cooks had done a marvellous job. Turkey, pork, Christmas pudding, beer . . . and afterwards we all cheerfully joined in a sing-song. We had two Jewish boys in our troop, Jacobs and Herschel Schneiderman. I sat next to Jacobs, and as I didn't like turkey I swapped him my turkey for his pork.

[75]

Jacobs was a strange sort of boy. He wore glasses, had black curly hair, and would spend hours sitting, elbows on knees, head bent and resting on his knuckles, deep in thought. He had very little to say, never took part in games or social activities and was the butt of much teasing which sometimes I thought went too far. I felt sorry for him. He did have a camera though, and was responsible for taking the few pictures we had of life in the desert. Once when he sent a parcel of negatives back to Cairo, they were lost. He was most upset and it was a tragedy for all of us.

Herschel was just the opposite to Jacobs, always bright and cheerful. Once when we came across a knocked-out German tank he got into it wearing a German helmet (there were a lot of them about) and Jacobs took a series of three photographs, one with Herschel looking out of the side of the tank giving the Nazi salute, one with Paddy Flanagan wearing an English helmet standing on top of the tank and hitting him on the head with a rifle butt, and the third, Colin, Ron Grist and myself dragging him out of the tank. Herschel was a keen card player too, but when playing three card brag you could always tell when he had a good hand. He'd pick up the cards, put them down nonchalantly (with shaking hands) and say, with an attempt at further nonchalance, 'I'll brag.' Every few seconds he would nervously pick up the three cards again, glance at them furtively, and brag again. As others dropped out, he looked at his cards more often and became more agitated – you *knew* he had a good hand. He was hopeless . . . but a real good sport.

Paddy was from Barry in South Wales, a real tough guy with a bristling moustache, always ready for a fight if anyone wanted one. I really liked him though, and we got on well with each other as most of us did. I can only think of one or two men I wasn't keen on. The comradeship between all of us was a real strength; I've never known anything like it before or since. Perhaps it was because of the situations and conditions we had to endure together.

Christmas Day had been cold but sunny. On Boxing Day the heavens opened, and we suffered the worst deluge yet. Our Christmas Day trenches were flooded, the sand turned to mud, and we thanked our stars that this hadn't happened the day before.

Sometimes the officers attended conferences to be briefed on what was happening and what was expected to happen next. They in turn passed on some of the information. But there were always rumours going around, generally that we were moving tomorrow, or next week – 'Blue lights' we called them. They came to nothing: 1942 ended and we were still in the same camp.

Ted Wanless had been sent back to Cairo on a course and I'd asked him to send me a new diary from there. It arrived just before the end of the year and my first entry on 1 January 1943 was: 'Well, here is the New Year, all being well it will be the year which sees us home . . .' It wasn't.

Occasionally Arabs came drifting by. We'd see two or three, sometimes with a camel or two, miles away. They'd come up to our tent and we'd pass the time of day. At least we would use the few Arabic words we had picked up, phonetically:

'Saeeda.' ('How do you do?')

And they would answer: 'Salama-leekum.' ('Peace be with you.')

There were no apparent tracks or paths, and we'd wonder just where they had come from, and as they disappeared in the distance, where they were going.

It took us a couple of days to put up a big entertainments tent. It was a little late really – we had after all been here about two months – but it served as a mess-hall, on Sundays as a church, and a place to spend some time in the evenings. Someone conjured up some housey-housey (bingo) cards so we held regular housey sessions.

Around the time of El Alamein we were told that the Americans would be landing in Algeria at Oran and Algiers. They were to move east and then push south, and we, moving west, would join up with them in Tripoli. But now Tripoli had been taken, and the Americans were still bogged down east of Algiers. There was heavy fighting going on west of Tripoli and on 18 February 1943 we were told to be ready to move next day. So on the 19th we took down the tent (we weren't going to leave *that* behind), fastened it on to a tank, and loaded the tanks on to transporters for the long journey ahead.

A thousand miles to Tripoli.

11

1943: Battle of the Mareth Line

The first day we didn't go far, staying near Tmimi; the next day we covered 166 miles. The country was becoming greener, a welcome change from the drabness of the desert, but it was extremely cold as we rode on the transporters. We moved south of the coast road, bypassing Derna, and stopped for the night eighty miles from the coastal town of Barce. Next day we headed down Barce Pass, then Tocra Pass, and south into the desert country again; then west through Benghazi and south along the coast. After crossing the desolate salt flats west of El Agheila, we came into greener countryside again, and more populated. We bought or bartered eggs and tomatoes from the Arabs, and fried them for breakfast with the tinned bacon we already had. We'd run out of bread, so it was back to biscuits.

One day our transporter sank into the soft sand and we had to unload the tank to get it out. Another day, 26 February:

> Travelled well till 3 p.m. when we had to stop – burst two tyres ... Am now writing sitting at the roadside waiting for them to be mended. The sea is a grand sight across the road, well-named the 'blue Med' ... Well, tyres are worse than we thought, had to pull off road.
>
> 27th: Stayed in same place all night and now it's 11 a.m. and we're still here! The transporter drivers went about 8 a.m. to get new tyres and aren't back yet. Had bacon for breakfast and now Buck, Harold and I have just come back from a bathe in the sea. Water rather cold but enjoyed it. Very hot day, and flies are *terrible*. Finally moved off about 1 p.m., but after only 25 miles broke down again. This time the tyres caught fire!

We had more trouble with that transporter because there were a further two punctures next day.

The weather was cool at night but very hot during the day. In the evening the mosquitoes took over from the flies: between them they made life very uncomfortable, although we had regular inoculations and were also issued with anti-malaria tablets, and chlorine tablets to put in the water. They didn't improve the taste, but no doubt kept us reasonably healthy.

The transporters reeled off the miles along the good coast road. Because of our tyre problem we had to be up extra early, but soon caught up with the rest of the Regiment. We watched the big white kilometre stones, simply a number after the name of the next place – Nufilia 150, Nufilia 100, 50, 10. Nufilia 5, 4, 3, 2, 1, Nufilia 0! But we never did see Nufilia.

At Sirté the scenery changed completely – trees, date palms and more towns and villages. The weather was hot and we were enjoying the ride. But we weren't moving fast enough. On 1 March we were told to be ready to move at 3 a.m. the next day. We actually left at 4 a.m. and travelled till 11.30 p.m. We were in bed by midnight, but up again at 2.30 a.m., moving off at 3 and travelling all day. The next day we were allowed to sleep in till 8.30 a.m.

At last we knew the reason for the mad rush. There was heavy fighting at the Mareth Line in Tunisia, about 150 miles west of Tripoli, and a counter-attack was expected from the Germans as they desperately fought to hold their positions. This was the heaviest fighting since El Alamein. The 8th Armoured Brigade were going into action and we handed over our tanks to them. (We kept our tent.) Next day we moved by truck to a few miles short of Tripoli and learnt that we would be here at least for a few days and would be re-equipped with new tanks. We immediately pitched our tent in a pleasant area of trees and grass. The whole Regiment was around us, the cookhouse was set up, and we no longer had to make our own meals. We were near the sea too, so were able to go swimming. And we got some mail. I had twenty-three letters!

The Regiment ran lorries into Tripoli for the next two days. Ronnie and I started 'walking the town'. 'Perhaps it was OK in peace-time but now there's very little there and everything is dear. Had coffee and cakes, ice-cream and sweets, that's all we could get to eat except dates and peanuts . . .'

Next day some of us, including Nobby and Colin, were sent to workshops where our new tanks were waiting. We found they were painted dark green instead of the usual sandy colour. The rest of the squadron moved over to join us, so we never went back to collect our tent, which was quite a blow. We spent a day cleaning the guns and giving the tanks a good going over, then next morning filled up with petrol and ammunition before loading onto transporters. We were away by 4 p.m., travelling all night, and at 7 a.m. passed through Ben Gardane on the Libyan-Tunisian border. We had travelled hundreds of miles in a westerly direction, but once in Tunisia, still following the coast, we headed north.

Next morning the transporters left us. We went out and fired the guns, then moved on and came to a halt just before dark on top of a hill, from where there was a wonderful view. There was a glorious sunset, followed by a lovely moonlit night.

On the coast was the town of Gabes. There were mountains about fifteen miles due west of the town, stretching to the west and gradually petering out. The area between the sea and the mountains was known as the 'Gabes Gap'. Nearby was the town of Mareth, and it was here that the Germans had dug in and were holding the Mareth Line. Although our Air Force was bombing the German positions repeatedly, the ground forces were making no progress.

Next day we moved forward about six miles and were ordered to dig trenches for protection in case of attack from the air. We had hardly started to dig when, at about 3 p.m., transporters arrived and we were told we were moving immediately. We travelled all night, going west and finally stopped at 7.30 a.m. Next morning at 3 a.m. we moved off again, travelling till 2 a.m. next day – 'Feeling tired,' my diary says unsurprisingly. Next morning: 'Up about 7.45 a.m., made breakfast. Not much variety left in rations now, couple tins of bacon, plenty bully. Bacon, bully and biscuits for breakfast.'

Later we learned the reason for our hurried move. A Scottish infantry regiment had tried to storm the Mareth Line. They were crossing a deep wadi when it started to rain heavily, turning the wadi into a rushing torrent. Some of the infantrymen had crossed it but couldn't get back. They were annihilated. The ones left on the south side had to withdraw. We understood now the reason for our surprising move west, for the new plan was to go round the mountains and catch the enemy from the rear. We, the 2nd Armoured Brigade, were about to make history.

The transporters had taken us the length of the south side of the mountains, and now for the first time tanks were to be used to advance during the night. As the Regiment moved round the mountains we ran into an area of almost impassable sand: 'What a journey, thick heavy soft sand, and the tank rolled just like a ship. Terribly dusty.' I think this area was one of the worst we had ever attempted to cross; and to make matters worse, there were in addition, locusts flying about in thick black clouds. With great difficulty we made our way through the sand and started the journey east along the northern side of the mountains. We moved and stopped, moved and stopped, and then on Friday 26 March we sat and waited for the full moon to rise. I later wrote to my mother saying I had always liked a full moon but that night I hated it – something she never forgot.

Our objective was the village of El Hamma behind the Mareth Line. We had the 9th Lancers with us, and the New Zealand infantry, who at first were in front but then we moved through them. After advancing several miles we ran into a contingent of German troops and vehicles. They were taken completely by surprise. As we attacked with guns blazing, soldiers jumped out of their blankets and ran in every direction. We shelled their vehicles; there was complete chaos, with fires everywhere.

In the moonlight a tank appeared about 300 yards ahead. 'Let him have it, Jackie,' yelled Nobby. I did, and it went up in flames.

The noise was deafening. We pushed on, right into the middle of the enemy encampment where there was utter confusion. Vehicles were running about not knowing which way to turn, some even coming towards us. We fired at everything in sight. We sent up more vehicles and tanks in flames and completely overran an anti-tank gun position. The crew ran past us to give themselves up. Tracer bullets raced across the sky. It was fierce, intense, yet, in the moonlight an eerie experience that left one with a feeling impossible to describe.

And then we were through them. Our squadron thankfully had suffered no casualties, though two tanks and their crews had been lost from other squadrons. Hundreds of enemy soldiers had given themselves up to the New Zealand infantry mopping up behind us. This part of the operation had been a resounding success, but our objective was still El Hamma.

As dawn broke we found ourselves moving across a wide grassy plain. Our squadron was leading, two troops in front and two behind. We ran into opposition, but nothing too serious and we overcame these pockets of resistance without much trouble, with no losses of tanks or men. We could see El Hamma ahead now. Between us and the village were trees and dense undergrowth. We trundled slowly and cautiously forward, our troop and No. 3 Troop in the lead. One of their tanks, commanded by Corporal Jim Nolan, was to our left and slightly ahead, I could see it through my periscope. Then the quiet was suddenly shattered by a terrific bang. Anti-tank guns hidden in the trees ahead opened fire. I saw Jim's tank hit and it immediately burst into flames. He and his turret crew baled out, all three of them on fire. They ran about screaming . . . and all died. The other two crew members never got out of the tank.

Then we were hit too. I found myself covered with blood, but it wasn't mine, it was Nobby's. He'd been hit on the head and he dropped straight down into the turret behind me. Our wireless operator lay on his back on the floor in a state of terror, beating the floor with his fists and his heels. Colin, our driver, shouted over the intercom: 'My periscope's shattered, I can't see where I'm going.'

Without stopping to think, I jumped up, took Nobby's seat and, half out of the tank, saw we were still heading straight for the trees. Shells were flying everywhere. Any minute I expected we'd be hit again.

'Jink, Colin, jink,' I shouted.

Colin zigzagged but we were still going forward. I yelled at him: 'Pull on your right stick as hard as you can.'

He did as I said, and we made a complete U-turn:

'Put your foot down. Let her go.'

Colin kept his head, did as I directed and we kept going until it was safe to stop. We were all very shaken. Nobby had a bad cut on the head. We saw a Red Cross vehicle not far away and handed him over to the people there, then turned to assess the damage to the tank. The shell that had shattered Colin's periscope had hit us on the track. Part of it was sheared in half, the pins broken at one side and just holding the track together at the other. We were amazed that after the jinking and U-turn the track had still held – if it had broken we wouldn't have lived to tell the tale. The tank had been hit all over the place, probably by shrapnel from the same shell. Looking up the gun barrel we could see bumps inside. If another shell had been fired through it, the whole gun would surely have exploded.

We moved back about twenty miles to a workshop and there they were able to repair the track, but couldn't do anything with the gun. They told us to go further back to the REME. We were glad to get there; we had hardly eaten anything for the last three days, we were nearly out of water, our bacon was used up and we only had bully beef left. At least now we could eat with the REME.

We heard that the attack behind the Mareth Line had been successful, and Gabes and El Hamma had been taken. Meanwhile our tank was beyond repair and they started to strip it to use some parts as spares. My diary for 31 March, written while with the REME says: 'Have to go to a different place for meals now, about a mile away, quite a tidy walk . . . Heard news on wireless. Things seem to be going OK out here. I hope and pray that it's soon over and please God we soon have a chance of going home . . .'

Ted Wanless came to REME and with him as commander in a new tank we rejoined the Regiment which was resting now. We were sorry to have lost Nobby Clarke: he had been a good courageous commander, who always kept his nerve – unlike another commander I once had who, when we surprised several lorryloads of German soldiers, ducked down in the tank and screamed: 'Don't shoot, don't shoot! If you do they'll shoot back.'

I *did* shoot and scattered them, and they didn't shoot back. That commander recovered his composure and we had no further problems.

We were still well over 200 miles from Tunis, and the enemy, though on the retreat, was fighting all the way, but Tunis was our goal.

12

1943: The Fall of Tunis

The Regiment had to have more tanks and men to replace those lost in the recent battle, so we stayed here for a few days to regroup. During this time we kept the guns clean and the tanks in good working order, and had an excellent lecture by a brigadier on fighting tactics in this type of country. I had the chance to write some letters, and we played cards. A mobile bath unit appeared and we all had welcome baths.

Some of us walked over to a nearby aerodrome and the RAF boys showed us around the planes. We watched one of them go off on a bombing mission, and waited till it came back. The pilot said he'd seen very little to bomb. In return, we invited them to look round the tanks. We got on well together.

There were a few empty shacks around, which we decided to explore – unwisely as it turned out, since we found ourselves covered with fleas. We caught a lot, but not enough. After a very uncomfortable night we sprayed our blankets with petrol, and hoped we'd seen the last of the problem.

Later in the day we loaded the tanks on to transporters and moved off next morning at 5.15, travelling north up the coast road. After fifty-seven miles we took the tanks off the transporters to continue under our own power, and at 10.30 stopped for breakfast. After breakfast we drove on all day with occasional stops. The countryside was littered with burned out vehicles, equipment, German helmets, – evidence of the retreat, we passed a knocked-out 60-ton Tiger tank, a massive thing.

On 11 April I wrote: 'Today we should have been in Tunis, but – well, we should be soon. Traded a couple of old shirts and a pullover for fifteen eggs. My bit of French came in handy.' Next day, when cooking the eggs for breakfast, we found three of them to be bad.

Trucks arrived from 'B' Echelon bringing rations, water, petrol and some mail, and there was Ronnie. His squadron office was always with the Echelon, usually a few miles behind the front line. Even so they were vulnerable to the bombing, and it was good to see him and know that he was all right. The trucks stayed overnight so we were able to spend a few hours together.

We continued on our way north. The troops ahead of us were slowly, oh so slowly, pushing the enemy back. We (the 8th Army) were now about to join the Americans and the 1st Army. We envied the Americans their good cigarettes – we often had to make do with Italian ones and they were terrible. We smoked constantly, and soon used up the tins of fifty English cigarettes that were issued from time to time. Sometimes we had the doubtful bonus of 'V' cigarettes. They were awful things – in a purple coloured packet with a yellow letter 'V' on the outside. They were made in India. The tobacco, if it was tobacco (which we doubted), was coarse and dark. But then they were cigarettes and better than nothing at all. Back in the Catterick days no naked lights were allowed within twenty yards of a vehicle. Here in North Africa we smoked *inside* the tanks.

On 14 April we were on transporters again. Besides its being a quicker way to move tanks it was also much cheaper, as the tanks only did about a mile to a gallon of petrol. We left about 8 p.m., after a very hot day, so that night we all slept in the tank, on the transporter. Bob Buckland, our operator, and I made reasonably comfortable beds in the turret, had a decent night's sleep and listened to the wireless in bed. We awoke about 5.30 a.m. to find we were still travelling. My diary says: ' . . . finally stopped at 11.30 a.m., so had breakfast and dinner at the same time. Got ten eggs (for tomorrow's breakfast) for an old shirt, slept in the tank all afternoon, then moved off again at 1 a.m.'

Next morning I awoke at 7.15 . . . 'still moving. Passed through a nice little town, Le Kef, about 10 o'clock. Finally left the transporters at 11.30 p.m. about eighty-five miles from Tunis. Got stuck in a stream but got out. Heard a cuckoo! Very nice scenery around here.' When the rest of the Regiment came up I could see 'B' Squadron about two miles away, so I walked over to visit Ronnie – making sure I was back before dark.

On Monday 19 April 'About 3.30 a.m. it started to rain, so Buck and I moved our beds into the tank, but Ted, Colin and Harold got wet outside . . . had cigarette issue (70 Vs). Then at dinnertime got "canteen goods", 96 Kensitas cigarettes, a bar of chocolate, a packet of P.K. chewing gum and a tablet of soap. Pay up at 2 p.m. Played solo in afternoon, won ten francs. After tea, in tank when Ronnie poked his head in. We listened to the news then I walked him part-way "home".'

Next day the tanks left but we went only a few miles before calling a halt at 2 p.m. in an olive grove. The weather was still hot, but there were often sudden showers. Harold and Bob were on guard that night and I slept under the tank. Guard duty came round very regularly and even after a tiring day it was always someone's turn to be on guard. When you came off guard duty you would generally brew up and get the breakfast ready. Many times there wasn't time for breakfast – we ate what we could, when we could. The occasions when we had time to cook eggs, bacon, or porridge were a treat.

On 23 April, Good Friday, I wrote: 'Reveille 4.30 a.m. Packed up and moved at 5 a.m. Now (8 a.m.) we're very near the front line and waiting to go in. May God see us through this day safely . . .'

Our objective was to take a ridge three or four miles ahead of us. As we pressed forward we saw German soldiers laying mines. They ran when they saw us, but one of our tanks took one of them prisoner. We had no accidents on the mines, and reached our objective without loss. We then pulled back a short distance to close leaguer at 7.30 p.m. and moved out again at 5 o'clock next morning.

Over the next three weeks or so, we made our slow progress towards Tunis. All the time we met with opposition but slowly and surely we pushed our way forward. The plan was for us to do six days in action and then three days off, alternating with the 9th Lancers and 10th Hussars. This was only a loose arrangement, because if all three regiments were needed, the one resting was called back into action – indeed this happened to us once. We weren't too happy about it, but there was no alternative.

My diary for 24 April:

Up at 4.30 a.m., no breakfast. Moved off at 5 a.m. and took up position where we left off yesterday. Now it's 10 a.m. and we've advanced another two miles or so. Were shelled heavily few minutes ago but quieter now. Shell landed about ten yards away, punctured a couple of water cans – and *frying pan*. Easter Saturday, I could think of a better way to spend it, though next year . . . Had jam and bread (a bit we had left –

rather dry) and water. Shelling got heavier so didn't move further forward.

Our progress was painfully slow.

At nights when we came back to close leaguer we'd put a tarpaulin over the top of the tank so no light could be seen. Then one of us inside would get our little stove going and brew up, surrounded by 75 mm shells. So much for no naked lights within twenty yards of a vehicle.

One night the members of No. 4 Troop showed us a little pig they had picked up. They kept it in their tank as we continued the fight.

'B' Squadron were in front of us one day, and we watched as they were engaged in a tank battle in a valley below. To our dismay 'B' Squadron lost two tanks and their crews, although the Germans fared worse. There was a lot of air activity and a German plane came down right in front of us.

No. 2 Troop were ordered to take a ridge in front. Our troop moved up in support then fired smoke shells from our mortars to cover them and they took the ridge without loss.

On Wednesday the 28th:

Up at 4.30 a.m. Moved out of leaguer at 5 a.m. Cooking breakfast, half a dozen shells dropped fairly close so we ate it in tank. Afternoon pretty quiet. Buck and I chased some cows with the idea of catching one and milking it, but no success, we could only get within a few yards of them. Jerry planes over. Had a few shots at them – very low. There's a big hill about a mile away, we're more or less at the bottom of it. Jerry has guns up there. Our artillery gave them a pasting. Ready to move at 6.45 p.m. (now) to go into close leaguer and take over from 10th Hussars in morning.'   [Next day:] Reveille 4.30 a.m., moved at 5 a.m. up to ridge where 10th Hussars were. Very quiet. Few shots fired at us. Sat in same position from 5.30 a.m. to 7.30 p.m. Couldn't get out of tank. Brewed up inside. Read a couple of books. Moved into close leaguer at 7.30 p.m. Had a stew . . .

Next day it was a different story. We had to push on. We were shelled and we retaliated but kept moving forward. Our Troop Leader's tank was hit but the crew baled out and thankfully escaped unhurt. We were lucky to get away with the loss of only one of our

[87]

three tanks; the fighting was heavy and we could easily have been further victims. When we close-leaguered that night, quite shaken after the day's events, our commander, Ted, was sent back with Lieutenant Saunders's damaged tank and Lieutenant Saunders took over our tank.

Colin, our driver, had gone sick a few days before with a swollen arm, and his place was taken by Walker, a very rough and ready young man from Sheffield, but, like Colin, a good driver. Now he too went sick with a sore hand, and was sent back to 'B' Echelon to be replaced by a driver named Joyce. Meanwhile another tank was hit and the commander, Sergeant Stan Webber, hurt, but not seriously.

Sunday 2 May: 'Reveille 4 a.m. (this is getting a bit monotonous), could have slept for a week . . . Still here . . . The big hill on my right, which is so near yet so far, for Jerry still holds it, is Kurnine and we are at a point between Medjez El Bab and Pont Du Fahs . . .'

Occasionally a canteen wagon would come with sweets, beer and soap etc., while every night wagons came up to our leaguer bringing rations, petrol, ammunition, water and much-awaited mail. One night I had yet another marvellous parcel from Cape Town. The drivers of these trucks had a hazardous job, particularly 'Jock' Davidson who drove the petrol and ammunition – there was always a danger from shelling or bombs.

We advanced a little, and down in a valley came across a knocked-out German Mark 3 Special tank with the dead driver still inside it. But things appeared to have reached a stalemate. We had expected to be in Tunis long ago. Every day hundreds of our bombers went over and we could see the German ack-ack bursting around them.

Then during our rest period, when it was raining heavily and Buck and I were sleeping in the tank, we were awakened at 6.30 a.m. and told to be ready to move in fifteen minutes. Jerry was on the run! We passed Kurnine: the Germans had been blasted off it. We only covered twelve miles that day but we felt we were at last on the move. We ran into pockets of resistance but overcame them without loss. In spite of being heavily shelled and temporarily held up by anti-tank guns we still moved forward. Orders came for us to mop up anything in our way, and we proceeded to do so relentlessly. There were hundreds of refugees now on the roads and they were suffering casualties too. We stopped at a farm, filled up our water cans and pushed on.

'In bed after midnight – up at 4.10 a.m. and moved off at 4.40. About 11.45 a.m. two German officers came walking towards the tanks waving a white flag. Say they have 700 men who want to give themselves up. Two of us got out of the tank, waved them in, and then herded them back to the infantry behind us.' Then hundreds more soldiers, both Italian and German, started to stream down the road. When taken prisoner they would never mix with each other. The Germans in general were quiet, sullen, and obviously despised their allies, who on the whole were more cheerful and glad to be out of the war. Equipment was discarded everywhere, a real shambles.

We kept going and were needed to help the 10th Hussars who had come under heavy fire. One shell landed just behind us and some of the shrapnel went through the locker on the side of the tank. Later I discovered it had also gone through my mess tins and my mug. A major disaster.

Then it came over the wireless that on the hill in front of us were some German soldiers and a troop of tanks was to be sent over to get them. Our troop went. As we climbed the hill six Germans came running down waving their arms. We picked two up and had them on the back of our tank. They had a broad band round one arm inscribed 'Hermann Goering Panzer'. They were part of Goering's crack Panzer Division – his top tank fighting unit. One was a sturdy, red-haired, good-looking young man in his early twenties. The other, a blond boy, looked very young and we asked his age.

'Sixteen,' he said.

Both were quite cheerful. Then the older one pointed up the hill and said: 'Officer.'

I jumped off the tank, pistol in hand, and climbed the hill. At the top the ground sloped into a hollow. I went down – perhaps foolishly as I was now out of sight of the tanks – to where there were some bushes. I walked towards them, gun in hand. They suddenly parted and out came the German officer, frantically waving a white handkerchief, his face the same colour, and shouting: 'Kamerad, kamerad, kamerad.'

I saw he had a gun in a holster. With my pistol in his ribs I took the gun, turned him round, marched him out of the hollow and down the hill to the tanks. He said in broken English that he had only been in North Africa a few days, having been rushed there from the Russian front. We loaded him and the other four onto our tanks

[89]

and took them back to hand them over to the infantry. As we went, the roads were packed with German and Italian lorries, driven by Germans and Italians, full of thousands of their own soldiers, giving themselves up. It was an amazing sight.

Tunis fell on 11 May 1943. On the 12th there was fighting around the town but by the 13th there was no more resistance. Altogether over a quarter of a million prisoners had been taken and thousands killed. Thousands more were killed as they were bombed mercilessly by the Air Force while trying to escape by sea from Cape Bon. The area for miles was littered with vehicles and equipment, and the war in North Africa was over.

13
Return to Tripoli

Weapons taken from the enemy were supposed to be handed in, but I kept the gun I took from the German officer. It was a small neat Mauser. The bullets were not in a revolving chamber as they are in a pistol, but in the handle of the gun. A spring in there pushed them up as they were fired. It probably held about twenty bullets, but I found just eight inside. After the war I brought gun and bullets home – and my mother had a fit. She wanted nothing to do with the war, least of all a gun and bullets.

The Government knew thousands of us would have brought guns home. It was against the law, but they declared an amnesty. Anyone who had a gun should hand it in to a police station, and no questions asked. At this my mother insisted I get rid of the gun. So I handed it in – but kept the bullets. This wasn't good enough: she couldn't rest. To keep the peace I had to get rid of them; so one day when we went to Bolton Abbey, I stood in the middle of the bridge over the River Wharfe and dropped them one by one into the rushing water below.

On the morning of 12 May the squadron was in an olive grove near Tunis. We were told that two men from each tank could go into the town. Buck and I were chosen and a truck took us in at 11 a.m., coming back to collect us at 5.30 p.m. My diary has little to say about those few hours: 'Big place, but could get nothing to eat there. Had some wine. Plenty girls!' There was much evidence of the fighting: the town had only been taken the day before.

Tunisia was a French colony. The population was mainly Arab but most spoke French besides their own language. I had been pretty good at French at school so once again this came in useful. The Regiment moved to a pleasant area just outside Tunis, near a small village and by the sea. The squadrons were close together again, so Ronnie and I were able to see each other. We went to a concert in the village put on by the local people. There were lots of girls in it, singing and dancing, and we enjoyed it very much.

From my diary of 20 May: ' . . . Today is the Victory Parade through Tunis and most of the boys are there, only me left on our tank. The boys got up at 5 a.m. to go. I'll bet the place is crowded. Washed a shirt. Filled up with diesel. Wrote letter home . . . went to concert again tonight. Same as last night, a few different girls, enjoyed it again . . .'

My diary gives no indication as to why I didn't go on the Victory Parade, and I can't remember, but I don't appear to have been too perturbed or disappointed. To explain why I was filling up with diesel, some of the tanks we recently acquired had diesel engines instead of petrol. They were more powerful, and also no sparks were emitted from the exhausts as they were with petrol engines, so making them safer when on the move after dark.

No. 4 Troop still had their pig and were taking good care of it. On 22 May we went swimming, 'had lemonade and apricots in village'. The 23rd being Sunday there was a church parade and afterwards: 'Went swimming. Stan, Des, Hersch and I walked down to village – had beer and bread and rissoles. Grand day out . . . At night drank some cold water and a drop of wine.'

The 'nightcap' had a disastrous effect on me for I hardly slept a wink and was sick twice. Nevertheless I went into Tunis and met Ronnie there. 'Walked round and round then bought a loaf, found a seat beneath the trees and had salmon and bread. An old lady gave us a couple of glasses of Muscat each. I wasn't feeling too good.' I suppose there was little wonder but: 'In afternoon went to ENSA show *Laughter for Tonight*. Excellent show, really enjoyed it.' The ENSA concert parties were made up of professionals who, as their contribution to the war effort, travelled round entertaining the troops and were much appreciated.

Our short 'holiday' was soon over, and now we were to move – back to Tripoli of all places, 500 miles away. The tanks weren't going with us, but could follow on later. We left one driver with each tank, and the rest of us packed up and piled into trucks.

27 May: 'Rained very heavily during the night and everybody got wet. Up at 5 a.m., and on our way by 6.30 a.m. At 12.30 stopped and had a brew, and bread, jam and bully. (Buck and I supplied jam, tea, sugar and milk – now none left.) Moved on, but only for another hour or so. About two o'clock stopped for the day just outside Kairouan. Dried our bedding. A lovely day.'

We continued south, bypassing Sousse and Sfax. Once we stopped to pick lemons to make lemonade, another time we 'bought' apples from an orchard with cigarettes. We were always near the sea, so at every opportunity we went in for a swim. We spent one night just north of Gabes, after being on the move from 5.15 a.m. to 5.30 p.m., and as we passed next day through Gabes and Mareth there was still plenty of evidence of our activities a couple of months ago. Then we left the green of Tunisia behind and crossed the border into Libya, and back to the sand.

When we were in Egypt, our money was in Egyptian pounds and piastres; in Palestine, mils. In Tunisia we had francs, and now in Libya it was back to British Military Authority money in shillings, made legal currency.

All this moving back and forth meant that we were constantly passing through different time zones, and were often an hour 'across' when we either forgot, or didn't know, the time had changed.

On 30 May we arrived where we were destined to stay for a while, about twenty miles from Tripoli, close to where we'd been about two months before. There was 'plenty of sand about' but 'tons of mail'. We were issued with 'mosquito-proof' bivouacs, one between two men. Stan and I decided to share. We were a mile or two from the sea, but there was a swimming pool nearby where we swam at every opportunity – even at night, for there were lovely starry evenings.

One day, nine men per troop were allowed to go into Tripoli, and Stan, Des Darch from Somerset (a recent addition to our troop) and I went together. The town was very different from the last time we were here. We were given tickets to go to a cinema and saw the film *Mrs Miniver* which was very good. 'Had ice-cream, cakes and lemonade. After film had more cakes and coffee.'

Our Squadron Sergeant-Major was Ronnie Strutt, a stern unsmiling man. On muster parade on 6 June, he announced that three men had been promoted to lance-corporal. I was one of them. In my diary: ' . . . I don't know whether I'm glad or sorry. Reckon I'm sorry really. Paddy sewed my stripe on for me.' I suppose I felt sorry because once you get a stripe you are no longer 'one of the boys'. I wasn't sure I wanted that, though the stripe didn't alter me at all. However, it was a promotion. Afterwards I had to go to a lecture given by the Regimental Sergeant-Major entitled 'Now You

Are an NCO'! Ronnie meanwhile had just been promoted to sergeant.

That night Stan had a bad earache. I had some olive oil, so I put some in his ear and then plugged it with cotton wool. We lay there in our bivvy, sharing a bottle of beer ... and talked about home. Like me, Stan didn't have a girl friend. He was younger than I, twenty-two, where I was now getting old – twenty-four. But oh how we missed our homes and families. It was nearly two years now since I'd last seen them.

Next day Stan's earache was much better but I had toothache. I went sick and had the offending tooth pulled out. Otherwise we kept in good heart, except that with the temperature rising to well over 100 every day, we both managed to catch colds.

'Bivvy' life was hardly luxurious. One night when we were in bed I felt something crawling up my leg. I yelled out and Stan struck a match as I threw back my blanket to reveal a dark green centipede, about three inches long. We had been warned against these creatures: their feet were suckers and they had to be knocked off in the direction they were going, otherwise they would pull the skin off. In a great hurry I carried out these instructions, then clobbered the thing. It was a while before we went uneasily back to sleep. Fortunately, we saw no more centipedes.

We had no tanks yet but still had training, mostly talks. To keep us fit, we had 'swimming parades' where we piled into trucks and went to a nearby beach. This was one of the hottest areas on the North African coast, and the sea was wonderfully inviting. On one of these trips I was surprised to see Nobby Clarke. He had fully recovered from his head injury but had been given an administrative post instead of returning to the tanks.

Our tanks arrived, but we didn't have them long. After cleaning them up we handed them over to the 7th Armoured Brigade and returned to our makeshift military routine. We had lectures and talks on everything imaginable, including 'Crime in the Diamond Trade' and 'Frozen Meat'. The weather continued hot, sometimes reaching 125 degrees, and the flies drove us mad. Sometimes, too, the wind would blow, and the sand got everywhere. We read, played cards and went swimming. There were trucks to take us into Tripoli where a NAAFI had been set up, so it was somewhere to have tea and cakes and lemonade. There were a few good cinemas, showing the

American films we liked, featuring Gary Cooper, James Cagney, Ann Sheridan and other favourites. Back in camp a mobile canteen came round regularly so we were able to buy chocolate (to be eaten quickly before it melted), tinned fruit and cigarettes etc.

We were told that on 21 June we were to have a very special visitor, codenamed 'General Lion'. We duly lined up on each side of the road, and he rode slowly past in an open car, raising his hand in acknowledgement. To our astonishment we saw that it was the King. We had expected to see some high official but not the King himself. It was a boost to morale.

After the King's visit the whole Regiment moved – just a few miles, but it was a welcome move for we were in the midst of a heatwave and now the sea was right on our doorstep. We were burned to a cinder. My hair went blond.

On 10 July we heard news of the invasion of Sicily. This set us wondering, but a blue light was going around that we'd be leaving soon for England. Paddy Flanagan said: 'Jackie, mark the 13th of September in your diary, that's the day we'll be going home.' So I duly marked it with four crosses and we all started to place bets as to whether or not that would be the date, and where we would be sailing from.

Stan and I came back from a swim at 7.30 p.m. on Saturday 17 July to be met by SSM Strutt. He was waiting to congratulate me on the news that I had been awarded the Military Medal for saving the lives of our tank crew at El Hamma. Next day Major Streeter, formerly our squadron leader but recently promoted to second-in-command of the Regiment, came over and said: 'Many congratulations on your award, it is something you deserve.' I felt proud and happy, and the rest of the troop were very generous with their congratulations.

We were told that soon some of us would be sent back to Cairo to collect a hundred jeeps and drive them to Algeria. Among the men chosen to go were Stan, Colin, Paddy, Ted Wanless, Jimmy, Sid Aster – and myself.

14
1943: The Jeep Trail

I had to go sick with a boil on my arm, which required treatment and dressing. I was afraid I might miss the Cairo trip, so asked the M.O. to put me on M. & D. (medicine and duties), which means 'fit enough to work but needs treatment'. He agreed to do so, and gave me some ointment and bandages in case I needed to have the boil dressed while I was away.

Then – it was rumoured that the Cairo trip was off. While we waited, we played cards, swam, picked grapes to make 'wine', picked lovely ripe figs, and I, now an NCO, was ordered to take our troop on PT. 'Just went for a short walk,' comments the diary. Finally the trip was on again. We packed our belongings and moved in trucks to a dreadful place just outside Tripoli: nine of us in a roasting tent, which was swarming with flies during the day and mosquitoes at night. The only redeeming feature was that it was near the sea. There was a NAAFI and a library where 'all the books were at least fifty years old'. Stan had to cut out the swimming, it affected his ears and gave him a lot of trouble. Here we kicked our heels for twelve long days, then on 12 August we boarded the *Talma*, and sailed from Tripoli.

The *Talma* was an old Indian ship, reputed to have been sunk three times and looking like it. She was rusty, and badly in need of a coat of paint. We chugged out into the Mediterranean.

13 August: 'Stan and I went on deck. Hanging on the rail we suddenly sighted land, and it turned out to be Malta!' We had thought it odd that we were sailing in a northerly direction. We dropped anchor in Valetta harbour, and the Maltese came out to greet us in their little boats – we weren't allowed ashore. We were there for twenty-four hours, and then joined a big convoy sailing eastwards, our destination Alexandria.

Slowly we ploughed on our way. Our money was changed once again to pounds and piastres. We passed through a time zone and actually knew about it! My boil cleared up but I had developed a couple of painful desert sores. The food, meanwhile, was on a par with the ship – awful. But the sea was 'flat as a mill pond' the most beautiful deep blue, and we saw lots of flying fish. I started a letter home on the boat which I posted in three stages, from there until we rejoined the Regiment, twenty pages at a time.

The 1,000-mile journey from Malta took another five days. We were very impressed with the size of Alexandria when we docked there at 5.30 p.m. on 18 August, and we weren't sorry to see the last of the *Talma*. We were given a meal on the docks, then immediately picked up in trucks and transported to the station. There we boarded a train, our carriages being, as expected, the usual cattle trucks, and rattled on all through the night, reaching Cairo at eight o'clock next morning. We climbed off the train and straight onto trucks, which took us to a camp near Mena. Across the road from us were the Pyramids. The jeeps weren't ready, so we were sent to Cairo on four days' leave. Stan, Colin, Sid and I went together and found a good, small hostel called Liberty House. On arrival we washed, shaved, changed, and ate. Freedom!

21 August: 'Got up about 8.15 a.m. Oh it's great to be on leave, a *bed*, sheets and a pillow! We decided to buy presents today, and had a good morning's shopping. Colin and I sent telegrams home. Had our photographs taken. I bought an MM ribbon. Had dinner and tea, eggs, chips etc. Went to the pictures at night, then to the By-stander for supper and a drink.'

Our first job next morning was to post all our parcels, after which we looked round the shops again. At this time there were many Service Clubs in Cairo, and particularly good ones were the New Zealand and Tipperary Clubs where we indulged ourselves in the luxuries of eggs, chips, lemonade, ice-cream, sandwiches and cakes. We were still bothered by the little bootblacks, but they were only a minor irritation. We decided to go to the museum, but were disappointed to find on arrival that it was 'Closed for the duration'.

On the third day Colin and Stan had to go back to camp to do guard duty, of all things. Sid and I went and collected the photographs, and they were excellent. I had also had one taken wearing my MM ribbon – the verdict in my diary 'Not bad, but I look to be sulking.'

On 24 August 'Glad to see Stan and Colin roll in about 9 a.m.

Walked round. Went to the YM, bought some cigars, then to Tipperary Club. After dinner went to pictures.' So our short but most enjoyable leave had come and gone. We hitchhiked back to camp, arriving at 9 a.m., to be told that we could go out again till midnight; so we did a U-turn and spent another day in Cairo. That night Ted Wanless and some of the other boys gave us lurid descriptions of some of the night life they had seen on their leave. The pornographic displays were a bit too much even for some of the most hardened members of our party.

Next day we travelled by truck to Amariya where we spent the night. The jeeps were here, and we were allocated one each. Mine had twenty-eight miles on the clock. Stan and I wanted to drive together, so he followed on behind me and we set off in convoy on the long drive of nearly 2,500 miles to Bône in Algeria.

With a strange feeling we reached a now peaceful El Alamein, and relived the terrible battle we had fought there. There was a huge cemetery at the spot, with long lines of neatly kept graves, each marked with a cross and the name and rank of the soldier buried there. It was an emotional experience to walk between the graves and find friends and colleagues we had lost.

Then on we went – the same dusty, dry desert: 178 miles one day, 104 miles another, 135 another. West over Sollum Pass ('I was carrying the jam, it spilled, what a mess'), leaving Egypt behind, and into Libya. Through Capuzzo, and into Bardia to fill up with water – memories of the Grants. We were beginning to feel almost at home. Generally we finished travelling for the day during the afternoon.

We were following the coast road, built by the Italians years ago. Normally it was very good but it had suffered some damage because of the fighting, and occasionally we would hit a bad patch. There were times when we had difficulty making our way through soft sand; even the jeeps, with their four-wheel drives, needed the occasional push. From time to time, too, we had to change the engine oil, because it became thick with sand. For most of the way the road ran right by the sea, so at nights we were able to swim to get rid of the dust and cool down. Once there was a lovely beach just across the road from where we parked for the night. We wasted no time in running onto the beach and into the sea. It was only when we were returning to the jeeps that we noticed a sign: KEEP OFF THIS BEACH – IT IS HEAVILY MINED. Fortunately there were no casualties.

We continued through Tobruk yet again, now peacefully settling down. Two Sudanese were hitchhiking to Derna. I picked one up and Stan the other. Unfortunately for them we stopped for the night about twenty miles short of the town, so they had to pick up another hitch. It rained very heavily that night, but next day it cleared up and we had a wonderful view as we descended Derna Pass into Derna. The country now was greener and less austere. Twenty miles south of here was the bare and sandy place where we had spent the months around Christmas, now safely a memory.

Next morning Stan and I picked up two more Sudanese who were bound for Benghazi. The Army now had troops and bases in these coastal towns, and in Benghazi we filled up with petrol and water, drew rations, and I had my desert sores dressed by a medical orderly. We stopped for the day just fifteen miles west of the town to do maintenance on the jeeps. Some of the boys took a trip into Benghazi but Stan and I decided not to go: there really was little of interest, and we took advantage of the stop to do some washing and letter-writing.

The following day we were on the move again, and I picked up yet another Sudanese, who asked for a lift to Agedabia. When we stopped for the night on the way, I dropped him off to get another lift, but he turned up again later and stayed the night so he could travel on with me. Next day we did 101 miles and my mileometer passed the 1,000 mark. My Sudanese friend had decided he wanted to go further than Agedabia so he was with me as we drove through El Agheila, then right off the road to the seashore where we parked for the night on the beach. My passenger was enjoying this. He slept there too and was with us when we left next day.

Then it was on down the long, long road we'd travelled on the transporters months ago ... The kilostone still said 'Nufilia 0' and we still never saw Nufilia. My friend and I were now on first-name terms – 'Jackie' and 'Rehab'!

7 September: 'Went down to the sea and had a swim (eight of us in one jeep.) Got some eggs. Cigarette situation rather bad now ... plenty Arabs here and *millions* of flies.' We were bound for Tripoli, and stopped in Homs where Rehab finally left me after being my passenger for five days.

In Tripoli we filled up with petrol and attended to necessary repairs. I had a puncture mended. Then we stocked up with rations, including fresh meat, and had fried steaks that night for supper. Just west of the town we stopped for a couple of days. During the night Ted Wanless was taken ill, the cause appeared to be a sardine sandwich he had bought in the NAAFI. However, he recovered by the time we were ready to move.

There was an army hospital now in Tripoli, and I went there and asked if by any chance Sister Furnival was on the staff. Unfortunately she wasn't. They told me she was now on a hospital ship. I was very disappointed at this, I should have loved to have seen her again.

A couple of months before, I had marked 13 September in my diary with four crosses. This, according to Paddy Flanagan, was the day we should be going home. As we crossed the border once again into Tunisia, I showed the diary to Paddy and reminded him of his forecast. Poor Paddy, somehow he must have got the wrong information. He was a great man, tough on the outside but for me always had a soft spot. There was never a wrong word between us.

Ben Gardane is in Tunisia, near the Libyan-Tunisian border. We stopped there for one night, and the only thing I remember about it is the flies. Flies were no novelty, but Ben Gardane's took the biscuit. As we ate, we had to keep waving our arms to fend them off. Ron Grist and I were standing one on each side of a jeep with our food on the bonnet. Ron put some jam on his bread. He turned to talk to me and in a split second his bread was a mass of flies – you couldn't see the jam for them.

We passed once again through Mareth and Gabes, reliving the awful memories of those places, then north through Sfax and Sousse. 17 September: 'Bound for Tunis through small towns and villages. Through Grombalia where we were a few months ago after our last day of action, and through Hammam Lif where we used to go swimming.' We only did fifty-four miles that day. One of the officers had gone ahead to the Regiment to collect the mail. There was great excitement when he arrived back with a jeepful. I had thirty-four letters!

18 September: 'Reveille 5 a.m. and moved off at 7 a.m. Stan and I made the breakfast as usual. Through Tunis and Medjez El Bab, through beautiful scenery on very good roads. Up mountains and round thousands of corners with picturesque villages here and there. Finally arrived at La Calle, a lovely little Mediterranean fishing village. Walked round the village and had some wine.'

We were now in Algeria, nearing the end of our journey, and on 19 September parked the jeeps in a field on a hillside on the outskirts of Bône. My mileometer read 2,329, which meant I had done 2,301 miles in the twenty-three days since we left Cairo. We slept there that night, bitten by mosquitoes. With no reveille next morning we slept in. About twelve o'clock, lorries came to pick us up and take us back to the Regiment. I had enjoyed those three weeks, and said a sad farewell to my jeep.

15
1943–44: Life in Algeria

We spent the night of 20 September 1943 in a transit camp near Bône. Reveille was at 4.45 next morning and at 5.30 we left for the railway station. There we boarded cattle trucks and moved off at 7 a.m. It was very hot, our truck was crowded, and progress was extremely slow. We travelled all day and all night, with sleeping almost an impossibility. We had brought what was left of our rations, and occasionally when the train stopped for a while, we'd jump off and brew up. At one stop we used the last of our tea, sugar and milk. Our journey ended when we arrived at Medjez El Bab about 5 p.m. We were back in Tunisia.

When we left on our trip to Cairo, the Regiment was near Tripoli. Now all the Regiment including the cookhouse, had moved all the way back to Tunis, and we were picked up at the station by trucks to rejoin them.

Our SQMS was 'Topper' Brown. He and I were quite friendly and he had asked me to get a certain book for him in Cairo. He was delighted when I handed it to him. Topper was always with the Echelon, never up with the tanks, but I'd see him when we were all together like this. He was an extremely good musician, and could play a number of different instruments, one of them the accordion, which he carried with him. Strains of music could often be heard coming from his tent at night, and sometimes I'd call in there and listen to him play. He had written a few good songs, a couple of which I learned by heart, and still remember.

The Regiment together again meant that Ronnie was here. He had been promoted to SQMS and moved to 'HQ' Squadron, so now instead of handling the affairs of just one squadron he was in charge of the paperwork for the whole Regiment. During his time in Tunis he had made friends with a French family by the name of Leautaud, and having the use of a pick-up he took me to meet them. They were nice friendly people and had a lovely daughter about twelve years old, called Lucienne. They invited us to spend the coming Sunday with them. We went in the afternoon, took Lucienne swimming in the sea, then returned to their house for a meal. They had invited some of their friends, and after we had eaten we had a singsong – in French as no one spoke English. It was after midnight when we left. It had been a most enjoyable day.

We were due to leave the area in a few days' time, so Ronnie and I went into Tunis again to say goodbye to the Leautaud family. Lucienne asked if we would write to her and we promised we would. I'm sure Ronnie did, and so did I for several years.

On 1 October we moved to the railway station. Four cattle trucks had been allocated to 'C' Squadron and all the kit we had packed up the day before was loaded into them. Dave Beauchamp, Ted Wanless, Ted Ryan and I were left on guard. Then the rest of the squadron (except the ones who were going by road) arrived, and we all piled into the trucks along with the kit. The train finally moved off at midnight, bound for Algiers.

2 October: 'Moved and stopped all night, then more stops than moves all day. It rained during the night and some came through the roof. I think this truck has square wheels or else one has a lump on it the size of an ostrich egg. When we came to a halt, the cooks made breakfast, stopped at Soul El Arras at 9 p.m.'

Next day we were still on the train. At one point the railway ran near the road and we passed some of our road party. Then we came to a halt at a station and were there for twelve hours – from 3 p.m. to 3 a.m. I bought a bottle of Muscat at a buffet, and we passed the time between meals made by the cookhouse playing cards, reading, and drinking wine. It was a very cold night, and was still cold and raining when we got under way.

During the day we came to a steep gradient and the engine didn't have the strength to climb it pulling all those trucks, so the train was divided into two halves and the engine pulled up each half separately. Even this was a big effort, and as the engine strained up the hill it produced a considerable amount of soot. When both halves reached the top they were joined together again. Perhaps to compensate a little for our discomfort, the French Red Cross served us free cups of tea. The 500 miles from Tunis to Algiers took us four days. We were as glad to leave that train as we had been to leave the *Talma* at Alexandria.

Our squadron were taken by lorries to a farm near a small town called Chebli, about twenty miles from Algiers, and we were billeted in some of the farm buildings. Other squadrons were spread around in various farms in the same area. Ronnie, in 'HQ', was six or seven miles away.

The owners of the farm, a French family by the name of Greco, lived in a big house beside the main road. Across the road was a dirt drive which ran through a citrus orchard for about 300 yards, then through an opening in a big wall into the farmyard. On the right-hand side were stables, next to them the saddler's workshop and next door was a big, square room which was to be the billet for our troop. We gave it a good spring clean, scrubbed the stone floor, then arranged our beds in there. Some army electricians arrived, and soon we had electric lights. There was a fireplace inside and, just around the corner outside, a water tap. Back to back with us and the stables was a huge barn, and the cookhouse settled in one end of it. We were provided with benches and trestle tables, so we ate in the barn. At night it served as a recreation room.

It was a working farm, horses in the stables, and cattle, sheep, and poultry in the fields all around. No. 4 Troop still had their pig – which had now grown considerably – and they made a sty for it. Killer Wyatt was put in charge of it and took it for a daily walk. He guided it with a long stick. You could tell the pig liked him, it was like a faithful dog as it trotted alongside him, and I think Killer felt a certain affection for it. He himself looked anything but a killer: he was much older than most of us, a small man with big features, very much like a gnome. All the same he was a pretty tough customer. He used to do all the odd (and dirty) jobs but didn't seem to mind, indeed he was very conscientious.

The foreman who ran the farm was a Spaniard, a small, swarthy, rough-looking man with a wife to match. Their name was Ferrando and they had three children – a boy, Jean-Claude, aged eight, and two girls, Marie, fourteen, and Suzanne, sixteen. They lived next door to us. Their house was separated from our room by a broad track which went out of the stable yard and into the fields.

All the workmen were Arabs, and M. Ferrando, besides his native Spanish, spoke fluent French and Arabic. In fact all the Arab workmen were fluent in French, which helped a lot. I was often called upon to act as interpreter.

I developed a boil on my finger but didn't want to go sick, so Stan dressed it for me. I then got desert sores on my arm and knee and was forced to see the M.O. as they were very painful. I wasn't the only one to get these desert sores, which were something like an open boil, probably caused by the way we lived and ate. I had to go sick regularly to have the sores dressed, and this meant going over to 'HQ' as the M.O. was there. It was a nuisance, but as Ronnie was at 'HQ' we saw each other a few times. Stan was a kind and thoughtful young man, very easy to get on with, and on Sunday morning, because I was feeling off colour, he brought me some tea in bed. After about a week going sick the sores began to get better and the M.O. gave me M.& D. for which I was very glad.

We saw our neighbours and the workmen every day, and as time went by got to know each other pretty well. The Ferrando children were always around. Jean-Claude, who soon became known as 'Young Claude', was not a very friendly little boy, swarthy like his parents, and not particularly good-looking. Marie was a quiet, pleasant girl and Suzanne was in her element with all these soldiers around to flirt with, though her flirtations were rarely, if ever, responded to. She was on the heavy side, had long black hair and wasn't too attractive. They were a very poor family and I felt sorry for the children, especially Marie. I wrote and told my mother about them and she said she would send one of my sister's dresses, now too small for her, for Marie.

Up to now we had no tanks, but a few began to arrive at Brigade 'HQ' some miles away, and some of the gunners among us were sent to strip down and clean the guns. They were thick with mineral jelly which was pretty difficult to get rid of. Then we started to get tanks, Shermans, in twos and threes until we were finally at full strength. We parked them on an open space alongside the French people's house.

The nearest town of any size was Blida, though there wasn't a great deal to see there. One nice thing about it was that many of the streets were lined with orange trees, and when the fruit was ripe it wasn't picked but left on the trees looking very decorative.

We were able to get to Algiers often. It was very French so far as the shops etc. were concerned, although it was populated mostly by Arabs. Some of the shops would send parcels of fruit home, and occasionally I had some sent to my parents; though when the trees in 'our' orchard bore fruit, a few oranges and lemons were never missed and some of them found their way to England. The lemons were especially welcome at home as it was impossible to get them there. Sometimes I'd buy mushrooms, and the cook would fry them for me to eat with my breakfast. There were colourful outdoor markets – and there was the Casbah, a sleazy area, narrow streets lined with outdoor shops, and little back alleys with dubious reputations. It wasn't advisable to stray away from the main alleyway.

Ronnie and I wrote to each other and would arrange to meet in Algiers, usually at the YMCA. We'd go round the shops and to the pictures at night. There were always popular American films showing.

We were of course training all the time out in the country with the tanks, then back at the farm there were talks, lectures and PT. I was put on a tank commander's course. We were on guard regularly, but otherwise our evenings and weekends were free. At nights the mess-hall was turned into Las Vegas. Harold Balson and I got hold of some housey-housey cards so we ran housey nights, number 88 incidentally being dubbed 'Rommel's Special'. Harold gave out the cards and collected the money and I called out the numbers. When there was a shout of 'House', Harold checked the card with me, then paid out the winner. For our trouble in running the game, we naturally kept a small percentage of the takings for expenses!

A canteen was set up in the mess-room. As wine was needed, I was given the job of going into Algiers with a pick-up truck, bartering and arguing with the wine merchants, and bringing back wine for the squadron. We also built a stage and concerts were arranged. We still had a very good band, based at 'HQ', and they would come and play. Some of the more talented members of the Regiment sang songs or told jokes, not usually for the most sensitive of ears. Topper gave accordion solos, Jock Spence, a wild Scotsman, revelled in singing 'The Road to the Isles', and after a few glasses of wine could really let it rip.

And so the weeks went by.

16

Bachir and the Farm

One evening when I was talking to Marie, her father came out of the house and invited me inside. It was rather bare and not too comfortable, but we sat and talked the whole evening. They seemed to like my company, and we became quite friendly.

The man who I liked best, though, was the saddler. His name was Bachir. I had never been keen on the Arabs, but I really took to Bachir and in time we became very good friends. He was forty-two, a corpulent little man with a fat round face, and lived with his wife in a tiny house in a corner of the yard at the opposite end of the stables to us. I would go into his workroom in the evenings and we'd talk for hours. He was completely ignorant of anything that was happening outside his own little world. 'M'sieur Jackie' he called me, and questioned me constantly about England, the outside world, and particularly about the war. He couldn't read and could only write his name, and even this he did tongue between his teeth and with great difficulty. We did, however, have a language in common – French, and talking to Bachir my French improved daily. He also started to teach me Arabic, so that after a while I was able to pass the time of day with the men working on the farm, which delighted them.

One evening, talking about the war, I told him the Russians were advancing. At this he showed some alarm, so I asked him why.

'But, M'sieur Jackie, surely this is bad news?'

'Bachir,' I said patiently, 'it's *good* news.'

'But why?' he asked, 'Are they on our side?'

He brightened up considerably when I explained that the Russians were fighting with us, and not against.

One evening he had to go home for something, and hesitantly invited me to go with him. We walked across the yard, through the little door into the house. His wife was there, heavily veiled. He told her this was M'sieur Jackie; she didn't speak and we only stayed a few minutes. That was the only time I saw Bachir's wife in all the weeks we were at the farm, and I had the feeling that he thought perhaps he shouldn't have taken me there.

Sometimes Bachir would saddle horses and teach me how to ride. In the stables was a big fiery stallion called Bijou. He was a stud horse and we used to try to ride him – without a saddle. Once when I got on his back he suddenly made a bolt for the stable door. I slid off just in time, or I would have lost my head on the low doorway.

There were some promotions. Ron Grist got his first stripe, Ted Wanless his second, and Dave Beauchamp was made our troop sergeant. Dave didn't understand why 'these thick Arabs' couldn't get into their heads what he was talking about, so he would get hold of one, put his face very close to the Arab's and talk very slowly – in English. Somehow the man still wouldn't understand!

In a hall in Algiers they put up a boxing ring and we'd pile into trucks to go and watch the fights. We had some good boxers – Dave of course, Harold Balson, and another popular sergeant, 'Boxer' Blythe, among them. They fought against men from other regiments, and naturally we were there to cheer them on. After one particular fight I noted in my diary: 'Dave lost, but it was a magnificent fight (and a doubtful verdict). We're proud of him.'

The village of Chebli also had its own football ground and team, and matches were arranged between them and the squadron. The Chebli team were a very excitable lot – one wore a beret, and if things weren't going his way, if he missed a goal for example, he would throw his beret to the ground and jump on it. Ted Wanless, who played for our team and was always ready for a bit of fun, would egg the Chebli players on, making them more excitable than ever – and the matches even more entertaining.

October was orange-picking time. The Arab workmen were up ladders collecting the fruit, and nobody objected when they passed some on to us. Quite a lot of them I boxed up and sent home.

I was seeing Ronnie quite regularly. He had use of his squadron pick-up truck and came over to visit me from time to time. Sometimes I'd be in charge of a party going into Algiers, and so would Ronnie. We'd try to arrange this duty on the same day, go in and park our lorries next to each other, and spend the day together. On one of these trips I bought a bunch of roses for Marie. Nobody had ever given her flowers before, and it was worth the price I paid for them just to see the look on her face.

After one trip to Algiers our truck wouldn't start. Twelve of us pushed and got it going, but it stopped again, and after another couple of efforts we pushed it into a garage, where we stayed all night – sleeping uncomfortably in some taxis. Next morning we got the truck started but it only went a mile or two before giving up the ghost again; so eight of us hitchhiked back to the squadron, arriving in the early afternoon. Some men from the REME eventually diagnosed the trouble: it was an electrical fault.

On 11 November 1943 we had an Armistice Day parade in Blida. We marched along the decorated main streets with bands playing, to much hand-clapping, and flag-waving. It all went down very well with the local population.

It was getting colder now and the snow was creeping down the mountain sides. We scavenged around to collect all the wood we could to keep a good fire going. Once Dave and I were chased off by the Frenchman who owned the land. But we had to have wood.

One day Ronnie came over to tell me he had been promoted and was moving to Maison Carrée, a town about twenty miles east on the coast, where he would be working in an office building. After he'd moved, he hitchhiked over to see me, and said he hated the place. I couldn't get to Maison Carrée and he didn't have a pick-up now, so from hereon we unfortunately saw less of each other.

Into December. The Regiment were playing the 10th Hussars at football in Boufarik. There was also to be a dance that night. Practically all our troop, dressed in our best, went to the match and then to the dance afterwards. Ronnie was playing for the Regiment. It was a good match, ending in a 2-2 draw, and the evening at the dance afterwards was a big success.

Marie's parents had sent her out to work in service in Chebli, but she came home on Sundays. Bachir and I often spent some time together on Sunday afternoons. It was a unique experience to be learning Arabic from him in French, then translating it to myself in English. One afternoon Marie poked her head round the door and asked if she could join us. Naturally we said she could. We sat and talked over some wine and this became a regular Sunday afternoon occurrence. My French improved by leaps and bounds. They wanted to know all about the war, about England, my family, our way of life, so unbelievably different from theirs. They also wanted me to teach them English words. Marie asked if she could look at my 'book' (my diary). She couldn't read what it said but liked to see her name there.

One afternoon Bachir said: 'M'sieur Jackie, I have an idea.'

'What idea is this?' I asked.

'Why don't you marry Marie and stay here?'

I said it was a very nice idea, but I felt that Marie, being only fourteen, was perhaps a little young. In any case I couldn't leave the Army, and what about my family at home? He was disappointed that his idea wouldn't work, but hoped at least I'd go back and see him when the war was over. I said that I would, and that I'd bring my sister too. At the time I really meant it, but he said sadly: 'M'sieur Jackie – you'll never come back.' He was right. I never did go back, but I often wished I had, if only to surprise him.

All this time 'blue lights' were flashing. One young man by the name of Archer told them so often that he earned himself the name of 'Blue Light Archer'. He had always overheard a conversation, or seen a letter in the squadron office, or 'had it on good authority' that we were going home 'soon', or 'next week', or 'next month' – but *definitely* by Christmas. All his predictions came to nothing. Christmas came, and we were still on the farm. Our third Christmas in North Africa. Meanwhile, with some trepidation, we followed the progress of the fighting in Italy.

On 23 December a group of us went into Algiers to do the rounds of the cinemas. In the afternoon we saw *Three Cheers for Miss Bishop*, after tea Betty Grable in *Springtime in the Rockies*, and then to yet another cinema to see Mickey Rooney and Judy Garland in *Strike up the Band*. Betty Grable, Judy Garland, Mickey Rooney – they really brightened up our monotonous lives.

On 24 December we trimmed up the mess-hall and gave a party for the local children. They enjoyed themselves eating, drinking and singing (a mixture of French and Arabic), and all went home with a little present. They had a happy time and it was fun to entertain them.

Christmas Day started with a church parade for the whole Regiment, held at 'B' Squadron. We sang carols and thought of home. After church parade, it was back to our own squadron for Christmas dinner. There was no turkey this year, they were apparently in short supply (which didn't worry me) but we had everything else, and as usual the cooks did a first-class job. As usual too, the officers and sergeants served us at the tables, and the wine flowed freely. In the evening M. Ferrando invited me into the house where I had a meal with him and his family – and naturally more wine. Fortunately Boxing Day was a holiday, for most of it was spent getting over Christmas Day. Ronnie missed the Christmas Day church parade but had got hold of a pick-up truck, and I was delighted to see him turn up on Boxing Day and stay a few hours.

I had asked my parents to send me a new diary. It arrived on 31 December, just in time for me to christen it on 1 January 1944 with a New Year resolution – to write more legibly. This was in the days before ballpoint pens, which meant I wrote with pen and ink. Merely trying to keep a supply of ink was a problem, but I also wasn't helped by the fact that my pen nib was damaged and I had to locate a new one. However, my resolution held for a while.

As we still showed no signs of moving, an entertainments committee was formed. I was elected chairman, which meant I had a pick-up at my disposal to go round to the other squadrons and regiments, arranging football and rugby matches and other events. I ran a football sweep, organised whist drives, darts competitions and concerts. Sometimes I took our 'indoor games' team to other regiments. We had some good evenings – and there was always plenty of wine. It was essential to have something to do during our spare time.

Another trip to the boxing matches, and this time we took Bachir with us. Oh, he thought this was great, and how he enjoyed himself.

The pig was growing big and fat on the waste from the cookhouse. Killer still took it for walks, but now someone decided we should have pork for dinner. So one morning the poor thing with its back feet tied together was hung head down from a hook in a lean-to outside. I ran a sweep on how much it would weigh once it had been killed and cleaned. 'Kipper' Herring had been a butcher so was given the deed to do. Mme Ferrando asked if she could collect the blood in a bowl. The poor pig screamed as Kipper cut its throat and I left, not wishing to see the rest of the operation. Next morning when I went for breakfast I saw half of its head in a bucket of water and felt sorry for it. Killer was quite upset, the pork was good, but because of the circumstances perhaps not quite so appetising as it might have been.

Nineteen new recruits joined our squadron, three of them to our troop. It fell to me to go over the guns with them, answer their questions, teach them how to T. & A. sights etc. On 8 February 1944 I was awarded my second stripe and became a paid lance-corporal.

Some of the boys decided to print a squadron newspaper and I became sports correspondent, writing up articles on rugby, football, darts etc. *The Good Timer* came out every two or three weeks. The paper was really quite good, and I sent copies home occasionally, though unfortunately not one of them has survived.

M. Ferrando invited me into the house quite frequently and sometimes I stayed for supper. When the Regimental Band came over to give a concert, the Ferrando family and Bachir and a few of the Arab workers would be invited.

The dress had arrived for Marie and one Sunday afternoon I gave it to her. From my diary: ' . . . after dinner I gave her the dress. Oh dear, what a commotion and was she *delighted* to put it mildly.' Marie asked me to write a letter to Jessie for her, thanking her. I did so, and she signed it.

The weather had turned very cold now; we had heavy rain and hailstones, and there was more snow on the mountains. Dave came back from a conference, to say that it was to the mountains we should soon be heading.

17
1944: Training in the Mountains

Two days after Dave's conference we were briefed on the latest plans. We were to go up into the mountains, then carry out manoeuvres in the rough terrain the other side. We would be there at least a fortnight, then come back to our farm for a week or so before moving on. We weren't told where we would be moving to, though Blue Light Archer had it on the best authority that it would be Fez in Morocco.

We packed up our kit and loaded the tanks on to transporters. As we headed for the mountains, it started to snow heavily. We carried on through the mountains, the snow now thick on the ground. After travelling about eighty miles the transporters left us – about a mile from the town of Aumale, which to our disappointment was immediately put out of bounds. We were to be here three days, then use the surrounding area for the next couple of weeks or so as a base, going out on schemes and practising fighting in the sort of hilly country we might encounter in Italy. We cleared the ground as best we could and put up our bivouacs. In an effort to keep warm we lit petrol fires inside but these were very smoky. We stayed where we were for a day when a few of the Echelon people joined us.

On a hill across the road was a farmhouse. I walked up there and found the occupant to be a very pleasant old lady. She was French, invited me in, gave me a glass of wine, and we talked a while. When I left she gave me six eggs. Having nothing better to do the rest of the day, a group of us were in our bivvy playing cards when a fair-haired little French boy appeared in the doorway, clearly excited to have found all these soldiers here. Being the only one who could speak French I asked his name. He said it was Yves, he was eleven years old, and lived on a farm just down the road towards Aumale. He stayed a while, very interested in the card-playing, then said he'd better be going home, and left.

There was more snow in the night, and next morning it was

bitterly cold. We moved off at 10 a.m. taking our bivvies with us, though they were difficult to dismantle as the ropes were frozen. We drove over a 3,000-foot mountain pass, then dropped down to lower but very rough country, negotiating an often dangerously narrow road with numerous 'S' bends. After various exercises we spent the night near Sidi Aissa then returned to our base next day.

'Titch' Hughes was sent back to Chebli for some equipment as well as some wine. He brought back two letters for me, one from Marie and one from her sister Suzanne. They both said they hoped we wouldn't be away long and looked forward to seeing us back at the farm soon.

We were in this area for over a fortnight, once out on a regimental scheme 'fighting' other regiments, on another occasion travelling 100 miles south as far as Bou Saâda on the edge of the Sahara Desert. There had been a time when we couldn't touch the tanks because they were so hot, now we could hardly bear to touch them because they were so cold! My diary of 29 February 1944: 'Out on regimental scheme all day . . . bitterly cold wind. After tea had kick-about with football. Wrote to Lucienne. Fried eggs for supper . . . strong rumour that we're going home.'

At this time Lucienne was my most prolific correspondent. I had letters from her every few days, and answered them straight away. She was learning English at school and when she wrote in French I'd answer in English, she'd then reply in English and I'd answer in French. This English/French correspondence continued for months, and consequently her English and my French benefited accordingly.

Reveille was usually about 7 a.m. but once it was decided we'd have an early start. My diary for 3 March: 'Reveille at 3 a.m. Oh what a time to get up – bitterly cold. Moved on and stopped by wadi and watched the sun come up. After a while had breakfast, and it was certainly welcome. Finally came back about 10 a.m. On maintenance for about an hour.'

After these manoeuvres we always returned to an area near Aumale. Then on 11 March three trucks were laid on to take some of us back for a weekend 'leave' at our farm. We arrived to great rejoicing from all our friends – it was like coming home. Having left our frying pan with the tank, I borrowed one from the house to fry breakfast. We managed trips to Algiers and Blida and on Sunday Bachir and Marie couldn't wait to have one of our afternoon sessions. Marie said she had given up working, because her employers expected too much of her.

Our leave was over all too soon, and it was back to the tanks and the mountains and more manoeuvres. Ted Wanless went sick. 14 March: 'As Ted has gone into hospital I now have to take over his tank. Would rather stay on our tank and do gunner than commander on another tank. Still it can't be altered.' We camped by the side of the narrow road. About 200 yards away, towards Aumale, was a bridge over a stream with big trees growing on either side of it. The bridge was on a very bad bend, and one day a tank missed the corner, crashed through the bridge and landed upside down in the trees. It was a long drop but the trees broke the fall. The crew, although bruised and very shaken, escaped serious injury, but it took several hours, with chains and ropes and other tanks pulling, to recover the tank.

On 20 March we found ourselves in exactly the same place we had been a month ago, on the outskirts of Aumale. We were told we would be here a few days, and then be returning to Chebli, the exercises concluded. This was very welcome news for it had been a miserable, cold and tiring month.

The morning after we arrived, while we were eating breakfast, Yves appeared, delighted to see us again. He said his grandma lived at the farm on the hill across the road, and would I go with him to see her. I had of course already met her, but was glad to go and visit her once more. She really was a lovely old lady, and we stayed quite a while. She produced two copies of the *Illustrated London News* dated 1860 and 1870 – souvenirs of bygone days.

Later in the day Yves arrived at the camp again, to be followed shortly after by a man riding a big grey horse. It was Yves's father, M. Hugnit. Yves excitedly introduced me to him as 'my English soldier friend,' and we shook hands. M. Hugnit said Yves had been telling them all about me (this in French, for he couldn't speak English either), and would I like to come and have a meal with them that evening. I was pleasantly surprised and willingly accepted. They both left, only for Yves to return yet again with the news that his sister had baked a cake especially for my visit.

'Oh – you have a sister?' This was interesting news.

'Yes, her name is Suzette, and she is sixteen.'

At about six o'clock I walked the half mile or so down the road, through the little gate, up the path, to be greeted at the door by M. and Mme Hugnit, Yves – and his sister. When I saw Suzette I took a deep breath . . . She was gorgeous! Blonde hair, blue eyes, fair skin, the most beautiful thing I'd seen for years. Suddenly Aumale wasn't the miserable place I'd thought it was. A few hours ago I'd been delighted at the prospects of returning to Chebli. Now I wasn't looking forward to going back at all.

I don't remember what we ate for the meal, but I do remember the cake, decorated with white icing. What could I say except that it was the most delicious cake I'd ever tasted – a remark which brought a blush to the cheeks of Suzette!

M. Hugnit was a large, friendly man. He told me they had come from Marseilles some years ago to settle on this farm. Suzette played the piano, we sang songs, and I returned to camp thinking how lucky I was to have spent the evening with such a happy family, but above all to have met Yves's lovely sister. Before I left, M. Hugnit said I *must* come and spend a week with them sometime if I possibly could. I said I'd love to and really meant it, but I knew the chance of that happening was extremely remote. Then next day, as we were packing up to leave, M. Hugnit rode up on his horse again. He said he'd come to say goodbye. We shook hands and he repeated his invitation to come to see them, any time.

Now it was tanks on transporters and back to our farm, once again to a warm welcome from our friends. There was mail waiting for us, a note from Ronnie too, saying he'd been over to see me the previous Sunday and was disappointed to find I was away in the mountains. Bachir looked anything but happy. Soon, on the verge of tears, he told me his wife had left him. It appeared that they had had an argument about something, I wasn't sure what, and she had walked out. I was sorry; I didn't like to see him so downcast, but could only offer my commiserations.

My sister Jessie, besides writing to me, wrote to a number of boys in my troop and to Ronnie. She would also knit for them, running whist drives to raise money to buy the wool. The scarves, gloves and so on that she sent were much appreciated. She had left school at fourteen to work as an assistant in a high-class clothes shop in Huddersfield. When she was nineteen she wrote to say she had joined the Land Army and had been sent to work on a farm at Northallerton in North Yorkshire. It was hard, manual work, very different from a quiet shop, but girls were being recruited to release young men who were drafted into the Army. She was helping with the war effort like many other young women, but she continued both her knitting and her letter writing. We were always glad to hear from her.

Life settled down to the old routine, though my thoughts were rarely in Chebli, they were eighty miles away, up in the mountains. One of the sergeants, 'Smudger' Smith, had come up with a girl friend in Algiers and commissioned me to write letters to her in French, but I should much have preferred to be writing letters in French to Suzette. One day I tried, without success, to get a pick-up and take a trip to Aumale.

On Palm Sunday, 2 April, we went off to church parade – and Marie went off to Mass, proudly wearing the dress my mother had sent for her. She had had her hair permed and everyone said how nice she looked.

On Easter Sunday a cricket match was arranged between our squadron and 'B' Squadron. Ted, Jack and Harold played, I was scorer. 'B' Squadron made 63 but we were all out for 19 – of which Jack made 12, as well as taking seven wickets! In the evening Ronnie came over and Topper too, complete with accordion, to round off what had been – in spite of our defeat – a very enjoyable day.

On Easter Monday Stan, Sid, Harold and I had passes to go to the RAF station at Blida, but to our disappointment we were just too late to take a flight. We enjoyed looking round all the same. My diary for the next day says: 'The orange blossom and lilac in Blida was wonderful last night, and what a marvellous scent. A letter arrived from Jessie with a photo in for Marie, and Marie was delighted to get it.'

The days came and went; we were bored, waiting – for what, we didn't know. My diary says there was a mutinous feeling in the air as we spent monotonous hours cleaning our brasses and equipment, and all the time my thoughts drifted to that beautiful town with the lovely freezing snow – Aumale.

18

Suzette

My mother and sister had written earlier in the year to say they'd had their fortunes told and were assured that I would be coming home on 30 April. I put four crosses around that date in my diary. But – as with Paddy Flanagan's predictions – the date came and went, the crosses faded into the past, and we were still in North Africa.

I spent a fortnight going over to 'A' Squadron to teach a class of thirteen new recruits about the 75 mm gun. At least this was something different, but it was the end of April, the weather was already getting warm, and my pupils and myself found it hard to concentrate. I'm sure they were as glad as I was when the lessons were over. But at least Bachir was his usual happy self again. His wife had returned. Even so, I couldn't have known if he hadn't told me, because I never saw her.

On 4 May some of our tanks were to be taken to the docks, then the following day it was officially announced that in the near future we would be moving to Italy, but before doing so, the squadron were to be given a week's 'holiday' at a rest camp by the sea, near Algiers. We saw on the cinema news that Mount Vesuvius was erupting, and we knew that before long we wouldn't be far from there.

I asked our Troop Leader, Lieutenant Saunders, for permission to have an interview with the Squadron Leader, Major Hibbert. This was granted. On the appointed day I entered his office, with some apprehension, for he was rather a stern man, though I had a great deal of respect for him.

'What is it, Corporal Merewood?' he asked.

'I understand, sir, that we are to spend a week at a rest camp near Algiers.'

'Yes – that is true. So?'

'Well – er – I wonder if it would be at all possible that instead of going to the camp I could – er – have a pass to spend the week at Aumale?'

He looked at me rather quizzically, but I saw a twinkle in his eye as he said: 'What's the matter? Have they got a pretty girl up there?'

'Well, sir . . . Yes.'

'Right,' he said. 'You can have a pass; go and enjoy yourself.'

I thanked him profusely, and I think I floated out of his office.

My pass was from the 8th to the 14th of May and I still have it. I went to the QM and asked for a new shirt. 7 May: ' . . . Did some sewing, all buttons on my new shirt blinkin' well hanging off.'

Next day I left on what proved to be a hazardous journey to Aumale. I rode into Chebli on one of our trucks, then hitched a ride to Boufarik where I was to catch a train. The train was two hours late which didn't surprise me, but as a result I missed my connection at Maison Carrée. I had three different lifts from American soldiers, the final one dropping me off at the station at Menerville. 'Had terrible sandwich (which I couldn't eat) at canteen, and horrible cup of coffee which I couldn't drink.' From there I caught the train to Bouira, the nearest station to Aumale, this time riding in a carriage, not a cattle truck, having bought a ticket. I had left the farm at about 8.30 a.m. and when I finally arrived at Bouira it was midnight. The only person at the station was the station master *(le chef)*. It was a very cold night, I had no overcoat, but he had a big fire going in his office. He invited me to stay there, offered me some coffee, and I made myself as comfortable as I could. I hardly slept, and at 6.30 a.m., as it started to come daylight, I thanked him for his hospitality and set off on the road to Aumale – still over twenty miles away.

After a short while I flagged down a ramshackle old truck piled high with vegetables, and the Arab driver picked me up. A couple of miles later he stopped and got out with a can in his hand. I thought he was going to fill up with petrol, but instead he opened the bonnet to reveal fountains of water coming out of the radiator in every direction. He calmly filled the radiator, then we were off again. At 7.45 a.m. he dropped me off at the gate leading up to the farm – and charged me fifty francs!

Although they didn't know I was coming, M. and Mme Hugnit and Suzette gave me an enthusiastic welcome. Yves was at school. When he came home at noon and saw me, he cried out with delight and was allowed to stay at home the rest of the day. I was tired, but I couldn't believe I was here. No one could speak English, and I thought that was great. In the afternoon Yves and I climbed the hill to see his grandma. There was an aunt of his visiting her, a twinkling-eyed mischievous young lady in her thirties by the name of Nanette. I was fussed over and enjoyed it. After a few minutes of conversation she asked if I was married, and my reply of 'Pas encore' caused some amusement. I liked Nanette.

In the evening Suzette and Yves wanted to know the card games we soldiers played. I could hardly begin to teach them brag, so turned to simpler games like switch and rummy, and they loved it.

10 May: 'Got up at 6.45 a.m. after a good night's sleep, rather early rising, but I didn't mind a bit. After breakfast walked up to school with Yves.' In the afternoon, with Yves at school, I spent the time with Suzette and her parents. We talked incessantly, then in the evening played cards until ten, when I went to bed in a lovely bedroom with clean white sheets – and I felt I must be dreaming. The house itself was modern, nicely furnished, clean and tidy, and had the look of being owned by a prosperous family. The garden was full of beautiful roses.

Next morning M. Hugnit took me up into the town, where we went to a café for a drink, and he introduced me to some of his friends. We did this again on other mornings, an experience I enjoyed. Aumale was a grim-looking place, more like a walled fort than a town, and M. Hugnit explained that over the centuries it had changed hands a number of times, being fought over by Turks, Moors, French and others. The Turkish influence was much in evidence in the architecture. I thought to myself that if I had been looking for a beautiful French girl, Aumale was the last place on earth I would have expected to find one.

I went with M. Hugnit down into his cellar and he showed me his distillery where he was illegally making *anisette*. Perhaps this ex-plained some of his prosperity, though we didn't go into that.

A friend of Suzette called Paulette came, and both girls teased me about my French. I loved it – but they also wanted me to teach them some English, which they had never learned at school. Now it was my turn to tease them. M. Hugnit much regretted not being able to speak the language and encouraged me to try and teach them more. I did my best, but there was little time.

As for me, I was learning new words every day and to keep me on my toes I had regular prompting from Suzette. The back door of the house led into the farmyard, with some stables, poultry strutting about, and animals in the fields beyond.

'What is the name of that bird – in French?'.

Well, I knew the English name for it but how was I to know the French for guinea-fowl? But I learned it – *pintade*. Did any teacher ever have such a willing pupil!?

The weather was gloriously warm and sunny, and the snow-covered bleak mountains we'd known in the winter were completely transformed. Yves and I went climbing the hills. He had a gun and wanted to shoot rabbits, but though we saw plenty of evidence of them, we saw no rabbits to shoot.

Suzette played the piano, taught me French songs and wrote out the words for me. One I remember well was 'Le Bateau des Iles'. The evenings were spent playing cards, talking, singing, sipping *anisette*, and added to all this well-being was the excellent cooking of Mme Hugnit. One day, unbelievably, I suddenly realised that I was even thinking in French.

Mme Hugnit wanted to know more about 'Shurshille'. As I didn't understand at first what she meant, she repeated it a couple of times and I realised that she was talking about Winston Churchill. I told her that I thought he was a great man, and there was no one better to be leading us in this war. We had total faith in him.

All the time they asked questions which I was pleased to answer when I could. Questions about my family. How did I come to be in the army? What had I been doing in North Africa up to now? . . . and on and on. Nanette and other relatives and friends called – an English soldier with the family was something of a novelty.

I enjoyed these evenings with the family, but when I came back to Aumale it was because of Suzette. I wanted to see her again so much, to be with her all the time – and better still just on our own. I loved her impish sense of fun, and enjoyed being bossed about by her during the day – in the nicest way. She made me grind coffee, sent me out into the garden to gather radishes (which I then had to clean) and collect eggs from the chicken coops. We laughed, and I would have done anything for her just to be there. We could have known each other all our lives, for from the very beginning we were so much at ease together. As the days went by she and I grew closer: we loved each other's company, we had the same sense of feeling and the same sense of humour; and we loved it best when we were alone together.

The opportunities for this came in the afternoons when her parents were busy and Yves was at school. We went for walks in the surrounding hills, and I was in a different world. Tanks, guns, and war were a million miles away.

But time was desperately short, the afternoons too few, and on the last one we held hands, kissed, and promised to write to each other. She gave me a photograph to keep in my diary and it is still there.

For months I had wanted to leave Algeria – now I wanted to stay, for nothing mattered except to be with this lovely girl. I had never known such happiness.

The week was ending all too soon. I had enjoyed it beyond belief and there was no doubt that they had enjoyed having me there. M. Hugnit said I *must* come and see them again soon. He looked at the calendar, 28 May was Whit Sunday – would I come and spend another week with them then? Oh I would, somehow, if we were still here.

But now I had to leave. M. Hugnit advised me to catch a bus to Algiers rather than bother with the train. It was a more direct route and much quicker, something I now realised. We said our goodbyes, tearful ones from Mme Hugnit and Suzette, but in my heart I wondered when, or if, I would ever see Suzette again.

Yves and I walked up into Aumale for me to get the bus, but arrived to find that it was booked up. However, there was one in about a couple of hours, at 12.30 p.m., to the station at Bouira, so I reserved a seat on that. Yves begged me to go back to the farm. We did so, and in the ensuing excitement, Suzette almost burnt a cake she had in the oven. We said goodbye again and I caught the bus, an ancient vehicle, that gave us almost as bone-shaking a ride as the one from Bouira to Aumale in the vegetable truck. We covered the twenty-odd miles to the station in about an hour, then I had to wait until 3.30 p.m. for a train. This time I had no trouble with my connection at Maison Carrée, then Boufarik, and arrived back at the farm in the evening. The rest of the squadron arrived soon after from the rest camp.

I had been in heaven for a week, now it was back to earth.

Next morning we were to pack up to leave the farm for good. 15 May (Jessie's birthday): ' . . . got all kit packed, said goodbye to Bachir, Marie and the rest of the friends I'd made. I don't like leaving a bit. What with just coming back from Aumale, and now having to leave the farm, I feel pretty fed up. Oh dear, what a depressing atmosphere. Wish I could get back to Aumale.' Marie asked me if I would write to her and I promised to do so.

We moved to a transit camp just a few miles away. 'Told we would be here five days. The blinkin' bugle blew at 6.30 a.m. Oh I *hate* the bugle, and I hate this camp.' We were under canvas, Herschel was sleeping next to me, and in the morning he said: 'Jackie, I don't mind you talking in your sleep, but last night you were talking for an hour – in French! What were you talking about?'

'I don't remember – but if I did I don't think I'd tell you.'

The rest of the troop wanted to know if I'd had a good time in Aumale. 'Marvellous,' I said, and filled them in on most of the details. The consensus of opinion was that I'd enjoyed the week in the mountains much better than they had done at the rest camp. I knew I had.

Friday 19 May 1944: 'Came off guard duty at 7 a.m. Went on route march ... later going to Chebli but found we had to have a pass, so will go tomorrow. Oh I wish I could get to Aumale. Wrote to Suzette. Did some sewing and washing ... '

Next day I got a pass to go to Chebli and from there walked to 'our' farm. Marie and Bachir were surprised and delighted to see me, and I spent a few hours there before returning to the camp.

I saw Lieutenant Saunders and he asked whether I'd enjoyed my trip to Aumale

'Yes,' I said, 'it was great. Do you think there is any chance of me getting there again?'

He said he would ask Major Hibbert.

We had a 'full marching order' parade next day. The Squadron Leader accompanied by the SSM strode down the line.

'Sergeant Major, this man's kit is untidy.'

'Yes sir.' (To the soldier, through his teeth – 'Get that – – kit tidied up.')

'This man's boots are dirty.'

'Yes sir.' ('Get those – – boots cleaned.')

The Squadron Leader stopped in front of me. I wondered what was wrong with my kit. He looked me in the eye and said: 'I'll bet you wish you were in Aumale.'

'Yes, sir,' I answered, 'I certainly do.'

But later, to my great disappointment, Lieutenant Saunders told me he was sorry, but because the impending move was so close, there was no chance of my being given permission to go back to Aumale.

I wrote to M. Hugnit thanking him for the marvellous week I had spent with him and his family, but regretting that I would be unable to see them on the 28th. A few days later I had a letter from Suzette. She had been looking forward so much to Whitsuntide, now I wouldn't be there . . . she missed me . . . I missed her too.

I had asked the Hugnits, the Ferrandos, Bachir and my other friends to sign their names on an Algerian five franc note. It was a difficult task for Bachir, but with tongue between teeth he made it. I still have the note.

On 24 May we were up at 4.15 a.m. and after breakfast walked the three miles to Blida station carrying all our kit including a blanket: ' . . . all about collapsed when we got there, on train and soon at Algiers.' Next day we embarked on the *Durban Castle* and sailed for Italy.

19
1944: Italy

We had taken Tunis in May 1943, and six weeks later our forces made a landing in Sicily. They crossed the island and went on to invade Italy. We followed their progress as they successfully pushed their way northwards. The Italians had no heart for fighting, and it was with elation and relief we heard in September 1943 that Italy had surrendered. This could have been the end of the conflict in that country, but the Germans were more motivated and much tougher fighters. We soon realised that they had no intention of following suit.

In November 1943 the advancing army reached Monte Cassino, but here they ran into the most stubborn resistance they were to encounter and there was a tremendous battle for the town. Then, at the end of January 1944, a landing was made at Anzio, thirty miles south of Rome, the idea being to capture the city and link up with the troops driving from the south. The venture failed, for although a beachhead was established and held, our forces were unable to move forward.

At Cassino the Germans had occupied a monastery overlooking the town which they were using as an observation post, to deadly effect. One assault after another was launched on the town with disastrous loss of life, and Cassino was reduced to a mass of rubble. There were naturally reservations about attacking a religious building, but this monastery had been turned into a fortress and there was no way to advance until it had been destroyed. Our Air Force turned their full power and attention to the task. Day after day the monastery was bombed relentlessly. The Germans stubbornly continued to occupy it, but eventually, after suffering heavy casualties and with the building reduced to a shell, they pulled out, and our army was able to link up with the Anzio forces.

Now we knew why we had been held so long in North Africa. We were there in case we should be needed in Italy. Although our troops were advancing, the defiant German army simply would not give in, and our forces needed more strength and support. This is why the 2nd Armoured Brigade sailed on 25 May 1944 from Algiers.

I would never have dreamed in a thousand years that on the day we left Algeria I'd write in my diary 'Feeling miserable'. It wasn't because we were going to Italy, it was because I was leaving behind part of my life, and 'feeling miserable' was the understatement of the year. This terrible war – friends and loved ones torn apart – when would it end?

The *Durban Castle* was just the opposite of the *Talma*, she was clean, the food was good, and at any other time this would have been a pleasant journey. The weather was beautiful, so hot and sunny that during the day we played cards and wrote letters up on deck. I wrote to Suzette and M. Hugnit, and also to Marie. At night it was so warm we slept on the deck too.

We followed the North African coast eastwards and then turned north. We'd left Algiers on the 25th and docked in Naples harbour on the 27th; but though it was a hot and sunny Naples, my thoughts were in the cool hillsides of Aumale.

After disembarking we had a walk of about eight miles to Afragola on the outskirts of the city, and the camp was swarming with Italians, mostly children, many of them looking ragged and poor, and most of them trying to sell something.

'Cut your hair, soldier?'

'Do your washing, soldier?'

I bought a new pen and a bottle of ink for 150 cigarettes. One young lady was walking about with a tray hanging from a strap round her neck (like an ice-cream seller in a theatre), filled with nuts. Above the rest of the clamour around us we could hear her voice: 'Nuts-a very good. Nuts-a very good. Nuts-a very good.'

One of the boys called her over and said 'No, no. You've got that wrong. It isn't nuts-a very good, it's "Not so very good".'

'Ah, grazia signore,' she said and went on her way shouting 'Not so very good. Not so very good. Not so very good.'

We were surrounded too by dozens of budding Carusos and strains of 'O Sole Mio' floated from every corner of the camp.

Next day was the 28th – Whit Sunday. Only a couple of weeks ago I had drawn a square round day and date, and written 'Aumale!' I started the entry for the 28th: 'Today hoped and expected to be in

Aumale but instead I'm here in this camp, in Italy.' I wondered what Suzette was doing and wished so much that I was there with her.

'Harold and I walked the few hundred yards into the town. Plenty people about and very friendly. Feel sorry for the children, they seem so poor. Then hitched ride into Naples.' Our first impression of Naples was not very good, it seemed dirty and untidy, but the view across the Bay to the Isle of Capri and other islands was fantastic. A small cloud hung in the blue sky over Mount Vesuvius, and we saw plenty of evidence of the recent eruption – black rivers of lava down the mountain side and everywhere thick with dust.

Next morning, after an arms inspection, Stan and I hitched a lift to Pompeii. The truck driver said that a month ago the road we were on, between Vesuvius and the sea, had been two to three feet thick with dust from the eruption.

Pompeii was ' . . . a wonderful sight – need a book to mention everything.' I have been again in recent years, and more of the city is now unearthed, but in 1944 it was much quieter and less commercialised. We had a very good guide, for now the war had moved away it was 'business as usual' for these men, and they bore us no animosity. As we walked through the ruins it was easy to imagine what a thriving, prosperous, bustling city this must have been before it was disastrously buried in AD 79. The streets, many lined with shops, were well laid out, and some of the houses still had the original paintings on the walls. The amphitheatre was intact, and we walked in the enclosures where the lions and other wild animals had been kept before being turned into the arena. It was a most interesting day.

Normally guard duty came at night, but here we had to mount guard in the daytime as well – to keep the children out. 'Started guard at 6 a.m. What a job keeping children out of camp and then helping to feed them at meal times. Hot and dusty – poor kiddies. Not a bad guard really. Finished at 6 p.m.'

Although they were a nuisance, the children were very friendly, neither bad nor destructive. One ten-year-old called Carmelita took me home with her, and her relatives were very anxious to make friends too. A young man in his twenties could speak French so we were able to converse. Other relatives with 'Oohs' and 'Aahs' picked up the conversation here and there.

I called in and had a drink with this family a couple more times, and then after having spent a week in our camp, we packed up and moved. As we marched the two miles through the little town to the station, the whole population turned out to see us off – trying at the same time to sell us oranges, nuts and half-a-dozen other things.

The Italian cattle trucks were no different from the North African ones and so were no novelty to us – though there had been just once when I'd actually travelled on a seat in a carriage. We left in the afternoon and after a cramped, cold and uncomfortable ride, arrived at a station where we left the train, climbed into trucks, and after about fifteen miles arrived at Matera, 160 miles east of Naples.

This was very hilly, picturesque country, with Matera itself quite a big town, clinging to the hills. It was a clean, peaceful place, and the inhabitants were well-dressed, a complete contrast to Naples. We had been billeted in a variety of places over the years, but our new home was different yet again: this time we lived in a small monastery.

Some of the streets were no more than alleyways climbing up the hillsides, too narrow for traffic, and from the window of the room allocated to our troop we looked out on to one such 'street' below. It was as clean as if it had been scrubbed. Children played there and we leaned out of the window to talk to them in a mixture of English, French and the odd Italian words we'd picked up, accompanied by gestures. Unlike the poor children of Afragola, these were clean, well-dressed, well fed, and they weren't trying to sell us anything. Neither were there any aspiring operatic tenors around. In no time we were friendly with the children and one of the mothers offered to do our washing for a very small payment – an offer we quickly accepted.

Wherever we had been and whatever nationality they were, we always made friends with the children, and often I thought how tragic it was that they should be involved in this terrible war. They didn't want to fight us nor we them, we just wanted to be friends. There were five of them, all girls, ranging in age from about eight to sixteen, in the two houses below our window, and our relationship with their parents too was very good.

Matera didn't have a lot to offer in the way of entertainment. There was just one cinema, but there were pleasant cafés with tables and chairs set outside where one could sit with a glass of wine or cup of coffee in the warm evenings. However, these pleasures were denied us at first, for though we had been in Italy over a week, we hadn't yet received any pay. Nor had there been any mail. Fortunately the pay came a day or two after we arrived in Matera, so: 'I went into town, had a haircut, a hot bath, and then coffee and ice-cream. But no mail yet.'

Our tanks had not accompanied us on the *Durban Castle* but came on another ship a few days later. Now they had arrived at the port of Taranto about fifty miles away. Stan, Ron, Colin and a new man called Haley and myself were among the ones sent to go over them on the docks. Once again we worked hard cleaning the guns of mineral jelly (a kind of thick Vaseline), then coating the breeches with oil.

The combined British and American forces were on the move again, and on 4 June made a triumphant entry into Rome. On the 6th we heard of the opening of the Second Front. It was D-Day, and the landings on the Normandy coast had begun. Now the Germans were being squeezed from every direction. The British and American forces were advancing from the north and west, the Russians from the east, we were pushing from the south, troops had landed in southern France and were advancing towards Grenoble.

And – the mail was here! I always looked forward to the arrival of the mail, but this time I awaited its distribution more eagerly than ever. I was not disappointed, for among a pile of letters for me were *five* from Aumale. Not only had Suzette written but so had M. Hugnit, Mme Hugnit, Yves and Aunt Nanette. All were sorry I hadn't been able to visit them again at Whitsuntide and that I'd had to leave Algeria. They hoped I might go back someday. Suzette wished I'd be there soon, for she had loved those happy days we'd spent together, but they were too few. When did I think I'd come back to Aumale? I only wished I knew . . .

20

1944: Reluctantly to Hospital

I had been hoping for a letter from Suzette – I hadn't expected another four from her family, but I was delighted and sat down promptly to answer them all.

We had now to collect our tanks from Taranto. A few men had been left there to guard them, one of whom was Dave. On arrival we found he'd been mixed up in a brawl in a bar the night before, and had been stabbed and taken to hospital. We didn't know the details, but Dave was a pugnacious man at the best of times – one to steer clear of, especially when he'd been drinking. Even so, this was quite a shock, though his condition didn't appear to be serious.

We brought the tanks to Matera and parked them on waste ground on the edge of the town in an area abounding with fireflies. On guard at night the tanks appeared to be trimmed with fairy lights.

I had a letter from Ronnie – he was still in his office in Maison Carrée and not liking it a bit. Just like everyone else, he had hoped and expected that a move from Algeria would be to England. His wife Emily had had a baby boy, Ronald, in February 1941, who was only a few months old when Ronnie last saw him. Now he was over three.

After about three weeks in Matera we left our monastery. It had been pleasant there, I'd made friends with the family of the lady who did our washing and even went with them on a picnic. In those three weeks her husband taught me the words to 'Lili Marlene' – in Italian!

We didn't go far, just out in the country where we pitched tents. Once again it was the usual training but with the difference that now we were in a populated area, and were training for a different kind of warfare, where there were houses, towns and farms.

The CO gave us the usual pep talk: ' . . . all of which we've heard before, "Sooner we beat the Hun, sooner we'll be home" etc. etc . . .

it's the old story.' Then someone in the hierarchy decided that in this type of country, as we would be more involved with the infantry, it would be a good idea for us to experience something of their way of life – so we went on infantry training. 9 June: 'Advanced about three miles, everybody on their knees and fed up by the time we'd finished.' After a week we knew enough of infantry life to appreciate that it was tough, and that thankfully we didn't have to pretend to be infantrymen any more. We moved to an area where there were: 'some wonderfully coloured butterflies, dozens of different kinds; wrote to Jessie and told her about them.'

Dave came back after his spell in hospital. Of course the fight hadn't been his fault. He'd got into an argument and before he knew where he was, one of the Italian sailors there had knifed him. Well – that was *his* story. I wondered if perhaps the man hadn't been able to understand Dave's English, let alone his rather individual method of conversation. He had grabbed the man, pulled his face into his and started to speak slowly and deliberately – only to find this wasn't a timid Arab workman, but a roughneck with a knife. All the same it was good to see our fearless troop sergeant back with us.

I was busy writing letters in French now for about half the squadron who'd left various girl friends back in Algeria. Sergeant Smudger Smith's girl and I were still corresponding on his behalf. He was a tank commander in No. 3 Troop, an old regular, not good-looking by any stretch of the imagination, and with a wife and children back home, although this appeared to be of little consequence. I'd never met Smudger's friend, but if she was anything like him she might not have been much of a catch. I liked writing letters, but was much more interested in writing them to my own French friends than sending love letters to other people's girls I'd never met. However, I helped when I could. The mail was slow coming through, and I wondered how things were going in Aumale. It was time I had another letter from there.

When the mail finally arrived, among mine were two letters from Aumale, one from Suzette, and one from Mme Hugnit, telling me that life there was going on the same as always, and both wondering if we might be returning to Algeria. I was pleased to get a letter from Marie too, saying how much they missed us at the farm, it was so quiet now. Bachir wished he could write, but asked her to tell me he was thinking about me.

[131]

The American troops were lucky so far as entertainment was concerned, and a big show was coming to Bari. It was called *This Is the Army*, organised and directed by Irving Berlin, and he was in the show too. The Americans sent out complimentary tickets to some of the English regiments. We were limited to just a few for each squadron, names were put in a hat, and mine was one of the half-dozen drawn out. The show was in the fantastic, beautifully ornate, Bari Opera House. There were hundreds in the cast, all dressed in army uniforms, an excellent band, and they raised the roof singing 'This is the Army, Mr Jones', 'Ma, I Miss Your Apple Pie', and other popular and topical songs. Some they sang while marching on the huge stage, and Irving Berlin, a tiny black-haired man, 'sang' an amusing song asking what were we going to do with all the spam when the war was over? It was the best show I'd ever seen.

We had left Matera now, for an area near Bari on the Adriatic coast. The weather was very hot and we were glad to be allowed to go swimming in the sea. For town life we divided our time between Bari and Matera. Stan and I had made friends in Matera with our neighbours under the monastery window, so we visited them quite often. Stan was a good-looking boy, quiet and on the shy side, and all the girls loved him. Sometimes he was a bit embarrassed by their attention, but enjoyed it anyhow, and we had some good evenings with these people.

The weeks went by and life was getting monotonous – but I had letters regularly from Suzette and sometimes from her parents and her aunt. I looked forward so much to her letters and she to mine, and so often we said how we wished we could be together. Meanwhile my mother and sister continued to write regularly, as did other relatives and friends, and I was still hearing from Lucienne (English/French, French/English) and Marie, so there was plenty of variety in my mail. I wrote and received hundreds of letters. Ronnie wrote often too. He was over in Italy now, at a base somewhere near Naples, but we couldn't get to see each other.

We followed the progress of the troops advancing north. Besides British and Americans there were many other nationalities in the Allied Forces – Canadians, South Africans, Rhodesians, Australians, New Zealanders, Indians – and together they were relentlessly pushing the Germans back. Florence was taken, but then again the enemy began to dig in.

At the end of July we were told we would soon be leaving the area, but first were to have a week at a rest camp near Bari. Echoes of Chebli and Aumale, but this time there was no point in asking for an interview with the Squadron Leader. The rest camp proved to be right on the beach and we spent a relaxing week there. Also it wasn't far to Matera, and Stan and I went there to once again say goodbye to friends.

We left on 6 August, up the coast through Barletta, then to Foggia, and from there across country again towards Naples. We stayed the night in an apple orchard where the ground was covered in thick yellowish-grey dust from the volcano. Next day back to Foggia, back and forth as if we didn't know where we were going, and we weren't enlightened as to why. Finally back to the Naples area again and then north, bypassing Afragola by about fifteen miles.

For a few days I'd been having a lot of pain in my head, then 'got terrific pain in my eyes'. I endured this for more than a week and finally had to go and see the M.O. who gave me some eye drops.

We continued north through Caserta and then Cassino: ' . . . never before have I seen such a scene of desolation and destruction. The monastery on the hill is just one big ruin. Even all the trees are dead, and every house for miles past Cassino has been hit.' It was nine months since the Battle of Cassino, and, as if a huge earthquake had hit the place, there were still no signs of life.

In Northern Italy a number of rivers flow almost parallel to each other from the mountains across the Po Valley into the Adriatic. The Germans would dig in at one, resist attack as long as possible, then when they could hold the line no longer they would retreat to the next river. We were near the west coast, but now had to cross the country to the east to join the push north from there.

The pain in my eyes and head had become unbearable and I had to go sick again. The M.O. felt that all this trouble was the result of having been in the desert so long, and was probably caused by the sand. He insisted I go into hospital to have my sinuses drained and get other attention to my eyes and nose. This was the last thing I wanted, but he said there was no alternative, and I was sent all the way back to Caserta, to No. 2 General Hospital.

The hospital was an Italian one which had been taken over by the Army, and the nurses were all English. Only eight of the twenty beds in my ward were occupied, four of those by 'bed patients' and I was one of them: 'Ordered to bed and given some pills. Told to lie there and drink water. Wrote letters to Suzette and home.' Next day: 'Just about written to all my regular correspondents. Now written eleven letters since I've been here (four of them in French).' Two days later: 'M.O. says I've still got to stay in bed. Wish some mail would arrive. Can't smoke here. Still taking pills and inhaling. Wonder how long this will last . . . Got talking to the Sister. Asked me where I came from. She is from York and has worked in Huddersfield Royal Infirmary.' Also one of the orderlies told me he was from the Crosland Moor district of Huddersfield.

I became friendly with a Canadian boy, and we found we had something in common: he had spent some time in Sfax and had met a French girl there called Odette. I told him about Suzette and my week in Aumale, and we both sat there dreamy-eyed, talking and reminiscing about our lovely French girls. He said that before he left Sfax he and Odette had become engaged, and when the war was over he was going to take her home to Canada where they would be married. What were my plans about Suzette? Well, I didn't know. Although it seemed we had known each other for ever, I had in fact only spent one week with her. She was only sixteen and I couldn't tell what would happen. I just wished we could have had more time together. I loved her letters, and perhaps if we could go on writing like this, when she was a year or two older . . . well, all I could do was to wait and see how things might develop.

'Talking to a fellow from 2nd Echelon and they are only a couple of miles from here. Ronnie should be with them. I wonder if he knows I'm here.' Next day: ' . . . in middle of writing letter to Suzette when in walked Ronnie. Oh so glad to see him. Stayed till nearly dark and will come again in a couple of days if I'm still here.' I hadn't seen Ronnie for months, and now I was in hospital and he'd walked in, just as he had done almost exactly two years ago. Then, he had brought me the news that Bob Weightman had been killed. This time he had terrible news for me – Jimmy Turner had died as a result of an accident: 'Can't believe it. Oh God why do these things happen? Poor Jimmy, and his parents. Poor Doreen.' We had been abroad three years and Jimmy had been in the fighting all the time. The war must surely be ending soon, and to think that this had happened to him now. When I rejoined the Regiment I learned the facts. Jimmy's crew had been brewing up behind a tank, and for some reason someone had reversed it, knocked over the petrol fire, and Jimmy was engulfed in the flames. They got him to a hospital but he died two days later.

I had been writing to Jimmy's girl friend fairly regularly – from her letters she seemed a pleasant, friendly girl. Now I had to write and say how upset I was to learn of Jimmy's death, and I wrote to his parents too.

Ronnie said that the Regiment was getting near the front line and would probably be in action soon: 'I *do* hope and pray that all the boys are O.K. Waiting to hear some news of them. No M.O. again today. Looks as if I'll be in here for ever.'

I'd been in the hospital a week and was getting tired of this, but now had to go and see a specialist who took X-rays of my nose and eyes. They gave me innumerable pills and medicines but I wanted to be out: 'The M.O. didn't come round again today and I want to see him about getting back to the Regiment. Be in here for ever at this rate.'

Then, one day: 'I bumped into Sister Thomas, our blonde blue-eyed night sister of 1942. She recognised me and we had quite a talk.' Unfortunately she didn't know the whereabouts of Sister Furnival. She could easily have been at this hospital, and that would really have been a bonus.

My eyes were getting better. I was allowed out, and went to see Ronnie, having hitched a lift on the pillion of a motorbike. I went into the town too and bought a wooden jewellery box inlaid with mother-of-pearl and sent it to my mother (it has now been handed down to my daughter). I also sent Suzette a pair of shoes.

One day the sister put my name down to go on a trip to La Solfatara, a volcanic crater that had been dormant for hundreds of years. Cracks were appearing in the ground as we walked across it, and steam hissed from them. It was quite an extraordinary experience, and the guide delivered the line he'd no doubt used many times before: 'This volcano could erupt at any time – but not now.'

I had expected to be in hospital about a week and now I'd been there a month. Next time the M.O. came round I said I was better, and wanted to get out. He said: 'Right, you can go, but first you must go to a convalescent camp for a week.'

'But I don't want to go to a convalescent camp. Can't I go straight back to my Regiment?'

'No – definitely not. Convalescent camp.'

I was bothered about my mail, only a trickle was coming through. I felt the letters would be following me all over the place, and I didn't want to lose any. So I wrote to Corporal 'Ginger' Cudd, our squadron office clerk and asked him if he would keep my mail for me; I'd be back soon.

Ronnie came to see me once more and then, much against my will, it was off to convalescent camp. They kept me there an extra week, and I had no news of the Regiment, but heard there was heavy fighting north of Ancona. I felt sure the Bays would be in action now. I couldn't leave that convalescent camp quickly enough. Finally, after over six weeks away from the Regiment, five weeks longer than I had anticipated, I was dropped off by a wagon in the middle of 'C' Squadron. There was an eerie feeling about the place, it seemed deserted.

I walked to the tent serving as squadron office. Ginger Cudd, a man with a bright red face and hair to match his name, was standing outside. He was not a popular man, a stolid sort of person who hardly ever raised a smile. Today he looked grimmer than ever. I will never forget that moment, and the first words he said to me:

'You've lost all your mates.'

'What do you mean?'

'There's been a big battle. Most of the tanks lost, and a lot of men killed and wounded.'

I hardly dared ask the question.

'Who . . . was killed?'

He reeled off a dozen names of men I'd known, lived and fought with over the last few years: 'Paddy Deasey, Colin Hancock, Jack Hunter, Jack Adams, Ted Wanless, Stan Tatlow.'

'Oh no, not Stan.'

I was devastated. Ginger had saved fourteen letters for me – I couldn't read them.

I wandered over to my troop, and heard the story from the boys there. They had been advancing down a small hillside and had run into an ambush of anti-tank guns; they never had a chance. Herschel Schneiderman was badly injured, Titch Hughes, who had taken my place as gunner, had his foot blown off, Ron Grist missing, and more.

The last entry in my diary for that day says: 'Please God let me sleep tonight.'

21

1944: Reflections on Coriano

This had been the terrible battle of Coriano Ridge, fought over two weeks ago and I hadn't been there. The whole Regiment had suffered heavy casualties and 'C' Squadron had been hardest hit. The Regiment was resting, prior to being issued with new tanks, and more than sixty men were needed to bring it up to strength. When I rejoined them they were only a few miles from the site of the battle, the anti-tank resistance having finally been overcome. Many other regiments had taken part in the action and were now advancing.

They had buried all the boys except one, whose body was still in the tank, I don't know why it hadn't been recovered. The padre asked if I would go with him and three others to help to get the man out. I agreed to go, hoping and praying it wouldn't be Stan.

We went in a pick-up to the hillside. It was peaceful there now, with newly made graves on a ridge on the brow of the hill, each marked with a simple cross and the man's name. One was Stan's, and I couldn't hold back the tears.

On the slope from the ridge into the little valley below were ten broken and burned-out tanks, scattered about in unreal and unnatural positions. The one with the man still inside was at the bottom of the hill and partly burned. We went down there and looked inside. It was the driver, and his body was a shocking sight, crawling with maggots. The smell was nauseating. I got down in the tank beside him – and saw why he hadn't baled out. He couldn't, for his boot was jammed fast between the clutch and accelerator pedals, his leg twisted as he had tried to free himself. I pulled on his leg and his foot came out of the boot. We got him out, wrapped him in a blanket, carried him up the hill, and buried him alongside the others. The padre read a short service over his grave. He was a young, fair-haired, fresh-faced Scottish boy by the name of Jimmy Law, who just a few weeks ago had been shocked to hear from his parents that his twenty-one-year-old twin brother had been killed in action in

France. He'd said then that for his parents' sake he must come out of this alive.

I wrote in my diary: 'Jimmy's death was a great shock. Now Ted, Stan and Jack are gone. I'm just lost and in a maze. I suppose I should thank God that I wasn't here at the time. Why should such honest, good, young men die? Oh this war. But oh God, why did they die? It's unreal and unbelievable but the ghastly truth. I don't know what to say. Surely men will learn some day, and this useless throwing away of young lives will cease.'

I was back in my old troop in Dave's tank. Paddy Flanagan, Colin Rawlins, Buck, Harold, Ted Ryan and Jack Ryder were still there, but many of the other men were strangers. Every action in which we'd taken part, we had lost somebody, but never so many men whom I knew so well. Jimmy was with me at Catterick in 33 Squad five years ago, and had always been around. Ted Wanless too was always there and Stan and I had become inseparable since he joined the Regiment as a new recruit two years ago.

Jack Ryder and I used to play bridge regularly against Jimmy Turner and Jack Hunter. We'd lost them both now: 'Last night Jack and I played bridge together but oh how we missed Jack and Jimmy. So many new faces, it's not the same . . . '

I read the fourteen letters Ginger Cudd had saved for me. Twelve were from home and the other two from Jimmy's parents and Doreen. They were terribly shocked and thanked me for writing. Now I wrote letters to Ted's wife and to Stan's parents.

The graves are on the San Martino in Venti Ridge, about eight miles from Rimini in the direction of San Marino. I had to go to Regimental Headquarters, and while I was there the Adjutant asked if I would go up on to the ridge and tidy up the graves; I should take with me anyone I wanted. So I picked four men, including Jack, and we drove to the hilltop. There were some houses nearby, the people had returned to them after the fighting had passed.

31 October: ' . . . There all day. Italian people helping very much. Kiddies putting green leaves on graves. Haven't finished so hope to go tomorrow. Had five letters, mother, Jessie, Audrey, Suzette and Emily and another great parcel from Cape Town, socks, sweets, books, chocolates, shaving soap . . . '

1 November: 'This morning off again up to the graves. "Fiesta" for the Italians, but Pia our most industrious worker of yesterday

insisted on helping, and soon most of the kiddies too, particularly when it came to going and getting leaves – in the lorry. We took Pia and her mother and brother and some friends to church before coming back. They're having a service at the graves tonight and wished we could be there and so do I, but we must get back. The Adjutant came up as we'd finished and congratulated us on our work.' I haven't been there since the war ended, but know some of the Bays who have, and they tell me that the Italian people still take care of the graves, keep them tidy, and regularly put flowers on them.

We were billeted in some empty houses in the village of Santarcangelo, near Rimini. As the fighting came to these towns and villages, the people fled, hiding where they could, and then as the war moved away they gradually came back, often to find their homes in ruins. People were now returning here. We had a lot of rain, and the roads and fields around were flooded: we were glad, at least for the moment, to have the shelter of the houses. Besides being wet, it was cold and there was no heat in our house, until: 'Ted and I found an old stove outside so we washed off the mud and rigged it up with a chimney, put it in our room and it works O.K.!'

We had a new Troop Leader by the name of Lieutenant Lyle. He was straight from an officers' training college in England, and to quote my diary 'a real twerp'. He was a 'rookie' and after the Troop Leaders we'd had, this one had no idea how to handle men – especially some of whom had been abroad and had roughed it for years. 4 November: ' . . . On revolver inspection – got a rocket from our nice Troop Leader in spite of the fact that it's an old one and the marks won't come off . . . working on tanks . . . then all of us had a row with Lyle.'

On 5 November we were told we'd be moving on the 7th. That day: 'Up just after 4 a.m., had breakfast and finally left at 7.45. We'd made friends with some of the local people, and I particularly with an old man with whom I'd "talk" regularly. It caused some amusement when he kissed me goodbye . . . Through Cesena and finally stopped near Forli. Jerry's still there. The RAF is certainly giving him a pasting and we're sat watching the Spitfires dive-bomb incessantly. We moved on after dark – must have looked a very impressive sight. Civvies stood about watching us. Stayed overnight in houses in a village. Fine billet this – tables, chairs, cupboards, wardrobes, mirrors.'

The fighting was still just ahead of us. We'd had the Gurkha infantry with us, quiet, fearless men, for whom we had great respect, and now they were replaced by the New Zealand infantry. One of their sergeants came and said they'd just found eight Italian men down a well, all with their hands tied behind their backs and shot through the head. As we pushed on we also came to a well and we found another seven men down there who had suffered a similar fate – a gruesome sight . . . What sort of men were these we were fighting to commit such atrocities as this?

10 November: 'Snow on the hills not far away. We found spring beds and slept on them last night. Few shells landed. Should have advanced, but there is a river in front and it is swollen and we can't cross it. Stayed here another night – shells and bombs don't half rock this house.'

The rain poured, the fields turned to mud, and we came to the river. The flood had subsided a little, a survey was made, and a point found where a crossing could be risked. It was pretty deep and our hearts were in our mouths as our tank entered the swirling muddy water, but we made it to the other side and to our relief met no opposition – 'bit of shelling, that's all. Then crossed River Montone. We went a bit wrong with our tank and nearly ended up with Jerry. Haley and I caught two chickens – chicken for supper.' Next day: 'Did very well today, got a chicken and six cabbages.'

14 November: 'There's snow in the hills. Had to sleep in tank last night, frozen stiff in spite of being well wrapped up. At 5.30 a.m. we left in the mud and pouring rain and soon engaged the enemy. We exchanged fire, but though shells dropped around us we had no casualties and forced the Germans to retreat.'

We were now fighting from village to village, farmhouse to farmhouse, and in many of them we found people huddled, waiting for the war to pass. There were fields of mud, dead animals and poultry, and I felt sorry for the people, and especially the poor children. The rain turned to snow, and the conditions were atrocious. Still, for all this dreadful weather we continued to advance.

I thought about last winter in the snow, but we were only playing at fighting then. I thought about Suzette and the peaceful, happy farm at Aumale, and was thankful that she and her family had not been touched by this war. Suppose the fighting had reached Aumale, this would have happened to them. I couldn't bear the thought. But these were families just the same, their homes and farms in ruins, and we were part of this ruthless war. The Germans *must* know they couldn't win, and yet, even in retreat they continued to fight. Not only were the lives of our young soldiers being thrown away – so were their young lives too.

16 November: 'Had a first class bed last night – in a house ... Set off at first light and tried to get round the left flank, to relieve No. 2 Troop, but stuck a few times, and the area became impassable because of the mud. So in the end Squadron Leader recalled us, we returned to farm of last night, and the family there were very happy to see us back. Finally tried again, and we got up to 2 Troop.'

Next day: 'Had to sleep in tank again because so many shells about. Humphries killed a duck for dinner. In afternoon he really blasted us and we had to sit in tank all the time. Shells dropped everywhere and tank hit all over the place with shrapnel.'

18 November: 'Ration wagon got hit last night as he brought up supplies. We got out and helped him to unload. Took rations off in dark and no one hurt ... The ridge we're on is alive with Jerries and guns. Slept in tank again last night. Very cold and uncomfortable. Poles have been pushed back a bit on left, which leaves us in rather a dangerous position. We should have been relieved but can't get back. Jerry pounded us again at dinner-time. Dropped one right alongside us, shrapnel marks all along side of tank and big holes in idler.'

19 November: 'Still here last night which meant another cold and bone-aching night of attempted sleep in tank. He was dropping them all night, but no "Moaning Minnies" for a change.' The Moaning Minnies were a type of rocket, which when fired made a loud wailing sound like a siren. You heard them fired but, unlike a shell, you couldn't hear them in the air, so you crossed your fingers as you waited to hear where they landed. They were terrifying weapons.

The fighting continued fiercely. The Army rigged up searchlights and trained them on the ridge opposite and the RAF pounded it with bombs and machine-gun fire. Night and day there was no rest. The noise was deafening. It was like living in hell.

On 20 November we launched a big attack. We advanced with the infantry while the artillery fired over us from behind, and in front the Spitfires bombed and strafed. We played our part too. I knocked out among other things a self-propelled gun and hammered the village in front. 'Then he let us have it, and did everything but hit us. Edged forward 500 yards to next farm.'

After over two weeks of exhausting, nerve-racking fighting the 10th Hussars took over from us and with relief we withdrew. But the Germans were still showing no signs of surrender.

33 Squad, Catterick 1939. Ronnie Cross second from right, back row. Front row: Johnson, Jimmy Turner, Ray, author, Lin Wood, Ted Ryan, Brown, Wright.

With sister Jessie, 1940.

Tilford 1940. Standing on Crusader tank: author and Bob Weightman. Sitting: George Brooker and Sgt 'Boxer' Blythe.

With landlady Mrs Donald at The Studio, Tilford 1940/41. From left: Jim Emery, Bob Weightman, author, Findlow.

The author and Ronnie Cross, Palestine, August 1942.

With the tent kindly left by Jerry. From left, standing: Bob Buckland, Stan Webber, Ron Grist, Paddy Flanagan, Ted Wanless, Colin Rawlins, 'Track' Perry, Dave Beauchamp, Harold Balson, Des Darch. Seated: author (on chair), Herschel Schneiderman, Ted Ryan, Jack Ryder, Stan Tatlow, Wilcox. Libya, November 1942.

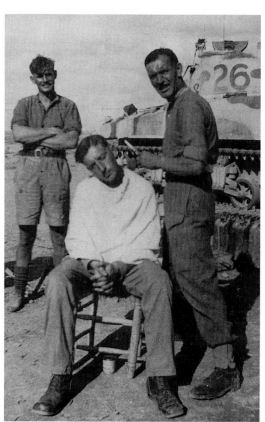

Barber! Sgt 'Nobby' Clarke with Paddy Flanagan standing and Bob Buckland in the chair. Libya, December 1942.

BELOW No. 1 Troop 'C' Squadron. Back row: Stan Betts, Paddy Flanagan, Colin Rawlins, Ron Grist, Bob Buckland, Foster, Harold Balson, Ted Wanless. Front row: Stan Tatlow, Jack Ryder, Herschel Schneiderman, 'Track' Perry, author.

ABOVE The cookhouse truck. BELOW Desert sandstorm.

LEFT Taking a 'German' prisoner. On tank: Paddy Flanagan. Prisoner: Herschel Schneiderman. From left: Colin Rawlins, author, Ron Grist. RIGHT South of Derna, Libya, January 1943. Sherman tank. Sitting on left: Herschel Schneiderman. On gun: author; Colin Rawlins, Paddy Flanagan, Ron Grist. Standing, from left: Wilcox, Ted Ryan, Harold Balson, 'Track' Perry. In front: Stan Tatlow, Foster, Dave Beauchamp.

Cairo, August 1943. Sid Aster, author, Stan Tatlow. In front, Colin Rawlins.

Suzette.   Ronnie Cross, Algeria 1944.

Memorial service, Coriano Ridge, 13 January 1945.

The author with Major Crosbie Dawson, Marlborough 1991.

LEFT The author outside Cardiff Castle, August 1995. RIGHT With Prince Charles.

22

Close-Quarter Fighting

As we pulled back from the fighting one tank hit a mine and Roy Heeler of No. 2 Troop was killed. He was a quiet well-liked boy and we were very upset to lose him.

21 November 1944: 'Through Dave's stupidity we half slung a track. Sid was driving but it wasn't his fault.' As the squadron retired to a village we were left with our tank, but as it was evening we couldn't deal with the track. Next morning we were able to get it back on and then rejoin the squadron. There was rabbit for supper that night but I didn't fancy any.

Next day some guinea-fowl were pecking around in the snow and clucking like a group of old ladies. With one shot from the tommy-gun Paddy killed one. (A tommy-gun could be used as either a machine-gun or to fire a single round at a time.) 'Cleaning up tank and did some repairs, having had new idler sent.' (The idler was a wheel that supported the track as it went round.) 'Plucked, cleaned and cooked the guinea-fowl. The Ities living below did our washing and they've made a fine job of it because everything was black.' It may be difficult to understand why the Italians were so friendly – after all, until recently we had been the enemy; but there was no love lost between them and the Germans, and in general they were glad to see the back of their former allies.

The mail arrived, but there was no letter from Suzette. I hadn't heard from her for three weeks, and I wrote to say that I hoped she was all right and that I'd soon have a letter. I had a wonderful parcel from home, 'best I've ever had, cigarettes, chocolates, razor blades, books . . . ' But I caught a cold and developed a bad cough, and I was grateful for some iodised throat tablets Jessie had sent.

The fighting had matured Lieutenant Lyle to some extent, and our relationship with him improved. But the weather was dull and cold and it continued to rain – some came through the roof on to Dave's bed. Now the Echelon had moved here and the cookhouse, so our diet of poultry (chicken, cockerel, turkey, duck and guinea-fowl) came to an end, but at least somebody else was making the meals for us.

Everybody suddenly began to get letters from home about 'Churchill Leave', and it seemed that all our families were expecting us back soon. This was the first we'd heard about it, but eventually we were given the news too, though it differed considerably from the publicity it was having in the UK. Soldiers were to be allowed home on a month's leave, and the impression being given was that this would apply to all of us. It did, but what wasn't explained was that only a tiny minority of us would be going on leave at a time. Our quota, for example, was to be only one man at a time from each squadron. At this rate, if your name was at the bottom of the list, you would be waiting for several years yet. Our squadron decided to put all the names of the men who were actually fighting in a hat and draw one out. There was an uproar ('almost a riot') when the first name drawn out was that of Corporal Harry Musgrave. Musgrave had earned himself the name of 'King of the Echelon', and had never been near a tank, let alone in one. He had a reputation of being a 'wangler' and somehow he must have wangled this. After the furore this caused, our squadron stuck strictly to the rules – fighting men only. In addition it was announced that a few men at a time would be sent back to Rome for a week's leave – so you watched the notice board hoping your name would be on it.

29 November: 'On guard with Sid and Jake, ground wet and muddy and boots wet through . . . still no letter from Suzette, wrote to her again to say I was getting worried. Rumoured that we may stay here a while. Three hour standby cancelled. Jack and I made a cribbage board and played most of day. Ended up "straights"!' We were 'resting' now, but the weather was so bad we were glad we had playing cards, most of them pretty thick, but sometimes new packs were sent from home. My mother sent a pack once – there were 52 cards, but when we started to use them we found there were two aces of clubs, two kings of diamonds and several other such pairs, but of some denominations there were none at all. The reason came to light; at home we had two packs of cards with identical backs and my mother had just sent 52 of them!

Our squadron was due to go back into action now but 'B' Squadron was sent instead, so we weren't unhappy about that. Some of us went into Forli. The town had only just been taken and was practically deserted, though there wasn't much damage to the buildings. There was a canteen but very little else. On the way back the driver ran the lorry into a ditch, and we had a walk of about a mile to the squadron.

It continued to rain, and for the first and only time ever, we were issued with gumboots. 'Not before time' was the general comment.

We weren't far from the front line, and could see and hear the battle for Faenza. 9 December: 'A barrage been going on all night, and what a barrage. We can see the guns flashing all along the plains. Infantry about a mile from Faenza. In the evening came the news that we were moving in the morning, but without tanks. Taking over 'A' Squadron other side of river. As Dave and others going on a few days leave tomorrow I have to stay here.'

The towns of Rimini, Cesena, Forli, Faenza, Bologna and Modena are in a line along the foot of the Apennines, the mountains being to the west, and to the east the wide flat plain of the Po Valley. This was the line the fighting was following.

Next day all leave was cancelled, and the squadron left ' . . . in lorries, leaving tanks behind, we're coming back for them some day. After journey over terrible roads, had lunch then transferred to Bren carriers which took us as far as they could get.'

Our troop was to take over the tanks of an 'A' Squadron troop so we left the Bren carriers and had a walk of about three miles along a track ahead, in places ankle deep in mud. We were taking over these tanks because some of them were so bogged down they were unable to move. 11 December: 'Last night we had a terrible walk. Done about two miles then Colin cracked up, said he couldn't go on, an extreme case of "shell-happiness".' Colin just broke down and was almost in hysterics. Sid and I volunteered to take him back to the Bren carriers, while the rest of the troop waited. With Colin's arms around our shoulders we squelched our way back along the track. Another driver was there, 'Busty' Ranson, so we left Colin, and Busty came with us to take his place. Once more, along with him, we trudged through the mud to rejoin the troop. It was extremely heavy going. There were scattered farms in the area, some occupied by German troops, and as it was now dark we half expected to end up as prisoners, but we kept to the track, and at 1 a.m. finally reached the farm we were bound for.

[145]

We had made it to a big barn, half-filled with hay. The New Zealand infantry were here, and the farm was shelled regularly during the night. When it came light we saw a number of bodies in the field outside, three or four Maoris and a Rhodesian with a huge piece of shrapnel embedded in his head. Some of the surrounding farms were occupied by our own troops, but it was difficult to keep in contact with them. That morning a patrol of four men had been sent out on reconnaissance but they never came back. They must have gone to the wrong farm and had either been killed or taken prisoner.

About 200 yards up the field in front of us one of the 'A' Squadron tanks was hiding from the Germans against the wall of a barn. Dave had gone up there the night before and relieved the tank commander. Tonight I had to go, taking three men with me to relieve the crew. My diary I think, puts it mildly, when it says that this was a 'pretty hair-raising experience'.

In the dark, Haley, 'Lofty' Crisp, Busty Ranson and myself prepared for the ordeal. We crawled up the field at the side of a hedge. Here it was grassy, and though wet there was little mud. We had to go slowly, because although we knew in which direction the tank lay, we couldn't see it, and didn't want to suffer the same fate as the earlier patrol.

We'd crawled about 100 yards, then I whispered to the others to stay there. I was going to go on alone; if I didn't come back they had to return to the barn and report me missing. I crawled on, and then to my relief the dark shadow of the tank loomed up in front of me. I went back, told the men to follow me, and we came to the tank. There appeared to be some bodies by the side of it.

Dave and the crew were expecting us. It was very dark and I tapped on the side of the tank, but Dave had seen us. The other crew quickly got out and we dived into the tank. A few minutes later we heard shouting and an explosion. Afterwards we learned that the crew had strayed off course on their way back to the barn and had run into a New Zealand patrol, who mistook them for Germans and threw a hand grenade at them. Two of them were hit in the legs, but immediately identified themselves. The atmosphere was extremely tense, and they could have easily been killed. As it was, the two men were not seriously hurt and the New Zealanders escorted them back to the barn.

There was a road not far away and in the dark we heard a

German vehicle come along it. It stopped and we could hear the men shouting. We guessed it was a self-propelled gun. It opened fire, but it was shooting over the top of us in the direction of the barn behind. It fired a dozen shells or so, there was more shouting, and the vehicle left.

Busty, the driver, and Haley, the scatter-gunner, had very little room to move and were cramped in their seats. Lofty, the operator, myself and Dave had a little more freedom in the turret, and took it in turn to be on guard half out of the top of the tank. To hand, for instant use if necessary, were a tommy-gun and hand grenades, and we were also wearing loaded revolvers. The two who weren't on guard could push their heads out to see what was going on and keep the driver and scatter-gunner informed. Next morning we saw that there really were bodies at the side of the tank, four German soldiers lying side by side and another a few feet away. We were only a yard or so from the wall of a barn, the tank parked parallel to it, and about ten yards away was an orchard. On the opposite side was a haystack.

Through the trees in the early morning mist we could see German soldiers moving about. The tank was facing away from the orchard. The driver and scatter-gunner could only see in front, but we in the turret could see all round. It was Lofty's turn on guard, and he whispered that four of the Germans were slowly and cautiously coming towards the tank, through the trees. They were carrying a bazooka, a portable anti-tank gun, very deadly, but only when used at close range. They were coming towards the rear of the tank, obviously hoping to get near enough without being detected. We kept very still and quiet. Lofty had the tommy-gun at the ready and let them come closer. Then he opened fire. One of them he killed, another was wounded, a third gave himself up and the other ran away. On the wireless we contacted the Maoris back at the barn, who had heard the gunfire, and with the gun trained on the two men, Lofty directed them to the Maoris who were coming to collect them.

It had been very cold and cramped all night in the tank, but we got the stove going and made some tea and opened some tins of stew to warm us up. 'Jerry in house only 100 to 150 yards away and we have to be alert all the time – rather nerve-racking. Bitterly cold and raining. Listening to Jerries talking.'

There were no further incidents that day, but when it came dark we heard the S.P. gun come up the road again, fire several more shells, then drive away.

My turn on guard came around as dawn broke, but things were quiet. Dave took over and after a while whispered to us to look outside. A revolting sight met our eyes. A pig had come up and was eating one of the dead Germans, pulling at his leg. We watched it for a few minutes then could stand it no longer. Dave killed it with a single shot from the tommy-gun. It sank to its knees on top of the dead soldier.

During the day the area was shelled heavily and the house adjoining our barn was hit numerous times, turning it into a pile of rubble. 'Things were hot – but about 7.30 p.m. they got even hotter because the haystack was hit, it caught fire and we had to evacuate *quick*.' The blazing haystack was too close for comfort. We jumped out of the tank and ran down the fields and to our surprise were joined by some Italian civilians who had been hiding under the haystack. We made it back to our original farm and luckily no one was hurt.

This farm was now full of New Zealanders, many of them Maoris. We got on well together, and they were really good fighters. That night they planned an attack to try to clear the area of Germans and advance. They left the barn, and we had little rest as they brought back some of the wounded and we helped with them. One young Maori died there as he lay on the ground in the barn. We covered him with a blanket and next morning helped to bury him just outside, in a corner of the farmyard. There was heavy shelling all day. We heard one land about thirty yards away and waited for the explosion, but it didn't happen, so we went to look for it. It was a huge shell at least a foot in diameter and if it had exploded it would have blown us to Kingdom Come. Meanwhile the Kiwi attack wasn't as successful as they'd hoped, but they brought back about fifty prisoners and had moved the enemy further away.

15 December: 'He shelled us heavily but we're lucky he didn't hit the house, troop going back, but some of us have to stop and try to get that tank out tomorrow.'

16 December: 'Sid, Dave, myself and a couple of men stayed behind last night and rest of troop left about 5.30 p.m. I lay on the straw with a couple of blankets – and slept for fifteen hours! – Wonderful! The Gurkhas attacked Faenza last night. New Zealanders advanced and now everything going well.'

[148]

It was quieter here now, and we went up to the tank. The haystack had burned out and the tank was undamaged. We drove it back to the barn, down the muddy track we'd recently walked, then back to the squadron a few miles away.

23

1944: Christmas in Pesaro

When we arrived back at the squadron there were 'loads of rumours going round that we're going a long way back, even that we're going home. All except two men per tank left at 4 p.m. to go to new billets – presumably at Forli. Sid and I stayed with "our" tank [the one belonging to 'A' Squadron]. We were going to move in two or three days' time, but tonight orders came to be ready to move at 11.30 p.m. as roads fairly clear.'

Next day, 18 December: 'Managed four or five hours' sleep last night. Wish I could get rid of this blinkin' cough – had it about three weeks now. Up at 3.30 a.m. and moved at 4 a.m. Just Sid and I on our tank. Through Faenza, at least what's left of it. Haven't seen a place like it since Cassino, just piles of debris and ruins. Down main road to Forli, our Squadron tanks and crews there, and we took over our own tank. Raining. Got to Forli about 7.30 a.m. and stayed there all day.'

Forli is south of Faenza, and we were now heading away from the fighting which was moving north. The Echelon was here and I saw Topper; he said he was thankful to see me because he'd heard I'd been wounded.

That night we loaded the tanks on to transporters, left after dark and at 4 a.m. arrived at Pesaro, twenty-five miles south of Rimini, after our transporter had had a puncture. We seemed to be fated with transporters having punctures. 'Slept till 10 a.m. then up and cooked breakfast. Tidied up tank a bit, then had a bath. We are in very good billets – seaside hotels. Sid, Jackie White [a new recruit], and I are in one room – tons of room. Tanks parked right on sea front 20 yards from sea.' After tea Sid and I walked around Pesaro. Most of the shops were closed, but the place had suffered little damage as it was on the coast and the fighting had mainly taken place on the outskirts.

Unfortunately our sea-front hotel was bereft of furniture, which meant no beds, and the marble floors were hard and cold to sleep on. We complained to our Mr Lyle strongly about this – after all, he had a bed in the officers' mess. After much argument he agreed to take a wagon and a few men to a naval base at Ancona, forty miles down the coast, to see if he could get some wood to make into beds. A few hours later they returned, empty-handed.

In desperation I asked if *I* could take a truck and some men the next day.

'No – a complete waste of time,' he said. 'I've been through the proper channels, they wouldn't listen. No chance.'

A heated argument followed between Lieutenant Lyle and the rest of the troop, not the first one we'd had with our Troop Leader, but eventually, after a great deal of pressure, he gave in.

'You can take a truck,' he said. 'And I can tell you before you leave you're wasting your time.'

Next morning, with six men aboard, I drove a truck to Ancona. The base was in a compound, the entrance closed by two big iron gates, with a sailor on guard at either side. We could see a huge pile of wood about 100 yards away, inside. I stopped in front of the gates. One of the guards came up. With heart in mouth I pointed and said: 'We've come for the wood.'

He seemed a little surprised, but they opened the gates anyway. We drove in and they clanged shut behind us.

At the wood pile, as nonchalantly as possible, we began to load the wagon. A number of sailors walked past, but took little notice of us. As soon as we had enough wood to make about twenty beds, we piled calmly back into the wagon. The gates swung open and we drove out.

'Thanks.'

'O.K. – So long.'

Out of sight I put my foot down and we flew back to Pesaro. When we arrived, Mr Lyle stared in disbelief. He appeared to have lost his voice. Eventually he found it, and croaked: 'How did you do that?'

'Oh, there was nothing to it – I just said we'd come for the wood.'

'Did you ask permission?'

'No.'

To give him his due, Lieutenant Lyle pursued the investigation no further. It worried him that we hadn't done the right thing – but the wood was there, we heard nothing from the Navy, and eventually he brought himself to congratulate us. We appreciated this, and our relationship with him continued to improve.

We got hammers and nails from the fitters and made a variety of different-sized frames. Across these we stretched pieces of canvas, 'borrowed' from the Echelon, and for the rest of our stay we no longer had to sleep on the marble floors.

21 December: 'Working on tanks after breakfast. Pretty cold down on the sea-front. Mail arrived – I had 20 letters, none from Aumale. Wrote 256th letter home. I was put in charge of decorating the mess-room for Christmas dinner. Four of us got cotton wool etc. and made designs, "Christmas Greetings" etc. – shall be doing this for next four days. Another name drawn out for Blighty leave, Trooper Marks, lucky man. Sid and I walked into Pesaro, got photo-frame for Jessie's photo; very nice.'

22 December: 'On mess-room decorating again. Had a fine time dyeing streamers with ink and mepacrine. Cold wind blowing this morning, and the sea very rough. I like it though, a bracing wind. We had a "paratroop scare" last night, but no paratroopers landed. Snowing when night came. Topper came and enjoyed him playing accordion.' Actually, the sea became so rough that we had to move the tanks further back as the spray was going over them.

23 December: 'Snow greeted us this morning when we awoke and very reluctantly crawled out of bed [there was no heat in the hotel] ... went to mess-room to help with adding decorations. Snowing all day, so looks as if we'll have a white Christmas.'

24 December: 'Christmas Eve, yet another one to be spent away from home and abroad. Surely we shall be home for the next. It makes me wonder. How things have changed since last Christmas, and oh that we could have back those boys we have lost since then.'

We had done a good job in decorating the mess-room and it looked bright and cheerful on the 25th as we sat down to Christmas dinner, which was up to the standard we had come to expect and as usual served by the officers and sergeants. But for many of us the day wasn't happy. The memory of last Christmas played on our minds. Stan, Ted, Jimmy, Herschel, Ron ... so many missing. Chebli, Bachir, Marie, the farm – it had been a happy Christmas there.

Pesaro was coming to life. They had a Rossini Symphony Orchestra, named after the composer, who was born in this town. On

Boxing Day Sid, Colin, Topper and I went to a concert given by this orchestra. The conductor was a little man with a mop of grey hair and the more the concert progressed the more agitated and excited he became. The final number was 'Dance of the Hours' and by the time they'd finished he was almost in a frenzy. His performance affected the audience so much that at the end we were all on our feet clapping and shouting 'Biz, biz.' This so delighted the conductor that he decided to give an encore – and they played the whole piece again! Any moment I expected him to collapse from exhaustion, but with arms flailing he once again made it to the end. If ever a man gave his all, he did. In between the orchestral numbers a very good choir sang. In my diary next day I wrote: 'Yesterday was the best day of Christmas.'

That night the sergeants had a party at which the drink flowed freely. One sergeant (not from our troop) was throwing his weight about, boasting how much he could drink, and in a drunken stupor said he could drink a whole bottle of cherry brandy at one go. He did so – didn't feel well, stepped outside, and dropped dead.

Our daily routine followed more or less the same pattern: drill parade in the morning, then work on the tanks. Not that they needed much work – like us they were 'resting' – but we were constantly cleaning and oiling the working parts because they were so close to the sea.

When we weren't on guard duty, we went into Pesaro for the cinema, the Symphony Orchestra, and to the YMCA or the NAAFI which had opened up. A pretty dark-haired Italian teenager called Anna worked in the NAAFI. One night I asked if I could walk her home and she said 'Yes'. So most nights after that I took Anna home. Not that I'd forgotten Suzette, but Anna was a pleasant girl and I enjoyed some congenial feminine company.

One evening she asked: 'Jackie, how old are you?'

'Eighteen.'

'Oh, you're not *that* old,' she said.

Not wishing to disillusion the young lady I changed the subject.

Three men from the troop could go to Rome for a week's leave. We cut the cards, and the winners were Ted Ryan, Jackie White and Jock McLeish. It wasn't usually my misfortune to lose a cut.

Into the New Year, 1945. 4 January: 'The mail was coming through very slowly but today I had a few letters, one was from

[153]

Ronnie, and another from Marie.' Ronnie and I wrote to each other regularly and I was always glad to hear from him. I had letters quite often from Marie too, and she kept me in touch with life on the farm and news of Bachir and other friends there. I answered Marie's letter and put one in for Bachir which she would be able to read to him.

We weren't far from the ridge where Stan and the other boys were buried. A memorial stone had been erected at the graves while we were away and on 13 January we went there to a dedication service presided over by the Padre. There was snow on the graves. The Colonel laid a wreath at the stone and Topper played the 'Last Post'. It was an extremely moving ceremony. Pia and the Italian friends I'd made earlier were there and were very happy to see me, as I was to see them. From the concern they showed, you would have thought the boys buried there were their own family.

Then it was back to Pesaro to be informed that in a couple of days' time we could expect to be moving, up to the front line.

24

Skirmishes on the Senio

On 15 January 1945 I walked Anna home for the last time. For the past couple of weeks I'd seen her in the NAAFI most days, then taken her home at night. I'd enjoyed her company but now it was goodbye yet again, for we were due to leave next day. She hoped we'd come back to Pesaro -- so did I, but Aumale was really where I wanted to be, and that night I wrote again to Suzette.

Only our squadron left Pesaro – at 2 a.m. on the morning of the 16th, arriving at Faenza at about 9 a.m. We were to take over from a squadron of the 10th Hussars, a few miles north-east of Faenza and south of the River Senio. 'Bitterly cold, plenty hard snow here and drizzling sleet.'

We took over an empty farmhouse. It was furnished just as the people had left it, with pictures on the walls, photographs and personal belongings in every room, and clothes in some of the wardrobes. The owners appeared to have taken nothing with them when they fled. There was a big fireplace and plenty of wood so we soon had a fire going. We slept in the various rooms, some of us on the beds, others making themselves comfortable wherever they could.

Other troops of the squadron were in different empty houses and next day the Engineers put in a telephone line so that we kept in touch with them and 'HQ' by phone, and not by the wirelesses in the tanks.

The farm was on the edge of a small town called Granarolo. The Germans were retreating from one river to the next, and the towns in between, such as this, were caught in the fighting. Some of the people had left their homes, but many had stayed and most of the houses were occupied. About 100 yards from the farm, towards the town, was a narrow canal and, quite near, a bridge across it. Then another 100 yards or so away were houses with families living in them.

We were gradually training our Mr Lyle and introducing him to our way of life. He began to realise that the only way to live in harmony was to be, to a certain extent, 'one of the boys'. We didn't take advantage of him, after all he was an officer and had a lot of responsibility as our Troop Leader; but it was impossible for him to try to live the life here that he'd been taught in an officers' training school. So at night out came the cards, and he joined us in a game of pontoon in front of a roaring fire.

The enemy were dug in on the north bank of the river half a mile or so north of us, and seemed unaware of our presence. 'Played cards, not much else to do. Few shells landed, not many. Made a couple of meat and potato pies. No mail up.'

19 January: 'Paddy got up and gave us all a cup of tea in bed! Cold outside but we've got a big stock of wood and a big fire. Had eight letters – mother, Jessie, Ronnie and Emily. Got some sugar from Italians for M. & Vs.'

20 January: 'Jerry dropped some of his blinkin' rockets last night and did they rock this house. Horrible weapon. Made meat pie and apple pie. This is about the easiest time we've had in action (touch wood). He's dropping some rather big shells fairly close, 300 to 400 yards away, but the main thing is we're sleeping in a house and have a fire. With this snow and cold we're thankful for it.'

The Italian people were eager to be on good terms with us. Many of them had been ill-treated by the Germans as they passed through their towns and villages and there was no doubt they hated the 'Tedeschi' as they called them. Giuseppe Balbi was the name of the man from whom I'd got the sugar. He invited a few of us into his home and I became friendly with the family. His wife, who volunteered to do my washing, was very cheerful and they had a little girl, Diana, aged about eight or nine.

Giuseppe introduced me to his brother, who had three children, two boys and a girl. He had been in some sort of an accident: his leg was scraped and bruised from top to bottom, an awful sight and extremely painful. His family had bandaged it as best they could but he was in bad shape. I got in touch with our M.O., who was in another building not far away, and asked if he could do anything to help. The man could ride his bicycle (though not without considerable discomfort), so the M.O. told me to send the Italian to see him. The family couldn't believe we'd go to so much trouble to help, but the brother went to the M.O. and came back with his leg properly dressed and covered with a clean bandage. He was given instructions to go back regularly, and by the time we left the area his leg was almost better. He and the family were eternally grateful; they couldn't do enough for me, I could have eaten with them every night if I had wanted to. As it was I accepted their offer occasionally. I was just happy that I had been able to help the man.

The Balbis couldn't speak English. I had picked up a bit of Italian, but we were only able to carry on a limited conversation. However, my Italian did improve as a result of spending time with them. When we left, Giuseppe asked if I would write to them and I said I would. I wrote in English and he had someone in the town translate my letters, but then he would answer in Italian, which I did my best to decipher. We kept up this correspondence even after the war was over, but it was difficult for both of us and gradually our correspondence waned and eventually ended. This was another family I promised myself I'd go back and see some day, but if Bachir had been there he'd have said: 'M'sieur Jackie, you'll never come back.' And he'd have been right again.

Some of us had made friends with families in different houses, and sometimes in the evening we'd walk over the bridge together before going our separate ways. One night, Dave, Paddy and I had all been visiting and we met to walk back to the farm. We were walking along a track by the side of the canal, and were talking, when suddenly a Spandau machine-gun opened fire. We heard the bullets whistling around us and whining away in the darkness as they hit trees, and we instinctively dived into a ditch at the other side of the track. We were all unhurt, but as soon as we started to move the gunner opened fire again.

We lay in the ditch for a long time. It was dark, and very quiet – until we moved, and then the bullets whistled through the air again. It seemed the gunner would never relax. We lay there another hour or so, hardly daring to breathe, but eventually we had to chance it. We edged our way slowly along the ditch towards the bridge. All was quiet. Then we signalled to each other to make a break for it. I've never run so fast in my life. We flew over that bridge and back to the comparative safety of our house, and fortunately for us no bullets followed.

Much of the time was uneventful – 'It snowed heavily and some of us, including Mr Lyle, did some snow shovelling around the building.' – but we were here basically to harass the Germans as much as possible. Our troop, with its three tanks, was on its own on the farm, and we now started to take it in turn to go up to our side of the river to wreak as much damage as we could to the German dugouts on the other side.

21 January: ' ... cooked breakfast – spam and tomatoes. Went out for wood. At twelve o'clock it was our tank's turn to go up to the river. We fired at some Jerry dugouts about 300 yards away, and blew them up too.'

We were making regular trips to different places along the river, sometimes during the day, sometimes at night – Lieutenant Lyle and his tank once stayed all night. I was in Dave's tank, and one day we were given orders to attack a particular point where there were a number of Spandau guns dug in. Spandaus were very heavy powerful machine-guns with a range of several hundred yards and these had to be removed before any attempt could be made to cross the river. We moved into position at dusk, but we could clearly see our objective. I opened fire and blew up a number of the Spandaus; then we quickly returned to the farm. Some time later, when our infantry took this point, we learned that that night we had wiped out six of the German positions.

However, we weren't going to get away with our river-bank trips much longer without trouble. We expected some retaliation, and sure enough the enemy eventually located our farm. We had just started the engines on two of the tanks one night (ours was one of them), when the Germans began to shell us and really let us have it. None of the tanks was hit, but the house was damaged. One shell hit the chimney and blew part of the roof off. When the barrage ended, we went up to the river, fired across and did some damage. They returned the fire but we came back unscathed.

Once the enemy had pinpointed our building they gave us a lot of trouble. The house was being hit regularly, and one of the bedrooms was uninhabitable, with snow coming through the damaged roof. When the owners eventually returned they would find a ruined home. Dave and Lieutenant Lyle went out, and found another empty house a few hundred yards away, undamaged, so we moved there.

Besides our squadron, other tank units in the area were engaged in similar tactics, and also some infantry regiments, but we were making no progress. There wasn't a great deal of activity from the

Germans either. They were sitting there, holding their line, firing shells haphazardly in our general direction, and occasionally sending over a few of their deadly rockets.

Our new location was still close to our Italian friends. I played with Diana and her three cousins of about the same age who lived nearby and turned up whenever I appeared. We played in the snow, and made a slide on the frozen canal – but . . . 25 January: ' . . . Had a fine time with the children, snowballing and sliding till Jerry sent over a shell, then we abandoned the games.'

27 January: 'Moving tomorrow, No. 4 Troop taking over from us. Our Italian friend came over and we showed him round one of the tanks – very interested in the engine . . . Played cards. In evening Sid and I went over to house. Had a nice time drinking hot vino and sugar, as usual. Very little shelling all week except one evening when Jerry gave us a hammering.'

On the 28th we only went about five miles, so in the evening Dave, Paddy and I hitched a lift back to Granarolo to see our friends. Next day we did a few more miles east, ending near Ravenna but still south of the River Senio.

'Through Ravenna, then whole squadron parked for the night at the side of a big house. Moved into billets. Paddy and I got a donkey to carry our kit. Echelon joined us here. People rather annoyed at having to move around but soon "came round". Told that tomorrow moving as reserve infantry, except No. 3 Troop, they're taking their tanks. Had no breakfast because on the way here cookhouse got lost! In afternoon Paddy and I went into Ravenna. Big place but we couldn't find much of interest so after an hour came back.'

Next day: 'After breakfast went down to the tanks and took off four Brownings per troop and tommy-guns. Loaded them on to lorry. Very cold. After about an hour's run arrived here – Villa Nova in Bagnocavalli, a small town thick with mud, miserably wet, muddy and dirty. Frozen. Billeted in a house – an ancient one. Of course we're infantry now but hope it's not for long and that we're soon back in our tanks. What mud in this place.'

The front line had extended west to this point and now, as infantry, we were here to hold the line in case there was a counterattack. I took some of our newly formed troop on instruction on the Brownings and tommy-guns, and then we dug in and mounted the guns ready to repel the enemy if need be. The action in which we were engaged was over the River Senio. The river had yet to be crossed, but there were others, the main one being the Reno, into which some of them flowed. The rivers and the awful weather were responsible for the stalemate in the fighting, and it was obvious that until conditions improved we could do no more than we were doing now. Other units were similarly set up, but in our area there were so few of us that we were on guard every other night.

8 February: 'Went up the river bank 200 yards and fired our Brownings this morning. Cold frosty morning, but the sun came out later and the ground thawed, back into the inevitable mud. On guard at night. Cold, wet and misty night, then it rained heavily.' It was an extremely tiring time, not helped by the mud, and there appeared to be a considerable amount of indecision by our command as to what action to take.

After over a week in this situation there was no sign of an attack being launched against us, and we were called off as infantry and returned, guns and all, to our tanks – with great relief.

Our mail was waiting back at the village. Among mine was a letter from Suzette, but the news it contained was not what I was wanting to hear at all . . .

25

1945: Leave in Rome

I saw the envelope from Aumale with Suzette's writing, and I couldn't open it quickly enough, but I read the letter with dismay. She was very sorry she hadn't written for such a long time, it was difficult for her to have to do so, but she must tell me now – she had a boyfriend, and not only that, they were engaged and he didn't want her to write to me any more.

I couldn't believe it. Engaged! She was only seventeen! For nine months we had been writing, and I'd hoped we'd be writing for a long time yet, and then somehow, sometime in the future we'd see each other again. If only we'd had the chance to spend more time together. If only I'd been able to see her again at Whitsuntide. If only . . .

I tried to be logical, but the frame of mind I was in wouldn't listen to logic, and I was in no mood to be practical either. Surely, I thought, things could have worked out, in time.

And yet – if the Regiment had never gone up into those mountains, and when we did, if Yves hadn't come to the camp, I'd never have met Suzette. Even after that first meeting I hadn't expected I'd see her again, let alone spend a week with her. I found some consolation in thinking that no matter what happened in the future, nothing could ever take away the memory of that blissful week. But I'd lost part of my life, and I was inconsolable. I hadn't heard from her for over two months, so perhaps I should have guessed that something like this had happened. Perhaps I didn't want to think so.

Suzette's Aunt Nanette wrote to me regularly those first few months we were in Italy. I had come to regard her as an ally, and I wrote to her saying that I was upset at the news from Suzette. I suppose I was looking for a shoulder to cry on. I wrote to Suzette too, saying how much I loved her letters, but now if she was engaged, I could understand her fiancé not wanting her to continue writing. I felt miserable for a long time and I couldn't get the thoughts out of my mind. But I had to put my mind to other things; tanks, mud, war, and above all, thoughts of home. I'd not seen home for almost four years. Surely this war must end soon, and some day, if I managed to continue dodging shells, I'd be back in England.

The 12th of February was my twenty-sixth birthday. I was having breakfast at 7 a.m. when I had a very nice birthday present. The SSM came and told me that my name had come up to go on leave to Rome, and I had to be ready by 9.30 a.m. I drew some pay – £20! – and then found that Topper was going to Rome as well.

Topper had been writing to my sister for some time. I got along well with him, though I sometimes felt he looked a little 'wild-eyed'. He was one of the regulars of the Bays, an excellent musician and a very active member of the band. The Bays were particularly proud of their band and had reason to be; before the war it regularly took part in ceremonial parades. Topper suggested he and I should go together. I didn't know anyone else in the party, so I agreed. We arrived in Forli in the afternoon.

13 February: 'On a lorry to Rimini where we caught a train, leaving at 1 p.m. Carriage uncomfortable, but not too cold. Travelled all night, uncomfortable to sleep, seven in carriage. Arrived in Rome at 7 a.m. Lorries waiting to take us to rest camp. Had breakfast there – served by Italian waiters! C.O.'s lecture at 11 a.m. After a very good dinner, Topper and I down to Rome on one of the many trucks provided.'

The rest camp, which was clean and had good food, was a few miles out of Rome, but lorries ran there often. Alternatively, if we wished, we could stay in Rome overnight. This we decided to do, and found a small hotel in one of the *piazzas* where we booked in for three nights. From here it was only a short walk to St Peter's, which is where we went first. Michelangelo's Pietà was just to the right after entering the Basilica. We knelt at a rail quite close to the statue, and gazed in wonder. We stayed a long time, looking at every detail, the folds in the dress, the lifeless arm of Christ, but every time we were drawn back to the beautiful face of the Virgin Mary. From that moment I was a Michelangelo addict. It was the most beautiful sculpture I had ever seen.

The rest of St Peter's was fascinating too. We marvelled at the wonderful paintings – then marvelled even more when we found they weren't paintings at all, but mosaics. It was only on coming very close to them that we realised the pictures were made from tiny pieces of stone and glass. The way the shading was achieved was miraculous.

We climbed up to the Whispering Gallery, where whispers at one side could clearly be heard at the other, then climbed steps and a ladder to get right up inside the bronze ball at the very top of the dome. Then next day it was to see Michelangelo's work again: this time his painting, and especially the ceiling of the Sistine Chapel.

We walked the streets of Rome. It was tiring but we were having a great time; and then we were lucky, for Captain Wilson, one of the Bays officers, pulled alongside us in his staff car, picked us up and drove us all round the city. We really enjoyed that.

There was a YMCA in Rome, where we spent some time and Topper played the piano. He loved music and wanted to go to the opera. I had never liked opera because in my home it was considered only to be of interest to the 'better off'. Really, it was unfair to say I didn't like it, because I had never seen an opera.

La Bohème was playing at the Rome Opera House. Topper was mad to see it, so, not wanting to be a spoilsport, I agreed to tag along. As the opera progressed I became more and more interested. I was thrilled by the brilliant singing and the scenery was fantastic. I think that evening I had one of the most marvellous experiences of my life. I had gone expecting to be disappointed and uninterested, I left with nothing but praise and enthusiasm for what I had seen, and Topper was delighted.

We decided to stay in Rome a couple more nights as there was still much to see. We went to the Colosseum, the Royal Palace (the Wedding Cake) not far away, the fountains and St Peter's again.

On our last day Topper said: 'I've got to go to St Peter's just once more to see that statue.'

I felt exactly the same, so we returned to St Peter's and again we knelt at the rail in front of the Pietà and took in its beauty. We were in no hurry, and we lingered a long time before finally dragging ourselves away. Outside St Peter's I bought an 8″ x 10″ photograph of the statue.

I bought a trinket box for Jessie. I had already sent Suzette two pairs of shoes, something she really liked, and now, in spite of her letter, I couldn't resist buying her another pair.

Our leave was over. It had been an unforgettable week, we'd seen and done so much, and needless to say, out of everything, the Pietà and *La Bohème* had been the highlights. We arrived back at the camp on the 20th, and next morning, after a game of billiards, were taken to the station. The train left at one o'clock, not the most comfortable of trains, but at least we travelled in a carriage and passed through some beautiful mountain scenery. We arrived at Rimini at 5.30 a.m., were served breakfast about 7.30, then left in lorries which had been sent to collect us.

22 February: 'Got to Forli about 9.45 a.m. and saw Dave there – his name had been drawn out and he was on his way home on leave. Put buckshee kit [extra kit given out to take on leave, clean shirts, socks etc. – to be handed in on returning] back in stores there, and an hour later left for 'B' Echelon at Ravenna. At 2 p.m. left for Villa Nova and straight from there up to front. Few shells, pretty quiet. Had a pile of mail, thirteen letters and four *Examiners*.'

I was glad for Dave, he deserved the leave and I wished him luck. But for me, it was back to guns and mud, and that night I found myself already on guard.

26
Crossing the Rivers

The week in Rome was like a dream, but now it felt as if I'd never been away. I was sent to join No. 4 Troop (my own troop having retired for a rest), not in a tank but once again up to the Senio. The position hadn't changed while I was away, but a number of listening posts had been set up along the river bank and four of us manned one of these. We were on the lookout for any enemy movement across the river. There was always the danger that they may decide to attack. We took it in turn, four hours each, to be on watch, and then after sixteen hours were relieved. Next day we in turn relieved our relief.

24 February: 'Sunny but cold. Apart from machine-guns pretty quiet. Jerry 600 yards away on river. Then quite a bit of excitement. Jerry started it by throwing over a pretty big barrage, our artillery retaliated, and I reckon we got the best of it. We on the post were in the middle of it. Still, it could be much worse up here.'

After another three days we fell back about 400 yards and No. 3 Troop took over from us. We were still on standby but after nine tiring days we returned to Forli and I rejoined my own troop. 'What a relief to have a good wash then an unbroken night's sleep. Didn't get up till 8.30 a.m. After breakfast packed up parcels, Jessie's present, and shoes and books for Suzette. Sent flowers to mother through NAAFI. Jack and I went to cinema to see Esther Williams in *Bathing Beauty*, but unfortunately the film broke down.'

I got a two-day pass to go to Granarolo, so could stay overnight if I wanted. We weren't far away and it was easy to get a lift. Everybody was excited to see me, and were disappointed when I could only stay one night. The children just loved me to come and were delighted to find I had brought them some chocolate (*caramelli*). We overcame the language barrier with my broken Italian and the few words of English I'd taught them. The empty spaces were filled with gestures.

Once, the four children were talking among themselves and by their glances I knew they were talking about me. Signora Balbi asked if I knew what they were saying. I didn't, and she explained. The conversation was going like this:

'I knew him first.'

'No you didn't, I saw him before you did.'

'I know him better than you do.'

'Oh no you don't . . .'

Signora Balbi intervened to tell them that it didn't really matter who saw me first or knew me best, for she was sure I loved them all.

I went for a walk with Giuseppe, and we called to see his brother, whose leg was now better. He was once again full of thanks, he thought our M.O. was wonderful and said he just couldn't believe the trouble he'd taken to help him. At night we had a good meal and as usual drank wine. The children drank only wine at meals too, which surprised me, but Giuseppe explained that it was wine well watered down.

I slept there that night, a peaceful one with no shells – and then I awoke next morning to find all four children in the bedroom, waiting for me to wake up: 'I was then immediately besieged!'

Everyone begged me to stay, but I left in the early afternoon with a promise that if I had the chance I'd come back again. I'd really enjoyed my stay with them, the children were so good, and I just loved them. In only an hour and a half I was back in Forli, and that evening Jack and I went to see *Bathing Beauty* once again, only to find that this time it had been shown at five o'clock not 7.30 as advertised – it seemed we were fated not to see it.

4 March: 'Moving again – always on a Sunday – only went about seven miles from Forli. Good billets in houses. Marked out a football pitch.'

The weather was improving and warming up. Over the next few days we played inter-troop football matches. Paddy's turn came round to go to Rome.

Now we were resting, and the time was spent maintaining the tanks, playing football, playing cards, and doing little else, so I asked for, and was given, a 36-hour pass to go back to Granarolo, where I was greeted with the usual enthusiasm.

Some of our troops were still in the area, for the battlefront was static. A few shells fell in the afternoon, but not near enough to the houses to do any damage. My Italian friends told me that shells were still coming like this, and only last night they had been frightened to hear Moaning Minnies. They had no intention of leaving their home, but they were living in a world of uncertainty. I tried to reassure them that soon something was bound to happen to get rid of the Tedeschi. The awful weather, coupled with the numerous rivers to cross, had virtually brought the war to a standstill, but when it improved our army would make a determined effort to bring the war to an end. It was sure to come.

In March we began serious training with the tanks, but we didn't endear ourselves to the local farmers. They were extremely upset – and I had every sympathy for them – because we were driving across fields of growing crops, cutting wires in orchards on which vines were growing and tearing up the cultivated land. The Italians stood and watched helplessly, protesting loudly, as we ruined their fields. We ourselves felt there were other areas we could drive the tanks instead of wantonly destroying the farmland. Sometimes we'd drive to the coast and fire our guns out to sea.

15 March: 'Out on scheme across country. I (and many more) think it's a terrible thing to do, to go round mowing down vines and crops. Wilful destruction. Some of tanks got bogged down. In afternoon watched a lot of twerps milling around.' Next day we found that some tanks had ploughed up our football pitch!

On Saturday 17 March I had a weekend pass, so spent the time again at Granarolo, where I had as usual an excited reception and handed out chocolate to the children. So far as the war was concerned little had changed since we were here. Our first farmhouse looked a sad place, for it was now in ruins, but I was surprised to see that our second one was occupied by members of 'A' Squadron. I imagined they were still carrying on the daily 'river run'. My friends told me with relief that there had been little hostile activity since I was there last. I stayed the night with the promise to come again if I could.

20 March: 'Reminiscing . . . Aumale . . . a year ago since I first met Suzette . . . a year already . . . On schemes, more destruction of vines, crops and ditches. What a mess we're making on these silly useless schemes.'

We'd straightened out our football pitch so resumed games when we could.

On the 23rd I had a wonderful surprise – Ronnie arrived. Although we wrote often he hadn't said he'd expected to come up to the Regiment, so it was a delight to see him. He was now permanently employed in an office block in a town several miles to the south, but he'd managed both to get away and to borrow a pick-up to come and visit me. The last time we'd seen each other was months ago, when I was in hospital in Caserta. A lot had happened since.

Among other things, it was Ronnie's job to notify people at home of the deaths of their relatives killed in action. He said this information was sent to him from the Regiment, and every time he got the list of names he dreaded to look at it in case mine was one of them. It was always upsetting for him when he saw names of boys he had known well. He knew how hard it had been for me when I learned of the deaths of Stan, Ted and the others.

While Ronnie was still with me there was some mail, and among mine were two letters from Aumale, from Suzette and Nanette. Had Suzette and her fiancé fallen out? – well you never know – but no, her letter thanked me for the shoes and went on to explain that the man in her life was a French soldier. Although Ronnie had never met Suzette he knew all about her, and now I had a friend with whom I could talk it over. Ronnie always turned up at the right time.

We considered the facts. Suzette certainly had no boyfriend when I was in Aumale, for she would have told me – or even if she hadn't *someone* in her family would have. In any case she would never have been so affectionate had there been someone else. She wouldn't have agreed to write to me either. A few months after we'd left Algeria, along came this soldier. She must have fallen in love with him and told him about me. They had got engaged and he asked her not to write to me again. So she stopped writing. But after two months, as she was still getting letters from me, she felt she must write and explain.

We read her aunt's letter. She was most sympathetic, for she knew how much Suzette meant to me, and how I looked forward to her letters. Ronnie thought it might after all be for the best, but the way I felt just then, I wasn't sure. Perhaps he was right, I didn't know, and I wondered . . . would she really marry her Frenchman?

Ronnie's stay wasn't long enough – after three days he had to go back to his office. It was impossible to get away to see him, so we didn't know when we'd meet again. We just hoped it would be soon.

After he left I wrote five letters, my 307th home, and the other four all in French, to Suzette, Nanette, Marie and Lucienne. The French correspondence to Smudger Smith's Algerian girlfriend and all the other squadron sweethearts left behind had long since petered out – to my relief.

While we were near Forli, an old man from one of the houses asked me if I'd teach him English; in return he'd teach me Italian. So I would go to his sparsely furnished living room where he produced pencils and paper and we gave each other lessons. It was something to do in the evenings, and we both enjoyed ourselves as we sat there drinking wine and writing and talking. When we left the area both he and I had benefited from our efforts.

Paddy had enjoyed his leave in Rome, and on Easter Saturday, 31 March, he and I decided to go and visit our families in Granarolo. We had weekend passes and first of all went to 'my' house. As usual there was excitement when we arrived, but they wanted to know why I hadn't been for a fortnight. Was I all right? They'd expected me last week. I had to point out that though I loved to visit them, there were other things I was obliged to do.

In the evening Paddy and I went for a walk. There were a number of soldiers about and I noted in my diary: 'At night Paddy had a fight with a 78th Div. fellow who deserved the hiding he got!' Paddy was a handy man to have around when there was trouble.

Next day was Easter Sunday: 'Could have spent it in a worse place.' It was several weeks since Paddy had visited his friends (we were each sleeping in our respective 'homes'), and when we left 'Paddy's people wept'. We promised to come again if we could, for we had both enjoyed the weekend, and no doubt Paddy had enjoyed the fight. But we explained that it was only a matter of time before we would leave the area.

I was pleased to find two letters from Chebli in the mail, one from Marie and one from her sister Suzanne. After all this time it was the first letter I'd had from her, and a pleasant surprise. They were still remembering us and thinking about us at the farm.

There was a tragedy in the village on 4 April, for a trooper in 'B' Squadron accidentally shot and killed a little boy with a tommy-gun. The children were always around the soldiers and accidents could happen, but there was enough death and destruction about already. This was something we could have done without.

Rumours were going around that we'd soon be on the move. It was no more than we expected, and we worked hard fitting 'platypus' tracks to some of the tanks, metal extensions to the sides of the tracks to give the tanks a broader base when they encountered mud in attempted river crossings. 'Hard, heavy work, with everyone tired and hands blistered.' 'Jake' Jacobs at least was in luck: his was the name drawn out for Blighty leave.

The area now was bustling with activity. We were briefed on the plan of action and moved up to the Senio in earnest. Thousands of troops and vehicles were massing just south of the river. The artillery bombarded the enemy and the Air Force pounded them ceaselessly. On 9 April a massive attack was launched. Bailey bridges were laid across the river and troops poured over them. We crossed the river over a bridge near Granarolo; our friends must have been terrified by all the noisy activity, but for them it would soon pass – we now had the initiative and were sweeping forward. The north bank of the Senio 'certainly had some dug-out positions there. Right on through Lugo which the Kiwis took yesterday and where they captured 640 prisoners. Civvies all waving and shouting and clapping.'

12 April: 'We heard that President Roosevelt had died. Once more into the thick of it – destruction everywhere. Dead German soldiers, dead Italian civilians, dead horses and cattle in the fields, a sickening sight.' Once again we were fighting house to house, village to village, but as we passed by and through them the Italians came running towards us, cheering us on. We passed a haystack and half-a-dozen people emerged from underneath it. One lady was brandishing a bottle of wine and they were all shouting: 'Nostri liberatori, nostri liberatori!'

The shells landed, the bombs dropped, the noise was ear-splitting. We attacked houses just in front of us in which were German troops, and I set a number of them on fire. As we moved on we found that the Germans had left booby traps – pens that exploded if picked up, doors wired with devices that exploded when they were opened – as well as laying mines in the fields.

13 April: 'Frank Brett and I slept in dug-out last night (Jerry one) near tank. This morning up road and stopped few minutes at San Maria Di Fabriugo. All Italians hysterical to see "Inglesi". Had to push on. Advanced two miles or so. Italians gave us a great welcome. Got to railway for dark.'

14 April: 'Before leaving this morning Paddy and I had a walk to nearby houses. People certainly seemed overjoyed to see us. Told us Jerry had fled yesterday.'

The Troop Leaders had been moved around and now Mr Lyle had been replaced in our troop by Lieutenant Ian Saunders, who had been with the squadron a long time as Troop Leader in another troop. I liked Mr Saunders, and had at one time been gunner in his tank. For bravery in an earlier action he had been awarded the MC.

'Flails' went ahead across suspected mined areas – manned armoured vehicles with flails attached to detonate mines before other vehicles ran into them, but they moved very slowly, too slowly, so in some cases we were given orders to try and get through the minefields anyhow. The tank commanded by Mr Lyle hit a mine, and poor Jock Bayter, his driver, was killed and another crew member wounded. We were running into stiff resistance, and another of our tanks was hit and put out of action, fortunately with no casualties.

A bridgehead had been established north of the Senio, but the enemy mounted a heavy counter-attack against it. 'A' Squadron had suffered losses and casualties and our squadron had to push on to reinforce the bridgehead. Our troop was leading, in fact we were the leading tank, but amid all the shelling we led a charmed life and reached our objective. Another of our tanks was hit and Lieutenant Read, the commander, was wounded. The light was failing, the German counter-attack was held and we leaguered among some houses about five miles south of the River Reno.

15 April: 'Reveille 3.15 a.m. and moved out at 4 a.m. Cold, misty, dismal morning. I had a sleep (of a kind) on turret floor as we went along. Dark outside and nothing to see. Crossed the Reno, the third river we've crossed this week. (Senio, Santerno, Reno.) Our tank sprang an oil leak. Stopped at 6 a.m. to work on it. Took off sprocket and worked all day.' The squadron was now about two miles ahead but we caught up with them. The enemy was on the retreat again but another of our tanks was hit and its commander, Lieutenant Perkins, was wounded: 'not badly thank goodness. Place here full of mines.'

17 April: 'Up about 2.40 a.m. and moved at 3 a.m. When it came light we were about a mile north east of Argenta. We pushed on with No. 3 Troop. Loads of mines about. Aircraft as usual doing

[171]

magnificent work, especially the Spitfires. Lot of prisoners coming in. A hard day's fighting. One of the 3 Troop tanks knocked out. Then we were hit, but no damage done and kept going. I missed one of his tanks, but someone else got him. Hammered a lot of houses. Took prisoners.'

The fighting was fierce and tiring and though we steadily continued to advance, the Germans fought for every inch of ground. The poor civilians were often caught up in the firing and many were killed. My heart ached for them and especially for the children. It was hard to understand this pointless suicidal resistance by the German troops; and now they brought up Tiger tanks to stiffen their line.

It had been a tough battle to cross the Reno, for it was a big river and the German fortifications on its north bank had been massive. But we *had* crossed it, and now our target was the town of Ferrara.

Wednesday 18 April: 'Dead tired this morning, but by dawn we were on the move again, steadily advancing, and with us the 10th Indian Infantry Division.' We battled on all day and it was coming dusk when we pulled into a farmyard, with our tank up close against one of the buildings. Unexpectedly, in a field in the direction in which our guns were pointing, and about 300 yards away, six German soldiers who had been hiding in the grass stood up and waved a white flag. Some of our infantry went out to get them. I had my guns trained on the Germans, when suddenly they threw down the flag and opened fire on our men. This proved to be a fatal mistake, for it only needed the press of a button with my foot and they were dead men. Our soldiers were unhurt.

All the tanks were in touch with each other and 'HQ' all the time on the wirelesses. We began to settle down for the night to sleep in the tank, when over the wireless came: 'A message for No. 1 Troop, 'C' Squadron. Corporal Merewood. Your name has been drawn out to go home on leave. Prepare to leave the tank in a few minutes. A scout car is being sent up with a replacement gunner, to collect you.'

'I'm going home. Oh God, I can't believe it.'

27

'Blighty' and V.E. Day

I couldn't believe it – right in the middle of the fighting my name had been drawn out. Within a few minutes the scout car arrived and took me back to our 'HQ'. Captain Crosbie Dawson greeted me: 'I drew your name out,' he said, 'and no one could have deserved it more.'

I thanked him profusely, then from there was taken by jeep to RHQ.

We all had kitbags, which were stored at bases many miles behind the lines, but moved up as we did. Mine was brought from Pesaro, 100 miles away, and I sorted out a few personal belongings and changes of clothes, put these in the kitbag to go on the boat, and packed the rest in a valise to be put back into storage. I then wrote a postcard home to give them the news, and sent cards to a few people, like Ronnie, to let them know too.

21 April: 'To transit camp yesterday – couldn't sleep last night, but reveille at 2 a.m. anyhow. Very hot and dusty but who cares. Breakfast 3 a.m., left in lorries at 4. Crossed the Reno, Santerno and Senio to Ravenna, and on to Forli. Railhead now here instead of Rimini. Train pulled out about 8 a.m. We're away! – roll on Blighty.'

As usual the train journey was uncomfortable. We stopped at Jesi and Asti for meals, and spent the night trying, unsuccessfully, to sleep in the corridor, regularly being trodden on by other passengers and bitten by bugs. Next day we arrived in Naples and were taken by lorry to a transit camp about four miles out of the city.

23 April: ' . . . Lire changed to English currency. Great to have £1 and 10/- notes again.'

On the 24th we boarded the *Orduna*, sailing next day from Naples. She was an English troopship, but unlike the *Empire Pride* not overcrowded, and we had plenty of room to sling our hammocks. However, it was so warm in the Mediterranean that many of us slept on deck. The food was good, 'fresh bread and best butter!' Few of us knew each other, but there were more men from my

Regiment, and it didn't take long to get acquainted – and join a solo school.

We saw shoals of porpoises and flying fish, the weather was beautiful, and three days after leaving Naples we dropped anchor off Gibraltar. We were there overnight and before sailing next evening took more troops on board. No doubt, like us, many of the other men were on 'Churchill leave'.

There was no training now and plenty of entertainment; whist drives, cribbage drives, housey-housey, and also a cinema where I saw Bing Crosby in *Going My Way*, among other films. A band played some nights, and we had a library and reading room; it was like being on a cruise.

We had sailed up the Mediterranean on our own, but at Gibraltar we joined a small convoy. Once into the Atlantic the sea turned from blue to grey-green, and began to get rough. Occasionally we heard the destroyers that accompanied us dropping depth charges.

I wondered how the Regiment was doing in Northern Italy, and hoped and prayed that we had no more casualties. We knew that our troops were still advancing there, and then, on 2 May, just a week after leaving Naples, we heard of the unconditional surrender of the Germans in Italy and that Hitler was dead. This was the news we'd been waiting for, and I just hoped all my friends in the squadron had survived. The war in Europe wasn't over yet, but surely now the end was soon to come.

3 May: 'Still no sight of land this morning. Raining and windy. Sea a pale green. Played solo in morning, after dinner went to whist drive and enjoyed it. Seems we're in pretty dangerous waters. Some depth charges dropped. Quite a lot of men seasick, but I escaped it.'

4 May: 'At last land sighted first thing. I saw it at 6.15 a.m. Reckon it must be the south coast of Ireland, as we're heading due east. Told will be in tomorrow at 4.45 p.m. Sighted land to starboard – must be Blighty! Blighty, I can't believe it. What a feeling. Went to community singing in evening.'

On 5 May 1945, eleven days after leaving Naples: 'Up at 6 a.m. to find we were sailing up the Clyde. Finally dropped anchor off Gourock about 10.30 a.m. What excellent news today, few more days should see end of the war with Germany. Hung about all day, trying to pass time playing cards. At 6 p.m. we finally left our ship, onto a lighter. Then we were ashore. It was raining, but what did it matter, it was Blighty at last. Were given tea, cigarettes, chocolates and cake. By train to Ibrox Park. Good system here. No going to bed, working all night with rations, pay, kit, etc.'

The last time I'd seen Gourock was 'to board the *Empire Pride*', in which I was to spend nine unhappy weeks. That was September 1941, three years and eight months ago, but it seemed like a lifetime.

Ibrox Park in Glasgow is the home ground of the Rangers and Celtic football clubs. There we were all 'sorted out' and next morning I left Ibrox station with a pass made out until 8 June. 'First stop Keighley, changed in Leeds, got to Huddersfield about 5.30 in the evening and just couldn't believe it. However it was true, for I got a taxi and was *home* for 6 o'clock.' My mother and father were in tears, and the neighbours turned out in force. Those emotional moments are difficult to describe, excitement, joy, relief . . . home.

Jessie was now out of the Land Army, and when I arrived was at a friend's house nearby. My father went to tell her I was home, and I hid behind the door as she burst in shouting: 'Where is he? Where is he?' Another emotional happy reunion.

7 May: 'Well I'm not dreaming. I'm really home.'

I had lots of aunts and uncles (my father was one of a family of seven, and there were eight in my mother's family), so the next few days were spent visiting and being visited: hectic, happy days.

Jessie and I walked in the quiet of Beaumont Park where in our childhood and teenage years we'd spent many happy hours, and I called in to see the men in the bakehouse where I had worked from the age of fourteen. I wondered if, after I left the Army, I would settle down again and work in a bakery? That was a difficult question, and I didn't know the answer.

I also went into town to see Jessie at George Hall's the same shop at which she had worked before the Land Army, and where she had now returned. The man in charge was a retired army officer, Mr McNee – and he gave me £1!

8 May 1945: 'V.E. Day and Jessie and Dad have holiday today and tomorrow. The whole country celebrating. Street parties, flags flying, and everywhere a feeling of joy and patriotism.' In the afternoon I went with my father to his local club where we had a drink and chat with some of his friends, then in the evening relatives came to our house and we held a party of our own.

14 May: 'Stan would have been twenty-four today . . . '

Jessie's twenty-first birthday was on 15 May, so we had a '21st/Welcome Home' party. My bakery boss, Mr Whitaker, supplied the cake and I decorated it; but instead of twenty-one candles I put twenty-one miniature Union Jacks on top. We actually held the party on the 16th as this was a Wednesday, and Jessie's half day off work. (All the shops in Huddersfield closed on Wednesday afternoons.) Mr Whitaker took the cake to Whiteley's Restaurant in town. Forty-two guests had been invited, some of whom I hadn't seen yet, so it was one big happy get-together. 'Had a marvellous time – wonderful.' I bought Jessie a rose for a corsage, and Topper Brown sent her a huge bouquet of carnations.

Jessie had a week's holiday from work and we went to our favourite holiday resort, Blackpool. We did everything there we always used to do – putting, dancing in the Empress Ballroom, Pleasure Beach and the Big Dipper. Jessie also had a holiday from work at Whitsuntide so she went with me to Alnwick to spend a few days with Ronnie's parents and Emily, and of course Ronald, now four years old.

I went to see Ada Ryan, Ted's wife, and Mr and Mrs Turner, Jimmy's parents, and Doreen his girlfriend. This was a sad occasion. Jimmy was the Turners' only son. To have lost him was bad enough, but Mr Turner couldn't get over the fact that he'd died in an accident, and couldn't stop talking about it. Was I there at the time? I wasn't, so I only knew what he knew, that Jimmy had died from burns. I felt so sorry for all of them. They were very grateful I'd been to see them, I just wished that there was something I could do to help them, but all I could do was to offer my sympathy. I had intended to visit Stan's parents, but they were going on holiday, so we wrote and postponed our meeting.

Jackie White's cousin, the Revd Mr Welsh, was vicar of the local parish of Crosland Moor, so at Jackie's request I called to see him, and spent some time there talking to him about Jackie and life in the Bays.

Since we had no cars, and no telephones in our homes, all our travelling any distance was done by train, and keeping in touch was by letter. Even if we wanted to contact a friend or relative two or three miles away we wrote a letter, and if we went to see each other it was by trolley, bus – or on foot.

Jessie had a lot of nice and attractive girl friends, and I must admit

I enjoyed being the centre of attention when we all went to dances. One young lady, Margaret, whose home was in London, was a student, and like many others had been evacuated to Huddersfield because of the war. She rented a room in a house of some friends of Jessie. Also two Canadian soldiers were staying there, and we all had a great time together. We bought a lot of records and nearly drove my poor father mad by playing them sometimes into the early hours of the morning – especially the record of Bing Crosby and the Andrews Sisters singing 'Don't Fence Me In', which we played over and over again.

Jessie had bought a record as a surprise for me. She put it on. Poor Jessie. It was to cheer me up, but it had the opposite effect. The record was 'Le Bateau des Iles' sung in French, the song Suzette had taught me and for which she'd written out the words. My family knew all about Suzette, and Jessie thought the record would bring back happy memories – it did, but they were still a little painful, and I was sorry for Jessie's sake that I'd been upset.

There were dances, cricket matches, we played Monopoly, cards, Sorry – and there was Yorkshire pudding. All too quickly my leave was coming to an end. It was 8 June, the war in Europe was over – and where was I to go from here?

Back to Italy, to rejoin my Regiment!

28

June 1945: Italy Again

8 June 1945 was a miserable day. I wasn't going back to the fighting, that was everything to be thankful for, but it was wonderful to have been at home for so long and I didn't want to leave, especially to go all the way back to Italy. I appreciated how lucky I'd been, but all the same, leaving home again was an unhappy occasion.

I caught the train from Huddersfield to Leeds, where a special train ran straight from there to Ibrox Park, carrying hundreds of soldiers like myself, bound for the Mediterranean. There was consolation in the fact, however, that overseas service for troops was now limited to four years, whether the war was over or not, which meant I should be on my way home again in three months. It seemed a bit pointless now having to go back to Italy.

Next morning we left Ibrox by train, straight to Greenock and onto a lighter, out into the Clyde where a French boat the *Felix Roussel* was waiting for us. There were a number of men with whom I'd become friendly on the way home, who now, like me, were on their way to rejoin their regiments.

10 June: 'Up at 6 a.m. (groan). Beautiful morning. Finished one or two letters as they had to be posted to leave the ship at 11 a.m. In charge of blinkin' mess table, saw about canteen etc. Played solo with "old school". Sailed at 4.45 p.m. and am I (and hundreds more) fed up. Thank God I won't be doing this journey again.'

12 June: 'Got out really hot and sunny and sea calm. This boat isn't too bad, very clean, food so-so, tea awful.'

The weather was warm enough to sleep on deck, which many of us did. There was now no fear of U-boats, so we were not in a convoy and were kept in touch over the wireless of our progress.

13 June (Wednesday): 'Told we'll be in Gibraltar at approximately 8 a.m. on Friday, and at present are sailing down the coast of Portugal between 50 and 100 miles from land. Went to lecture on navigation – very interesting.'

14 June: 'Slept on deck as usual last night. The old ship still rolling a bit, but not so bad as yesterday. Played cards most of day. Sunny but breezy. At 2.30 tomorrow morning will pass over where Battle of Trafalgar was fought; went to a lecture about it and enjoyed it very much indeed. Slept on deck, very windy but not cold.'

We arrived at Gibraltar at 7.30 a.m. on the 15th and a number of sailors disembarked. After being there all day we sailed at 4.15. surprisingly not for Naples – but for Algiers.

16 June: 'Beautiful sunny day today and the Med. the usual deep blue – just an ideal day for a cruise. Algiers sighted in the evening at 9 p.m. Dropped anchor in bay off Algiers, troops disembarking tomorrow morning. Algiers . . . 20 miles to Chebli, another 80 to Aumale. Oh I wish I could get ashore here for a day or two. Looks grand at night lit up – nothing like Cape Town did, but nice to see the lights. Suzette is just out there . . . and Bachir . . . I wonder what they're doing, if only I could get to Aumale . . . it's so *near*.'

17 June: 'Slept on deck last night as usual, the lights of Algiers twinkling on the shore. At 7.30 this morning pulled right into dock. Oh to think of Aumale – Suzette and all her family and I can't get off. I'd like to see dear old Bachir again. I'll come back again one day and bring Jessie.' We left Algiers at 2.15 p.m.

18 June: 'Following along the coast of Tunisia this morning, and left it about 3.15 in the afternoon. Later passed Cape Bon. Played cards, wrote, read and lazed in the glorious sun. Wonderful day and the bluest of seas. Went to lecture in evening about Italy and enjoyed it . . .'

19 June: 'Bright sunny morning, soon in sight of Malta, and just on 8 a.m. we dropped anchor off the harbour of Valetta. Malta looks very nice and picturesque from here. Plenty big buildings and what look like castles on some of the hills. Sailed from Malta at 3.40 p.m. after being alongside harbour since 8.30 a.m. Beautiful night.'

20 June: 'The Med. this morning is the calmest I've ever seen it, I doubt if it could be calmer, for there's hardly a ripple, it's just like a great lake. Passed Capri about 1.30 p.m. Dropped anchor in Naples harbour in the afternoon. Not disembarking till tomorrow. Went to horse-racing [a game played on board ship], won three races with No. 6 – changed money into lire.'

There was a considerable amount of confusion when we disembarked on 21 June, after eleven days at sea, for no one seemed to know just exactly where my Regiment was. The Bays were 'somewhere near Venice'.

We had a walk of four miles to the same transit camp we'd been before, and next morning, after reveille at 3 a.m. boarded a train at 5 a.m. going north. It was only sixteen miles to Caserta, but by 11 a.m. we still hadn't arrived there. I had been on some slow trains but never one like this. We were travelling in cattle trucks, which was nothing new, and as we passed through an orchard, we jumped off the train, walked alongside it picking pears, then just climbed back aboard. It was dusty as we crawled along, hot, though we had the doors open, and accompanying us on our journey were thousands of flies and mosquitoes. We picked up speed a little and eventually reached Rome at 8.15 p.m. where we stopped for an hour and had some food.

Next day, at 3 a.m. we came to a bridge which had been damaged and was unsafe for the train to cross. We could walk across, so unloaded our kit, carried it over the bridge and boarded another train, which travelled just as slowly as the first.

I awoke at 8.30 next morning to find we were in a station, so 'had a wash and shave'. We then transferred to an electric train, still in our cattle trucks. 'This railway is a wonderful feat of engineering, through mountains with wonderful views. It's the coaches (trucks I should say) and the timing which are at fault.'

We had travelled north from Naples to Rome, then right across Italy from the west to the east coast, through Fabriano and Jesi in the mountains and on to Ancona – the port on the Adriatic and the naval base where we'd collected the wood. The naval base was still there, but this time we weren't in need of any wood, and at 9 p.m. boarded a small boat and sailed about midnight. It was hot, so I slept on deck, and next morning had the interesting experience of sailing down the Grand Canal – the 'main street' of Venice. From Venice we went by road to a transit camp a few miles away at Mestre, then back to the railway.

25 June: 'Slept pretty well last night considering the circumstances. Had breakfast at Udine, then a little further on a lorry was waiting, thank goodness, to take us to the Regiment. Had dinner at RHQ and then to my own squadron and back to the tanks.'

It had been a hectic four-day journey from Naples by various trains, lorries, and boat, and I was relieved to be back with the tanks and among my friends, not far from the small town of Gradisca, and near a big river, the Isonzo, about eighty miles north east of Venice.

We talked for hours. I wanted to know what had happened after my hurried departure on 18 April, over two months ago, and above all, if everybody was all right. I was told that the Regiment had continued to be in heavy fighting, and 'C' Squadron was in the thick of it, in the drive to take Ferrara, but although we had lost some tanks, there were only minor casualties and our troop had come out of the battles unscathed. So Sid, Paddy, Colin, Harold, Dave, Buck, Ted and Jack were all there: what a relief to see them.

There had been many more regiments and thousands of troops involved in this final battle, but Ferrara fell and to the west the Americans took Bologna. Our Regiment was on the banks of the Po when the Germans finally surrendered. Altogether about a million German soldiers had given themselves up at the end of the campaign.

There were twenty letters waiting for me when I arrived, mostly from home and from people I'd already seen, all posted before anyone knew I was on my way to England. Also a kitbag had turned up, lost since I was wounded three years ago. Heaven knows where it had been all that time.

When the fighting was over, the Regiment had come to this very pleasant area abounding with orchards, and the local people were very friendly. The nights were warm and they held dances outside in the evenings. The dance floor was surrounded by trees with lights in them, a lovely setting, and there were plenty of good-looking girls to dance with (unfortunately usually chaperoned by their mothers). Sometimes our Regimental band played for the dancing, a big improvement on the local Italian band.

This northern part of Italy was like a different country compared to the south, and the people were quite different too, with fairer skins. They were well dressed and well fed, and inclined to look down on the people of the south. They would sometimes correct us when we spoke the language we'd picked up, pointing out that we spoke with a 'coarse' accent.

When I arrived, the cricket season was well under way which I enjoyed, and it wasn't long before I was asked to be 'sports editor' for the squadron magazine. I made up a cricket scorebook and scored for the squadron. Colin was nominated an umpire. Sitting there scoring, reporting, drinking lemonade and eating sandwiches in the hot sun – it was a great life. 'Picked figs and apples and yellow plums, can't grumble at the life here – little work, plenty pleasure.'

There was a lovely little island called Grado off the coast just south of Gradisca and Harold and I had a 48-hour pass to go there. We stayed in a very clean room in a 10th Indian Division hotel, the Eva. 'Grado quiet place, walked along front and had tea and cakes in canteen. To open air dancing in evening and then to open air cinema.' Next morning: 'On beach and in sea. Been a lovely couple of days.'

The tanks were here, but what a relief not to have to sleep in them, and better still not to fight in them. We had to keep them clean, which was almost a pleasure, for we didn't go anywhere in them – no driving or firing of guns. Guard duty came round regularly, but this only amounted to walking around the area and keeping an eye on the tanks. Things were very quiet, the people well behaved, and the last thing we'd have expected was for them to try to steal a tank!

Most of the time the weather was hot and it was only a short walk to the Isonzo where we spent hours swimming. It was a very wide river, but at present no more than a series of channels with islands of white pebbles between them. In places there were deep pools, and one we liked in particular had big rocks at the side of it from which we could dive into the cool crystal-clear water. The walk to the river was through fields where rows of tomatoes grew: 'Came out hot – really hot, hottest day I've experienced since I came back. Phew! it's stifling. Spent all afternoon in pool. Went down to river again in evening and Sid and I practised diving till after 11 o'clock.'

One evening Sid and I went for a walk and talked about what we'd do when the war was over. It wasn't over yet, the Japanese were still fighting, but the end seemed inevitable. What *would* we do? After all these years living outside, all the time on the move – could we ever settle down to a normal life again? The idea almost scared us. Sid back to working in an office? Me back to a bakehouse? Neither of us could imagine it. The terrible times we'd endured, the comradeship we'd shared. Would we ever be the same again? I unfortunately lost touch with Sid after the war, but for myself, I found settling down again in 'Civvy Street' a difficult experience, and no . . . I never would be the same again.

The weather was very hot, but sometimes there were heavy thunderstorms and occasionally hailstorms with hailstones 'as big as moth-balls'. Our tanks were parked in the field adjoining a farmhouse at the back of which grapes and figs grew in abundance. The cookhouse was here, but most of the time we practically lived on fruit. After the way we had lived and existed for nearly four years, it was as if we'd moved into the Garden of Eden.

We had heard that the Andrews Sisters were to give a concert at Gorizia on the Yugoslav border not far away, so, although we didn't have much hope, Stan Betts and I decided to try to see them. We got a lift to Gorizia and by one means and another found our way to a big field where a small stage was set up. The field was full of soldiers, mostly Americans, and they gave us a very friendly welcome. We worked our way forward and sat on the grass in front of the stage.

First of all Arthur Treacher, a well-known English actor, at the time working in films in the USA, came on the stage, did a bit of patter, then introduced the Andrews Sisters. They came out of a little tent onto the stage – and they were *fantastic!* The huge audience clapped and cheered as they sang all our favourites 'Rum and Coca-Cola', 'Apple Blossom Time', and many many more. We wouldn't let them go – encore after encore, but finally they had to say: 'This really is the last.'

The sun blazed down, and we crowded round them as they came off the stage – streaming with sweat. They talked to us, signed autographs, I couldn't praise them enough for the way they'd sung in that heat and stayed to meet us afterwards. Arthur Treacher heard my English accent and started to talk to me. He was most enthusiastic about cricket, and said he came over to England to visit his old mother whenever he could, and always went to the cricket matches. It had been a marvellous, unforgettable day.

The Irish Fusiliers, who were in Austria, had taken over a large house on the edge of a lake near the village of Egg am See, and our Regiment had arranged an exchange programme with them so that some of their soldiers could come and visit our area, staying with us, and some of us go to their house. A dozen of us, including Colin, Ted and myself, were lucky enough to go and spend five days there. 'Gorgeous scenery, mountains and lakes as we drove to Austria.' The gardens of the house sloped right down to the lake where there was a small landing stage and a rowing boat.

The village itself was on the edge of the lake and we walked round there, watching the children playing on the small beach and jetty. Lovely blonde-haired children, and they all looked happy. We were impressed by the fact that the people and the whole place was so clean, and we 'did a bit of fraternising'.

This village was between the towns of Villach and Klagenfurt and one night we went into Klagenfurt to see a performance of *Die Fledermaus*, which was excellent. Another day was spent riding a cable car up one of the nearby mountains: 'Quite a thrill going up there. Colin and I climbed higher, and what a glorious view. The air was thin and cool. There was a restaurant on top, and we had dinner there.' The rest of our holiday was mostly spent swimming in the lake and going out in the boat. There was an island in the middle of the lake, to which we swam on a couple of occasions and which we estimated would be about a mile away. Then on 5 August it was back to the squadron to find Sid just about to set off on 'Blighty leave'. Good for Sid. We also learned we were to move to another area in a few days' time.

There wasn't a great deal of mail coming these days. I had letters regularly from home and from Ronnie and Emily and other friends – but I wondered what had happened to Lucienne and Marie, and above all Suzette. I always hoped I'd hear again from Aumale – surely perhaps some day Suzette or her aunt would write again.

We were now into August but were waiting for September to come, for then we knew our four years overseas would be completed and we'd be coming home – for good.

29
Home for Good

On 7 August 1945 we moved to a new area – no explanation was usually given as to why we moved from time to time, and now was no exception. It rained the day we left, and on arrival the tanks were very muddy, so we took some time cleaning them up to make them look presentable again.

We were sorry to leave, but only went about ten miles. On our last evening at Gradisca, Jack, Ted and I went to a dance and didn't get back till 2 a.m.: 'danced with girl with up-swept hair.' We enjoyed these dances, which were held most evenings. Usually the same group of four or five of us went together, and we got on well with the girls. As we were now only ten miles away, it was no problem to get a pick-up and go there.

We had been living under canvas, but now our new billets were in occupied houses in the village of Campalogna near the lovely little town of Palmanova. Families had been persuaded to have soldiers billeted on them, and Ted and I found ourselves in a lovely house owned by two sisters, both in their late thirties. One was unmarried, the other, Signora Matarese, had four children, all beautiful little girls, Fiorella, Paola, Sylvia and Gabriella, ranging in age from five to twelve. Fiorella is the Italian for flower, a perfect name for the youngest girl. With her dark hair, big dark eyes and fair skin she was like a little doll.

We had a room upstairs and there was no doubt that this was the best billet we'd ever had. The door at the back of the house led into a large well-kept garden. The sisters, who besides Italian, spoke some English and French, were smart, gentle and intelligent, and appeared to be quite wealthy. (We didn't know what had happened to the husband of Signora Matarese, and she never mentioned him.) They had a piano, and were particularly knowledgeable about music. Topper was living nearby and naturally was interested in two good-looking, musical ladies. Soon he came round and we

[185]

introduced him. Some evenings he played the piano, to everyone's enjoyment.

10 August: 'Another glorious day. Harold and I went out in scout car to Gradisca and Gorizia and fixed up a couple of cricket matches for Tuesday and Thursday with 10th Hussars and MPs. Very good pitch at Gorizia airfield. At night went to dance. Enjoyed it very much mainly because 'she' was there – the girl with the up-swept hair (but now it's down-swept!).'

Besides the open-air dance floor there was an open-air theatre where the local operatic society performed. One night they put on *Cavalleria Rusticana* and *I Pagliacci*. Another evening it was *Rigoletto*. We couldn't expect them to be as good as *La Bohème* in Rome, but all the same they were most enjoyable.

There were quite a lot of Yugoslavian soldiers about. They looked uncomfortable in their ill-fitting dark, blue-grey uniforms, and were never very friendly. One night ' . . . just before the dance finished, load of Yugoslavs came in on lorries, and it seemed that there may be trouble. Someone fired a few shots, but no one was hurt, and shortly after, they left.'

A little mail was coming through and I was pleased to get a letter from Lucienne which I answered straightaway, and at the same time I wrote to Marie. I had been writing to Margaret, Jessie's friend, and there was a letter from her too.

Names were still being drawn for Blighty leave and now it was Colin's turn. Naturally he was delighted, but we wondered if we would still be here when he came back.

On 15 August there were great celebrations at the news of Japan's surrender. Now, after almost six terrible years, the war was really over.

These were happy days in Campalogna. Occasionally Harold and I went to a nearby racecourse, where I backed a horse once called Paola simply because of its name. It won. Paola was delighted when I arrived 'home' and told her. I loved these children, they were all well behaved although Paola was a bit of a tomboy. I taught the older girls a few simple card games, and Topper came and played the piano.

At last we heard that all the men who had sailed with the Bays were to leave on PYTHON. I forget now what the letters signify, but they stood for the period of four years spent overseas. So on 24

August a farewell Python dinner was held in a local hall. We had menus, which we all signed for each other, there were the usual speeches, and it was a happy occasion, but in a way tinged with sadness. The Regiment was not going home, only the men who had served four years abroad. I was leaving the Queen's Bays after five years, and leaving behind friends like Sid Aster, Jack Ryder, Jackie White, and Colin Rawlins, men who had joined the Regiment during the time we'd been abroad.

Major Rowlands had been replaced as our Squadron Leader by the recently promoted Captain (now Major) Crosbie Dawson, who was away at the time, so was unable to attend the dinner: but later we all received a letter from him. It was a typewritten duplicated letter thanking us for the help and support we had given him, and wishing us well. Across the bottom of mine he had written: 'P.S. We miss your cheerful face a lot. No one in this war has done a better job than you. Good luck.'

26 August: 'Definitely going home tomorrow! Wrote 376th letter home – and last from here! . . . Had letters from Jessie, mother and Margaret – and Marie.'

27 August: 'Said goodbye to the Matarese family and promised to write . . . Paola cried . . . In truck to Udine station. Flags flying, bands playing . . . train left about 11.30 a.m. In usual cattle trucks. Stopped at Padova for a meal about 6.30 p.m.'

28 August: 'At 2 a.m. we had to change trains (don't know why). After hectic half hour or more got in a compartment at Verona. Had uncomfortable night's sleep, and awoke to find us stopped in Bologna station. Bright and sunny, through Forli, stopped at Rimini for meal then Ancona. Followed coastline all way down.' This was the east coast, and we were heading for Foggia where there was a big air base. From here we were to be flown home.

On the 29th we were awakened at 4 a.m. (we always seemed to be up in the middle of the night). We had arrived at Foggia and were taken by lorry to a transit camp: 'First party went to aerodrome at 7.30 a.m. but none after that. Plenty of rumours but nothing doing. Very hot – flies – poor food – roll on the plane. Ted, Joe and I played crib all day long. Hot night.'

Thursday 30 August: 'No parties going today but ten going from Squadron tomorrow. Had to cut for it and Ted is going. Joe and I unlucky. Say we're going on Saturday. Went into Foggia and bought a couple of melons and grapes. Played crib rest of day. Very hot indeed.'

Saturday 1 September: 'Got up about 4.30 a.m., had breakfast and paraded at 5.30 a.m. Straight down to Foggia aerodrome (one of them). Canteen there. Got on plane (Liberator) about 7 a.m. and took off at 7.30 a.m., 25 of us in one plane – riding in bomb racks.' We couldn't see anything from the bomb racks but were allowed in turn to the back of the plane where we could look out. This was the first time I'd flown. 'Wonderful sensation – enjoyed it tremendously. Everything below looked like toys.'

Seven hours after leaving Foggia we landed at Glatton airfield near Peterborough and stayed there overnight. It was a marvellous feeling to be back in England – this time to stay.

Next morning we were taken in lorries to Peterborough Station – no cattle trucks this time, but where were we heading? Richmond Station in Yorkshire and from there in lorries and 'back to square one'. Catterick Camp of all places, where everything had started . . . a lifetime ago.

30
The End of the Road

So here we were back at Catterick, but only overnight. The next day we received ration cards, a canteen issue and other necessities, and then were sent home on a month's leave. I had been home three months ago, but for most of the boys this was the first time for four years.

I arrived in Huddersfield at 5.20 p.m.: 'To George Hall's, picked up Jessie and we came home in a taxi. HOME AGAIN, and you can't beat it – it's great to be home.' I spent the first few days visiting relatives and friends locally and I wrote a lot of letters telling everyone, especially my friends abroad, that I was now back in England for good. I wrote to Miss Store, Lucienne, Marie, Giuseppe, Signora Matarese, and I wrote to Suzette's aunt too.

I went dancing with Jessie. We gathered blackberries, something we used to do every year and take for granted. On Saturday I went to the rugby match with my parents. Then I had a busy week ahead. Audrey's parents had asked me to spend a few days with them, so I went to Tilford, first calling to see Major and Mrs Campbell, then to Audrey's – one morning taking a trip with her father on his milk round. Audrey, her mother and I went for a bicycle ride, and were excited to see Field-Marshal Montgomery in a passing car. He lived in the area.

After visiting Audrey I went to London to see Len Weightman. She was never a very exuberant person, but the war had broken her completely. Bob had been killed when baling out of his tank and I don't think his body was ever found. Then one day she arrived home from work to find that a bomb had fallen on the home of her mother, killing her and Len's young niece. She never recovered from these tragedies and I felt extremely sorry for her. I stayed with her overnight.

Jessie's friend Margaret had now moved back to London. I met her and her boyfriend Martin, and we had lunch at the Regent

Palace Hotel. It was the anniversary of the Battle of Britain, and we saw Mr Attlee, now Prime Minister, making a speech in Trafalgar Square.

Margaret, who had been writing to me since June, had photographs of a number of boys in her bedroom, and every night when she undressed for bed, she turned the photos round the other way! I stayed at her home overnight and next day we went round the usual London sights; then she saw me off at the station. We'd had a great day. Except for my visit to Len, it had been a very happy trip, and when I arrived home Jessie had bought a record for me, a lovely surprise for it was one of my favourites – 'Your Tiny Hand Is Frozen', from *La Bohème*, sung by Gigli.

Ronnie had followed me from Foggia, arriving in England a few days later and wrote suggesting we meet at Blackpool for a short holiday. We arranged it for Saturday 22 September, a local holiday (Honley Feast) when my father and Jessie both had Saturday to Tuesday off work. Not only did Jessie and I go to Blackpool to meet Ronnie, Emily and Ronald, but so did my parents and two of my aunts and uncles. We had four happy days together, dancing in the Tower, putting, visiting the Pleasure Beach.

Mr and Mrs Tatlow had asked me to go and visit them. This was another sad occasion. I was still feeling the loss of Stan, and I felt so sorry for his parents. Their home was as I had expected, a pleasant bungalow in a residential area of Solihull, Birmingham. I knew Stan had come from a good home and caring family. On the sideboard they had the photograph of Stan, Sid, Colin and myself, taken when we went to Cairo to collect the jeeps. They were lovely people, and I was sorry to leave them.

During this time I also visited Mr and Mrs Turner, who lived near Huddersfield. Ted Ryan and his wife Ada came from Wakefield and spent the day with us.

On 1 October 1945 I had a letter from the War Office to say I was to attend an investiture at Buckingham Palace on 13 November, to receive my Military Medal. Then on the 2nd a letter arrived from Aumale – with Suzette's writing on the envelope. I had always hoped I'd hear from her again. She was still engaged and enclosed a photograph of herself with her fiancé. She was sorry she had upset me months ago and wanted to be friends. Well – what would you expect? I could never have fallen out with her anyhow, and needless to say, I answered her letter straightaway. I felt happy just to be in touch with her again.

Then my leave was over, and it was back to Catterick, where I arrived late, as I should have changed trains in York but fell asleep and awoke to find myself in Newcastle! Within a day or two Ronnie and Ted were here, just we three survivors from the old 33 squad. Six years ago, and we felt we'd never been away because now we knew we were back among the *real* soldiers – MPs on the barrack gate and important-looking little sergeants strutting around shouting: 'On Parade.' . . .

'Get that tunic buttoned up.' . . .

'Put that cigarette out, no smoking within twenty yards of a vehicle.'

We hated the barrack rooms and kit inspections. All we wanted now was to be out of the Army for good. My boss, Mr Whitaker, wanted me out too – he wanted me back to work in the bakehouse, but of course the Army wasn't listening.

To be fair, it was a tremendous job to demobilise hundreds of thousands of troops, and in the meantime no one knew what to do with us. Then they decided to send 250 of us, including myself, Harold Balson and Ted Ryan, to Lincolnshire, to pick potatoes and sugar beet. Ronnie was left at Catterick, where he now had an office job.

We were billeted in a hall in Spilsby, a quiet little town, which at least had a cinema, and I finally got to see *Bathing Beauty!* Sometimes we went to a nearby RAF camp to play in whist and solo drives, and most weekends we could get passes to come home. In no time at all I knew the hitchhiking route off by heart.

A typical day – 25 October: 'Weather been wet, but out working today taking up and cutting sugar beets, oh what a job, thought I'd never straighten my back! Finished at 4 p.m. and got 7/-!'

One day Harold and I hitched a lift to Skegness, thirteen miles away, but it rained and the sea-front was deserted. There were still barbed wire defences around, and it was all a pretty depressing sight. We agreed that the day would have been better spent playing cards in our hut.

I was given a week's leave from 10 to 17 November because of the investiture on the 13th. At 9 p.m. on the 12th my parents, Jessie and I left Huddersfield for London and reached Euston Station at 5.45

a.m. From there it was to Lyons Corner House in the Strand for a wash and shave and breakfast. I knew the place, having eaten here before, but this was my parents' first visit to London. Jessie had been just once before, with a trip from school. So it was a day of great excitement; not only a trip to London, but a visit to Buckingham Palace too. My parents were overawed by it all. We only had two tickets for the Palace besides mine, but luckily we met Jim Davidson, who had a spare ticket which he gave to Jessie. Jim used to drive the truck bringing petrol and ammunition to us at nights when we close leaguered. He had been awarded the MM too, and well deserved it.

At 10 a.m. we walked into Buckingham Palace, my father being admonished for not removing his trilby – a hat he only wore on Sundays and special occasions – as we passed through the door. There were rows of chairs arranged in a large room, seating for our relatives, and facing a small raised platform.

I was ushered into a room along with about 100 other men. We had safety pins fastened to the breast pockets of our battle dress blouses. From the window I could see the two princesses, Elizabeth and Margaret, walking in the garden.

The King (George VI), was standing on the platform. We were lined up in single file and it was a very exciting moment when I heard my name called and I walked up to the platform. Someone was handing the medals to the King. He shook hands with me, asked what action I'd been in when I received the award and said 'Well done.' Then he hooked the medal on to the safety pin.

It had been a memorable day for all of us. My parents travelled home after the ceremony, and Jessie and I stayed the night in London with Margaret. Then it was back to Spilsby, only to learn we were about to move to Scunthorpe – perhaps we'd exhausted the local fields of their potatoes and sugar beet. Life was more pleasant in Scunthorpe than Spilsby, though they had potatoes and sugar beet there too, but it was a bigger town with a number of cinemas and dance halls and a YMCA.

The end of November came, the potato picking was finished, and the Army still didn't know what to do with us. They told us our demobs would come up early next year and sent us home on a week's leave. My boss came to the house and asked if I would go and work in the bakehouse. I wasn't keen on that at all, I didn't want to think about a future in a bakehouse, but I agreed to help out. So for three mornings from 5.30 to 1 p.m. I went to work, and he gave me 30/-. Then it was back to Catterick. Ronnie and I were finally together again, but we were so fed up – just waiting and waiting.

On 17 December I asked for Christmas leave, but was told by the Welfare Officer: ' . . . Sorry old man, etc. etc. Oh I wish they'd drop an atom bomb on this place and blow it to blazes.'

I tried again to get a pass for Christmas without success. Finally I decided that after having spent the last six Christmases away from home, pass or no pass I was going, I didn't care whether I got caught or not. So I left on the morning of the 24th and returned on the 27th and I was never missed!

On 9 January I had another letter from Suzette, this time to tell me she was to be married on the 30th. I wrote and congratulated her. I wondered if her marriage would be a happy one. For her sake I hoped it would. She was so young.

31 January 1946: 'I expect Suzette was married yesterday . . .'

Names were now being posted daily on the notice board of men who were to be demobbed. A big boil came up on my arm, but no way was I going to go sick, and soon, to my delight, there was my name. To his disgust, Ronnie wasn't on the list, but he was demobbed a few days later.

Reveille was at 4.30 a.m. – even on demob day. About 150 of us paraded at 6 a.m. and were taken to Richmond Station in double-decker buses. At Strensall Barracks in York we were issued with a new suit, shirt, tie and other clothes, and for the first time for years I was called 'Mister'. I was given a railway ticket to Huddersfield, and on 10 February, 1946, two days before my twenty-seventh birthday, I was out of the Army.

Envoi

Although I kept in touch with many of the people who wrote to me during the war, my correspondence with the friends I made in North Africa and Italy gradually faded away. Lucienne was the one who continued to write longest – until about 1950. I often wonder what happened to everybody. Bachir will surely have died now – if not, he'll be in his nineties. Lucienne, Marie and Suzette will be in their sixties, Suzette sixty-seven – no, she can't be; surely she's still sweet sixteen and baking cakes on the farm at Aumale.

Miss Store sent the occasional parcel from Cape Town even after I was out of the Army, and wrote until she died in the 1970s. Ronnie and I continued to be the best of friends. We both had two children, and our families often met at Richmond or Ripon to have a meal and then play cricket. In later years Ronnie, Emily, Sheila and myself enjoyed days at the races together. It was an awful shock to me when Ronnie died of a heart attack in November 1993. Over fifty-four years our friendship never waned. Emily and I still write to each other and talk over the phone, and occasionally we go to see her.

Mrs Campbell wrote and so did Len. Sheila and I visited both of them until they died in the 1970s.

I wrote to Paddy Flanagan for a few years and then we lost touch. Colin Rawlins and I remained friends and we visited him and his wife a couple of times in Bridport, Dorset. Then in the 1960s I had a letter from his wife to say he had died – the circumstances were obscure, but his body was found at the foot of a cliff near West Bay.

Bob Buckland and Ted Ryan wrote regularly, but both died in the 1980s. I still keep in touch with their wives, Joan and Ada. Harold Balson and I have visited each other on one or two occasions and we still exchange letters at Christmas. Audrey and I always remember each other on birthdays and at Christmas.

In 1991 there was a reunion held at Marlborough to celebrate the fiftieth anniversary of the sailing of the *Empire Pride*, and I was delighted to meet again, after all those years, Herschel Schneiderman – who had changed his name to Harry Taylor after the war, because having a Jewish name he was unable to find work. Since then we have written to each other occasionally and send cards at Christmas, and he and I met again at Cardiff when we attended the fiftieth anniversary commemoration of V.J. Day on 20 August 1995. I was one of the fortunate men honoured to meet Prince Charles.

Jessie's life too was changed by the war. She married an American airman in 1946, and emigrated to the USA. From 1954 to 1961 Sheila and I also lived in the United States, in Colorado, but then we returned home. Jessie continues to live there and we are *still* writing.

The memoirs were finished, but writing them had awakened a desire to go back and see some of those places again. In May 1996 we did so. I wanted to go to Italy, but first it was to France, to visit friends Sheila and I have in Maubeuge near the Belgian border. Pierre had been a French soldier and was stationed in Algeria when it was a French colony. He had even spent some time in Aumale. I told him I had written to the mayor of Aumale on two occasions, explaining I was an English soldier who had been there during the war, and asking if he knew anything of the Hugnit family, but even though my return address was on the envelopes I had had no reply. Pierre said he wasn't surprised, because in 1960/61 General de Gaulle had given Algeria to the Algerians who had then required all the French people living there to become Algerian citizens. Most of them objected to this and as a result over 80% returned to France. However he knew that those who returned had formed a repatriation group and at the moment he is looking into this with the hope of coming up with some information.

Next, south, where we have friends in Toulouse and Marseilles, both of whom speak excellent English and have read the memoirs. Suzette and her family were originally from Marseilles. These friends are also investigating, so who knows, maybe one of them will come up with news of Suzette and Yves.

Then along the French Riviera and into Italy. Pisa, Florence, over a narrow spectacular mountain road to Forli, through Cesena to the east coast and Rimini, for I wanted to find San Martino in Venti

Ridge and the graves of Stan and the other boys who had been killed in that dreadful battle.

We found the Italian people extremely kind and helpful, and were eventually directed to the military cemetery at Coriano. From the ridge where they were first buried, the bodies of the Bays killed there had been moved and were now in this cemetery along with men from other regiments. It was a most impressive sight. Row upon row of white headstones with flowers planted around them. Men were cutting the well-kept grass and cleaning the headstones.

Inside a small building is a register with the names and the number of the plot where they are buried. In one plot were the graves of twenty men of the Bays, most of whom I knew, the Bays badge engraved on every headstone.

I found Stan's grave and was completely overcome. I wanted to talk to him and tell him I was there. The times we'd talked together in the bivvy we shared, and dreamed of coming home. It didn't seem right he should be here. Ted Wanless is buried next to Stan, and I couldn't believe it was fifty-two years since I last saw them alive. I could see them as plain as if it were yesterday. We lingered there a long time.

I wanted to go up to the ridge and look down again into the little valley where the battle had taken place. But though we asked numerous people, nobody seemed to know where it was. Every time we were directed to the cemetery. We were about to leave there when we saw an old man and asked yet again, and this time he knew the place and drew a map showing us how to get there. It was evening. We decided to go the following day.

Next morning we went to the cemetery. I wanted to see the graves again and to say goodbye to Stan and Ted. Then we set out for the ridge. We found it, and it was exactly as I remembered, except that at the bottom there were fewer trees now. There were crops and grapes growing. Who would have known that here men had fought and died.

At the top of the hill is a monument to the memory of the men killed there. Nearby was an old shop and bar with a few people sitting around.

In my diary I had written of the day the Adjutant asked me to take some men to tidy up the graves, and I said that some of the children had helped us as we put green leaves on them. One I had mentioned by name – Pia 'our most industrious worker', and how we had taken her and her brother and mother to church one day.

I had the script of the memoirs with me. The two or three men sitting there could speak no English. My Italian is limited to a few simple words, but I mentioned the name Pia. 'Pia,' one of the men boomed, 'mia sorella' (my sister)!

Now there was a great buzz of excitement and animated talking and gesturing. A name was called, 'Francesca', and a charming young lady appeared who spoke some English and I was able to make her understand. Pia was her aunt and lived in Rimini. A phone call was made and I spoke to Pia's daughter Barbara whose English was excellent: 'Please stay there an hour and we'll come.' We drove a little way up the road, ate a picnic we had with us, and came back to find what seemed to be the whole family there. Pia and her brother Ivo, the one we'd taken to church, had arrived with Barbara and others.

Barbara read from the memoirs, translating as she went, and had a rapt audience of young and old. They were marvellous. Ivo had his arm round me and seemed he wouldn't let go. Pia beamed with pride when it came to the part where she was 'our most industrious worker'. Of course they remembered, and told the younger ones how the Inglesi had liberated them from the Germans. One lady said: 'We owe our lives to them.' I told them about the book and Barbara asked if I would send one to her and I promised to do so.

We stayed two nights at a hotel at the seaside resort of Miremare. When I told the young lady receptionist why we were here she was almost in tears. Later another receptionist, a young man by the name of Luigi, said he understood that we were there to look for the graves of my comrades, that I'd been in the fighting in the area, and he wanted to know more about it. I told him I had a few chapters of the script of the book with me. Could he borrow one and photocopy it? Next day he said he'd been so interested, did I have any more? I gave him two more chapters to photocopy. He said that he and many of the younger people there wanted to know more about this war that had taken place in their country. This was not an isolated case, and we were amazed at the interest shown by so many of the younger people.

We were packing the car ready to leave when Luigi came running out of the hotel and said: 'Wait – I want to give you a bottle of wine.'

A few minutes later he returned with two bottles. We felt quite humbled by this kind of attitude which we encountered so often.

Now I wanted to find Granarolo and the farm where we had made regular trips to the Senio. I wanted to see that river again, and I wondered if any of the Balbi family were still there.

Granarolo wasn't easy to find. I had numerous maps but it wasn't on any of them. But consulting the memoirs and asking in various places we finally found it. I made inquiries at a farm and the lady said yes, she knew the Balbi house. She got in her car and asked us to follow her. We drove half a mile or so and pulled up in the driveway of a house. The door opened, a lady came out, saw me and shouted 'Jackie.' I said 'Yes – Diana', for I immediately recognised her as Giuseppe's daughter. She couldn't believe it. Suddenly and without warning after fifty-one years I had come back. She was nine years old when we last saw each other. She spoke good English and said 'Come in, you're staying here with us tonight – no way are you going to go any further.' It was no use arguing. Giuseppe had died about ten years ago but astonishingly here was her mother. The Signora Balbi I had known was a bright, happy and friendly young woman of thirty-three, black hair brushed back and fastened with a comb. The Signora Balbi I saw now was an old lady of eighty-four but she still had a ready smile. Diana was married and lived here with her husband and mother. This was the same room where I sat and ate with them, at this very table all those years ago.

The house had been small and they'd built on an extension, but now Giuseppe had died, their daughter was married and lived in Rome, so they had plenty of room for us. And how about her cousins? One boy had died but Anna and Emilio were still alive. Their father, Giuseppe's brother, the one with the sore leg, had died only three years ago.

Part of the canal had been filled in and the bridge had gone, but the farmhouse from where we had made our daily trips to the river was still there.

In the evening we were joined by Anna and Emilio and other family members and also a lady, Orsola, who was extremely interested in the war and particularly the fighting in this area. She had lived in Granarolo all her life and was five years old when the Bays were here. She brought a video which she had obtained from the War Department in London, taken shortly before the Bays arrived. She knew all the history and was delighted now to have someone here who had taken part. We talked well into the night. I read a few excerpts from the memoirs which Diana translated to a full house – and they laughed about the children being in the bedroom waiting for me to waken, and were so interested in everything. Orsola left with the promise that in the morning she'd take us up to the river.

I was at the Senio again. Fifty-one years ago . . . what memories. I stood where we used to come with the tanks. It was easy to see now how the Germans were able to dig in at the bank on the other side. Where the road now crossed the river were the remains of the old bridge destroyed by the Germans.

Then we had to leave. 'But why – surely you could stay another day or two. Do you *have* to be in Venice by tonight?' We explained we had only intended to stay an hour or two and were still here a day later, we were getting behind on our schedule. We eventually got away but not until we had visited more of the family – cakes and wine every time. The people had been wonderful, and it was fantastic to have seen them again. Diana insisted I send her a book.

Now it was north to Venice, then an overnight stop in Grado, where Harold and I had spent that quiet weekend. We found a hotel which I think had been the Eva – but how Grado had changed. No longer a quiet little resort, but one with new hotels, bustling and busy with tourists. Next, to Gradisca and the Isonzo. The wide river with its islands of white pebbles was just as I remembered it. In the fields alongside grew crops, but the memory of just where we had been with the tanks and played cricket and swum in the river was hazy, and I wasn't sure of the exact locations. I wondered what had happened to the girl whose name I never remembered – but who had upswept (and downswept) hair.

On to Campalogna. A lady extremely anxious to help remembered the soldiers being billeted there, some even in her mother's house, but she couldn't remember the Matarese family.

We had been on the move two weeks now, another week yet through Austria with a couple of nights in Salzburg. A day in Berchtesgaden and to the Eagle's Nest – the mountaintop retreat that had been built by Hitler between 1936 and 1938. It couldn't have been more appropriately named. A drive of about three miles up a steep mountain road, then park the car and a further four miles in special buses, on another incredibly steep and spectacular road, leaving the bus, there to walk about 300 yards through a tunnel cut deep into the mountainside. Into a lift to the mountain top itself. Hitler's hideout has now been turned into a restaurant. The view from there is breathtaking.

Germany, France and Belgium for the ferry to Hull. It had been a marvellous, unforgettable three weeks, a drive of over 3,000 miles. Three weeks packed with memories.

Pierre had found the address of the repatriation group in Marseilles. I wrote to them asking if they had news of the Hugnit family. My experience here was the same as with the mayor of Aumale: there was no reply. But Pierre had also found out that there were three families with the name of Hugnit living in France. I said we were looking for a needle in a haystack, but he insisted, 'We'll find Suzette.'

So I wrote to the first on the list, a M. Hugnit of Mauvages. This time I had a reply, but a heartbreaking one. Yes, he knew Suzette, in fact they were cousins. She and her parents had returned from Algeria in 1960, her parents had died, and sadly so had Suzette. Yves, her brother, was married with a family, but he had lost touch with him long ago.

This was in October 1996. Then I thought about Yves; could I possibly find him? I still had two more addresses. At one lived Franck and Laurent Hugnit, so in January I wrote to them explaining who I was and how I'd met this family at Aumale. I had written to M. Hugnit of Mauvages and was shocked to hear from him that Suzette had died. Were they by any chance relatives of Yves? And I had a reply – from Yves and his wife Nicole. Franck and Laurent were their sons. Yves was delighted to have heard from me – and so were Suzette and Nanette! They were both going to write to me. Suzette's mother was alive, now aged ninety-six and living with Yves and Nicole.

I put the letter down. Sheila and I were in a state of shock. It took us a while to recover. Finally I felt composed enough to telephone. Nicole answered. 'Suzette is alive?' I asked. 'Yes, she is very well, she is going to write to you straightaway. She is a widow now, she and Nanette live in Romans. Everybody is so excited, we must get together.' But how about the man who had told me she was dead? Yves took over and said that this was a cousin whom they had neither seen nor heard of for years. The man had no connection with the family, and why he had told me this he couldn't imagine.

Suzette was alive! Incredibly, we had found the needle in the haystack.

A few days later the mail arrived. I always looked forward to the arrival of the mail; and I saw a letter with Suzette's writing on the envelope. . .

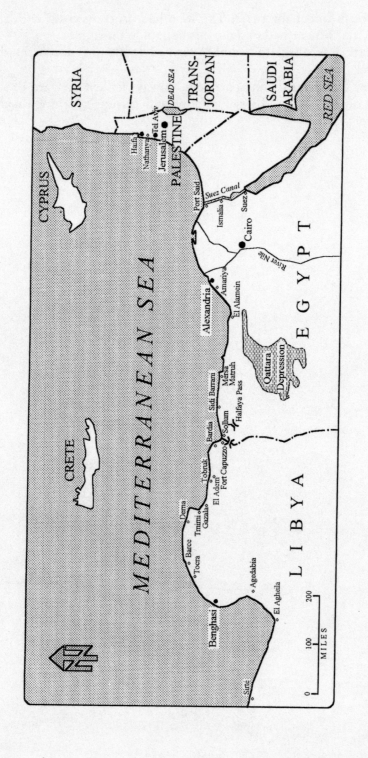

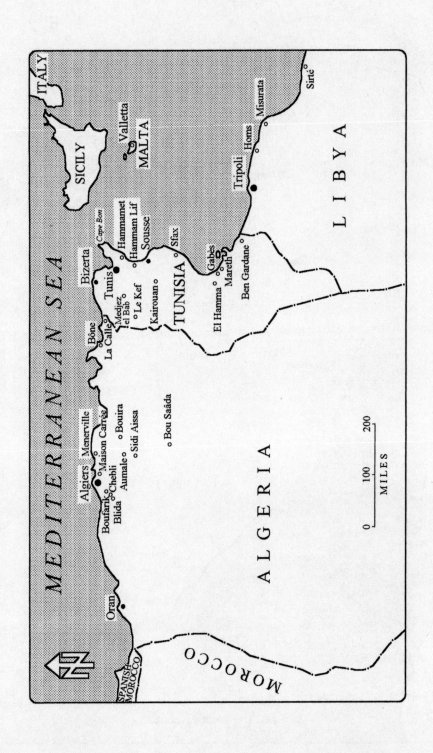

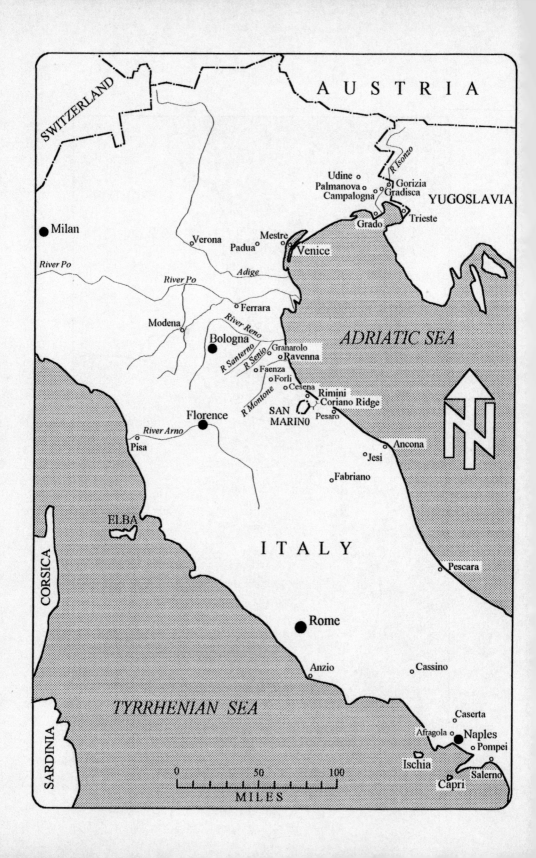

SWITZERLAND

AUSTRIA

Milan

Udine ○
Palmanova ○
Campalogna ○

R Isonzo

○ Gorizia
Gradisca

YUGOSLAVIA

Grado ○

Trieste ○

River Po

Verona ○

Mestre ○

Padua ○

Venice

Adige

River Po

Ferrara ○

Modena ○

River Reno

Bologna ●

R Santerno

R Senio

Granarolo ○
Ravenna ○

ADRIATIC SEA

Faenza ○

Forli ○

Cesena ○

R Montone

Rimini ○
Coriano Ridge

SAN
MARINO

Pesaro ○

Florence ●

River Arno

Pisa ○

Ancona ○

Jesi ○

Fabriano ○

ELBA

ITALY

CORSICA

Pescara ○

Rome ●

Anzio ○

Cassino ○

TYRRHENIAN SEA

SARDINIA

Caserta ○

Afragola ○ Naples ●

○ Pompei

Ischia

Capri

Salerno

0   50   100

MILES

Index

[207]

New Zealand Infantry, 61, 71, 81, 97, 140, 146, 148, 170
Nolan, Cpl Jim, 82
Norrie, Lt Gen Sir Willoughby, 54
North Africa, 17, 46, 51, 85, 89-90, 94, 110, 118, 121, 125-6, 194
Nufilia, 79, 99

Oran, 77
Orduna, SS, 173
Orsola, 198-9

Page, Tpr, 28
Palestine, 60, 93
Palmanova, 185
Patchett, Capt, 46-8, 50-1, 54
Pembroke, 29
Perkins, Lt, 171
Pesaro, 150, 152-5, 173
Pia, 138-9, 154, 197
Pierre, 195, 200
Pierson, Tpr, 68
Plymouth, 26-7
Po, River, 181; Valley, 133, 145
Pompeii, 127
Pont du Fahs, 88
Poole, 22
'Python', 186-7

Qattara Depression, 67
Queen Mother, HM The, 24, 44
Queen's Bays, 21-4, *et passim*

R.A., 11-12
R.A.C., 12, 19
Radice, Lt 'Joe', 51, 53, 55-6
Ranson, 'Busty', 145-7
Ravenna, 159, 164, 173
Rawlins, Colin, 66, 69, 72, 76, 79, 82, 85, 88, 95, 97, 129, 138, 145, 153, 181, 183-4, 186-7, 190, 194
Read, Lt, 171
Red Sea, 42
Reeves, Ned, 35, 39, 68
Reno, River, 160, 171-3
Repulse, HMS, 41-2
Richmond, 12, 18, 21-2, 27, 33, 188, 193-4
Rimini, 138-9, 145, 150, 162, 164, 173, 187, 195, 197

Rome, 125, 129, 144, 153, 162-3, 165-6, 169, 180, 186, 198
Rommel, Gen, 46
Rossini Symphony Orchestra, 152-3
Rowney, Dick, 46, 50-2, 55-6, 62
Ryan, Ted, 13, 21-3, 33, 52, 66, 69, 103, 138-9, 153, 181, 183, 185, 187, 190-1, 194
Ryder, Jack, 73, 117, 138, 144, 165-6, 181, 185, 187

St Helena, 39
Sahara Desert, 114
Salisbury Plain, 26, 28, 33
San Marino, 138
San Martini in Venti Ridge, 138, 195
Santarcangelo, 139
Santerno, River, 171, 173
Saunders, Lt, 88, 118, 123, 171
Schneiderman, Herschel, 75-6, 92, 123, 136, 152, 195
Scunthorpe, 192
Senio, River, 155, 159-60, 165, 170-1, 173, 198-9
Sfax, 93, 100, 134
Sherman tanks, 52, 64-6, 105
Sidi Aissa, 114
Sidi Rezegh, 46
Sierra Leone, 38
Sirté, 79
Smith, Sgt 'Smudger', 117, 131, 169
Sollum Pass, 98
Somme, River, 24
Sousse, 93, 100
South Africa, 40, 62
Spence, Sgt 'Jock', 106
Spilsby, 191-2
Store, Gladys, 41, 189, 194
Streeter, Maj, 95
Strensall Barracks, 193
Strutt, SSM, 93, 95
Stuart tanks, 16-17, 27-8, 49-51, 54-5, 65
Suez, 42-3; Canal, 42, 60
Suzanne, 104-5, 114, 169
Suzette, 115-17, 119-24, 126-7, 129-32, 134-5, 138, 140, 143-4, 153, 155, 160-1, 163, 165, 167-9, 177, 179, 184, 190, 193-5, 200-1

Table Mountain, 41; Bay, 41